S[illegible]at's Doct[illegible]2-2013

The Critical Fan's Guide to Matt Smith's Final Series (Unauthorized)

Steven Cooper
&
Kevin Mahoney

Punked Books

Published in 2014 by Punked Books
An Authortrek imprint

(www.authortrek.com/punked-books)

First Edition

ISBN 978-1-908375-24-7

Contents

Foreword

At over 90,000 words, this is the most comprehensive fan guide yet published to the 2012-2013 season of *Doctor Who*. After the first part of the season provided an emotional ending to the Doctor's travels with his friends Amy and Rory, Steven Moffat presented an innovative and intriguing new mystery, as the Doctor puzzled over the “woman twice dead” that is Clara Oswald, who had the most spectacular introduction(s) of any companion. This series was the most demanding yet for Moffat; no other *Doctor Who* showrunner had previously faced an assignment like writing a series finale, an anniversary story, and a combined Christmas Special/Doctor finale in quick succession. We are with Moffat every step of the way as he rises to this unique challenge.

The format of this book is the same as our previous *Doctor Who* guides. Steven Cooper has written excellent detailed analyses of each episode, which *Slant Magazine* published online in their *House Next Door* blog soon after each episode was broadcast. In this way, Steven’s reviews provide an invaluable record of how a long-standing fan reacted to each twist of the plot as it occurred. *House Next Door* published Steven’s 2013 episode reviews in abridged form; he then expanded upon his analyses, so this book contains far more of his insights than those published online. I then follow Steven’s analyses with my reviews, which I wrote from the perspective of having watched the entire series. This enabled me to gauge exactly how Steven Moffat had put this season together, and to assess the success of his various hoodwinks and sleights of hand.

In this series, Steven Moffat was just as ambitious as ever - perhaps too ambitious at times, when the scripting became uneven or the production team was not able to realize an episode as well as they might have done. Despite this, there were several episodes that rank among the best of the show’s achievements, which we applaud in this celebration of *Doctor Who*’s 50th Anniversary.

Kevin Mahoney
Publisher and Founder of Punked Books. July 2014

1: Asylum of the Daleks

Writer: Steven Moffat
Director: Nick Hurran
Originally Broadcast: 1 September 2012

Cast

The Doctor: Matt Smith
Amy Pond: Karen Gillan
Rory Williams: Arthur Darvill
Oswin: Jenna-Louise Coleman
Darla: Anamaria Marinca
Harvey: David Gyasi
Cassandra: Naomi Ryan
Voice of the Daleks: Nicholas Briggs
Dalek 1: Barnaby Edwards
Dalek 2: Nicholas Pegg
Photoshoot PA: Zac Fox

***Steven's Review*:** Opening a new season with the Daleks – pitting the Doctor against his oldest and most famous adversaries – has always been a temptation for the producers of *Doctor Who*. The audience-grabbing potential is so obvious that this is actually the fourth time it's been done in the show's history. *Asylum of the Daleks* also gives showrunner Steven Moffat his first chance to write a Dalek story, having deliberately rested the creatures last year – the first season since the show was revived in 2005 that the Daleks were not used (except for a one-scene cameo in the finale). Without the additional pressure of introducing a new Doctor or companion, or setting up a season-spanning arc plot, Moffat's season opener is a successful stand-alone adventure with several touches of horror that call to mind his earlier efforts during the Russell T Davies era.

A sombre mood is set from the outset as the episode opens on Skaro, the blasted, ruined homeworld of the Daleks. Inside a giant statue of a Dalek ("Hell of a choice of meeting place." "They said I'd have to intrigue you"), the Doctor has come to meet a woman, Darla, who wants him to rescue her daughter from a Dalek prison camp. As we saw in last year's Christmas special, the Doctor is now determined to keep a low profile following his escape from the Silence's attempt to kill him, and so he is not pleased that this woman has somehow managed to get a message to him.

Darla: "They say you can help."
The Doctor: "Do they? I wish they'd stop."

But he soon discovers that the whole thing is a trap – the woman is a Dalek agent, sent to capture him. Her human personality vanishes as a Dalek eyestalk erupts from her forehead and a Dalek gun from her hand. The idea of the Daleks employing controlled humans as slaves is certainly not new (it goes back as far as the 'Robomen' in 1964's *The Dalek Invasion of Earth*), but it's never before been shown in such a creepy and graphic fashion. On board a huge Dalek ship, the Doctor is reunited with his erstwhile companions, Amy and Rory, who have been collected from their lives on Earth by other Dalek agents. They find themselves in the "Parliament of the Daleks" – a massive amphitheatre filled with hundreds of the creatures, all chanting the last thing the Doctor expected to hear – "Save us! Save the Daleks!"

It was rather amusing to see that, after the poor reception given to the "new paradigm" Daleks introduced in 2010's *Victory of the Daleks*, they are very much in the minority here. The Parliament chamber is populated almost exclusively with the older bronze models, although the few representatives of the new design we see appear to have been given a face-saving officer status. In any case, the setup for the main story follows, as we learn of the Daleks' legendary Asylum – a planet where the Daleks dump all their failures: "the battle-scarred, the insane… the ones even you can't control."

The Daleks have gone to the trouble of kidnapping the Doctor because the supposedly impenetrable Asylum has been breached. In a deliberately disjointed scene (typical of Moffat) after the opening titles, we see a young woman named Oswin, apparently alone and under siege in the Asylum, who identifies herself as a crew member of a spaceship that crashed on this planet. She has been hacking into the Asylum's systems and disrupting them. Realising that this could open a way for all of the inmates to escape, the Daleks intend to beam the Doctor, Amy and Rory down to the Asylum, where they will be trapped until the Doctor can turn off the planet's protective force field, allowing the Daleks to vaporise it.

I enjoyed the confrontation between the Doctor and the Dalek "prime minister" – a wizened creature in a glass tank very similar to the one seen as the "Emperor Dalek" in 2005's *The Parting of the Ways* – in particular, the designation of the Doctor as "the Predator of the Daleks," and the following exchange:

The Doctor: "You think hatred is beautiful."
Dalek Prime Minister: "Perhaps that is why we have never been able to kill you."

It's also worth taking a moment to give credit to the contribution of Nicholas Briggs, who has single-handedly provided the voices for all of the Daleks (as well as the Cybermen, and various other aliens) since the series was revived in 2005. His ability to create different characters for the various types of Daleks is, I think, a very significant factor in the success the creatures have had in the new series.

As they are beamed down to the planet, Rory gets separated from the others, falling down a deep hole into a large underground chamber, while Amy and the Doctor encounter Harvey, apparently another survivor from the crashed spaceship. At this point Moffat rolls out an effective string of horror movie ideas, as Harvey takes the Doctor and Amy back to his escape pod, only for them to realise that his fellow crewmates are long dead… whereupon Harvey realises that *he's* actually dead and has become "Dalek-ised" (just like the woman Darla) by the Asylum's "nano-cloud" which transforms all intruding organic matter into Dalek material. Then, no sooner have the Doctor and Amy fought Harvey off than his zombie crewmates rise up and threaten them in the same way.

Moffat could be accused of recycling his previous concepts here – the nano-cloud is basically the same as the nanogenes from *The Empty Child*, and the idea of the walking corpse, unaware of its own death, harks back to the skeletons in spacesuits from *Silence in the Library*. But it's certainly a nicely macabre idea that anyone attacking the Asylum gets absorbed into its own security system. In order to protect against the effects of the nano-cloud, the Doctor and his friends are issued with special protective wristbands. These represent a rare failure in the show's design department – they are so large and bulky that Amy is left looking incredibly stupid on two occasions, when she fails to immediately notice that the attacking zombies have taken her wristband off her arm, and again later when the Doctor sneaks his own wristband onto her.

The direction by Nick Hurran lives up to the high standard he showed on his debut in 2011 with *The Girl Who Waited* and *The God Complex*. From the impressive CGI of the Parliament chamber, to the contrast between the vast snowy expanses of the planet exterior and the cramped, dingy underground tunnels infested with Daleks, the episode is full of memorable visuals. In particular, there's a lovely bit of dreamlike imagery when Amy, falling under the influence of the nano-cloud, sees a roomful of people, including a twirling ballerina, which then becomes a roomful of Daleks, with the ballerina replaced by a Dalek spinning serenely in place.

Once the Doctor and the others are all underground, they have the problem of finding each other in the maze of corridors and chambers while avoiding getting killed by the mostly dormant but still dangerous Daleks. It was lovely to see many of the older Dalek designs from the Classic Series in these chambers (although some of them were a little difficult to make out under the layers of grime). I also particularly enjoyed the neat trick the Doctor employed to use one Dalek's self-destruct impulse (automatically activated when it finds itself facing its greatest enemy without a working gun) to take out the others.

Meanwhile, Rory is doing his best to keep out of the Daleks' way, although eventually he has to be rescued by the watching Oswin. Which brings me to the big surprise of the episode… It didn't take long before I realised that Oswin was being played by Jenna-Louise Coleman, who (as was announced months ago) will be portraying the Doctor's new companion Clara, starting from this year's Christmas special. I can only congratulate Moffat on managing to pull off this surprise, which required the co-operation of the press and preview audiences in several different countries. Particularly ingenious is that the trick succeeds regardless of whether the viewer is aware of Coleman's significance – for those who don't know that she is scheduled to become the next companion, the surprise will come at Christmas when the Doctor meets someone who reminds him so much of the woman he encountered in this episode.

It remains to be seen whether there is any real connection between Oswin and the new companion, or whether they are simply being played by the same actress (as happened with Karen Gillan, who played a soothsayer in *The Fires of Pompeii* two years before she appeared as Amy). It's worth noting that, unlike Gillan's case (and earlier, with Freema Agyeman), Coleman's role in this episode would only have come about *after* she was cast as the new companion. So despite Moffat's stated intention to move away from last season's complex arc plotting, there are clearly still some connections being established between episodes. As if to remove all doubt on this point, Coleman gives a coy little glance directly into the camera as she delivers her final line: "Run, you clever boy. And remember…"

As for her actual performance, I was very impressed. She's a natural at handling Moffat's comic dialogue, and her flirting with Rory and fast-talking banter with the Doctor was a delight. At the same time, she managed to project enough confidence and intelligence to make Oswin's labelling of herself as a "genius" believable. And when given the chance to emote more deeply, as Oswin's ultimate fate is revealed, she was well up to the task. I've never seen any of her work before, but based on this episode, I'm very much looking forward to her joining the show permanently later on.

But enough about the companion-in-waiting; the relationship between the Doctor's current companions is the second major focus of this episode. The first five episodes of this season, leading up to a hiatus before the Christmas special, will bring the story of Amy and Rory to a close. In fact they are already partly out of the Doctor's life – their days as permanent travellers aboard the TARDIS ended in last year's *The God Complex*, and each episode since has faced the challenge of finding a way to involve them in the story. Here, they are collected by the Daleks to accompany the Doctor on the frankly flimsy justification that "it is known that the Doctor requires companions."

It's soon apparent that Amy and Rory's marriage is more than in trouble; when we first see them, they're actually signing divorce papers while exchanging barbed insults. Once on board the Dalek ship, Amy is annoyed at the realisation that the Doctor will inevitably notice the distance between her and Rory and try to do something about it. In a stark contrast to her dreams of her magic Doctor when we first met her two years ago, she now dismisses his desire to help:

Amy: "Don't give me those big wet eyes, raggedy man. It's life. Just life. That thing that goes on when you're not there."

When Rory realises that Amy has lost her protective wristband and decides to give her his to buy her some time, they finally confront the cause of their split. We find out that thanks to her experiences on Demon's Run (in 2011's *A Good Man Goes to War*), Amy can't have the children that she knows Rory desires, which has led to her pushing him away. Both Karen Gillan and Arthur Darvill are excellent throughout the episode – having played these characters for so long now, they really know how they tick – and this scene is very emotional, thanks in particular to Gillan giving it absolutely everything. Unfortunately, it loses some of its effectiveness simply because there has been no hint whatever of this plot thread before now. Rory's contention, "Basic fact of our relationship… I love you more than you love me," may be true, but all through the 2011 season they were shown as a very close couple, and it's very jarring to go from that closeness to the bitter acrimony on display here.

I'll admit it was a nice touch to show nothing more than a quick, wordless shot of the Doctor simply straightening his bow tie when Amy discovers he has put his wristband on her – a callback to her earlier annoyance on board the Dalek ship; nothing more is needed to get across the point that he has manoeuvred them into confronting the problem. I really hope that this isn't the last we hear of Amy and Rory's marital difficulties, though; such a quick solution to a dispute that went all the way to a formal divorce would be regrettably glib.

At any rate, while Amy and Rory are working through the repairs to their relationship, the Doctor continues making his way towards Oswin's refuge. Moffat's inventiveness continues with the idea of the "Intensive Care" area containing the Daleks which have personally survived previous battles with the Doctor, which allows him to have Oswin name-check various planets from the Classic Series – "Spiridon, Kembel, Aridius, Vulcan, Exxilon" – for the enjoyment of long-term fans.

In a lovely bit of plotting, the Doctor's repeated "Where do you get the milk?" question to Oswin's mentions of making soufflés turns out to be more than just a bit of whimsy – it signposts the solution to the mystery of Oswin's true nature. (On the other hand, I found the several "Eggs-terminate" puns to be painfully corny.) When the Doctor finally enters her chamber, he discovers not the woman we have been watching, but a chained up Dalek that still dreams of her human life. Matt Smith is especially good here, showing the pain in the Doctor's face as he gently explains to her what has happened.

The potent image of a Dalek breaking free from chains (first used in the memorable 2005 episode simply titled *Dalek*) is used as the story reaches its climax, with Oswin managing to help the Doctor achieve a victory despite her own fate. Earlier, she had saved the Doctor from the Daleks in the Intensive Care area by hacking into the Daleks' database and deleting their knowledge of him. Now, she drops the

Asylum's force field and the Daleks above wipe out the planet as planned, but the Doctor and his friends are teleported back up to the ship, into the TARDIS. The Doctor emerges, and discovers to his delight that the Daleks no longer recognise him – Oswin's deletions have reached even here (and possibly to all Daleks everywhere).

Oswin-Dalek: "We have grown stronger, in fear of you."
The Doctor: "I know – I tried to stop."

Realising that the endless conflict with the Doctor was actually helping the Daleks, Oswin has managed to break the cycle. It's an unexpectedly happy ending, in keeping with the now reconciled Amy and Rory cheerfully waving goodbye as the Doctor drops them off back on Earth – not only is the Doctor given the chance to extend his newly-desired anonymity, he doesn't have to keep re-fighting the great Time War which has loomed over him for so long. No doubt there will be more clashes with the Daleks in the future, but for the moment the Doctor no longer has to be "the Oncoming Storm," the "Predator of the Daleks." No wonder that the final shot is of him giddily dancing around the TARDIS console, on the way to all-new adventures.

Steven's Classic Who DVD Recommendation: Remembrance of the Daleks, starring Sylvester McCoy and Sophie Aldred, kicked off the 25th season of the Classic Series in 1988. The Special Weapons Dalek which made a very memorable impression in this story can actually be briefly glimpsed in *Asylum of the Daleks*, among the group of Daleks which wake up and attack Rory. It's a fast-paced, densely plotted story which shows the classic series attempting something different with the Daleks, and is well worth checking out.

Kevin's Review: *Asylum of the Daleks* kicks off the 2012 season and *Doctor Who*'s 50th Anniversary celebrations in excellent style. For long-time viewers of the show, it is very disappointing to see that Amy and Rory's marriage has hit problems. (Although when Amy does sign the divorce papers, she does so as "Williams" instead of "Pond", which means that she did adopt Rory's surname when she married, despite the Doctor's tendency to call her spouse "Rory Pond". This is perhaps an early indication of Amy's high regard for Rory, as it is no longer customary for a woman to adopt her husband's surname upon marriage. Of course this fleeting, "blink and you miss it" glimpse of

Amy's married name is a premonition of her and Rory's gravestone in the mid-series finale, *The Angels Take Manhattan.*) As the strife in the Williams' marriage develops, it becomes evident that Moffat only ever intended it to serve as this episode's *Star Trek: The Next Generation*-like "emotional high drama", which involves a nanocloud subtracting Amy's love for Rory while it turns her into a Dalek. Thankfully, it turns out that Amy does love Rory greatly, leading to the revelation that she has only turned him away upon discovering that she can no longer bear the children that Rory desires following Madame Kovarian's antenatal interventions during the events of 2011's mid-season finale *A Good Man Goes to War*. Although such scenes can sometimes be gratingly sentimental, Moffat has written them skilfully here, and Gillan and Darvill perfectly perform them, to the extent that they do not detract from the more powerful emotional drama that Moffat stores up for Oswin during the episode's resolution.

In the wake of his fake death during the previous series, the Doctor has become quite a messianic figure. Of course, the Doctor has been a messianic figure for a long time, since his first regeneration. However, Moffat may have been playfully referring to a more Biblical kind of resurrection here, especially since he intended to tie up this Doctor's eventual fate via the Papal Mainframe (the Church of the 51st Century and beyond). This Biblical overtone also pops up in the etymology of Oswin's name, which means "God Friend" in Old English. Since Oswin is the companion figure, it is evident that Moffat regards the Doctor as being the 'God' figure. "Oswald" has a similar etymology, and can mean "divine leader", "God Power", or "God Ruler". Now that we know from the season finale that splinters of Clara have shattered into the Doctor's lifecycle, it is likely that Moffat's intended meaning is "God Leader", as these echoes of Clara instinctively lead the Doctor away from danger. Even godlike beings like the Doctor, it seems, need the help of mere mortals to keep them away from danger. Indeed, "Clara" means "clear" or "bright", a fitting name for someone who will often subtly clear or illuminate the way for the Doctor throughout his life. It's apparent during the Doctor's encounter with Darla that his ambition to "step back into the shadows" (as he put it in 2011's finale, *The Wedding of River Song*) has not come about; he has not achieved the anonymity that he desired in the wake of his fake death, since mysterious forces are still calling him into action.

The Doctor bemoans the state of Skaro, the Daleks' home world, despite the fact that it has never looked pretty on screen following the

Kaleds' nuclear war with the Thals. The Doctor's contention that "Nobody escapes the Dalek camps" is also quite odd, as people were forever escaping Dalek prison camps during the Classic Series (admittedly with the Doctor's help though). Darla's conversion into a human Dalek is a startlingly effective innovation, as is the fantastic macabre horror of the later zombie Daleks; so it was great to see Moffat utilise this device again in Matt Smith's finale, *The Time of the Doctor*. One of the few things that looks disjointed in this episode is the sudden reappearance of the forest ship's glass ceiling from the previous episode, *The Doctor, the Widow and the Wardrobe*, in the Parliament of the Daleks. (Perhaps this is a subconscious allusion to the triangular wall pattern motif that was often recycled by *Doctor Who*'s set designers in the 70's!) A more definite style allusion in this episode is to *Star Wars Episode V: The Empire Strikes Back*, especially when our heroes crash land on the snow-bound asylum (which looks much like *Empire*'s Hoth), while the Doctor encounters an alien probe in the snow, and Amy meets Harvey, who is dressed like someone from the Rebel Alliance. As we discussed in our previous book, the 2011 mid-season finale *A Good Man Goes to War* also alluded stylistically to the best *Star Wars* film.

I am not sure that we really need a Parliament of the Daleks as an addition to their folklore, or a Dalek Prime Minister for that matter. The Daleks have never been democrats; indeed, their fascistic nature is entirely contrary to the ideals of such an institution that they would happily crush and destroy from any other civilization. One can only think that since the demise of the Cult of Skaro, the Daleks have adopted some of their practices (i.e. to think like their sentient enemies in their bid to defeat them). Hopefully, this will be the last episode that the Doctor encounters insane Daleks, as I do think it is a bit lazy (and not very politically correct) for *Doctor Who* writers to constantly depict Daleks as insane nowadays in order for our hero to have interesting conversations with them. (Just make them really evil – that worked well in the Classic Series prior to the return of the Dalek creator, Davros, in *Destiny of the Daleks*.) I guess the Parliament of the Daleks is ultimately just a device for Steven Moffat to break his previous record for having the most Daleks onscreen during the 1999 Comic Relief homage (*Doctor Who and the Curse of Fatal Death*), and it is very effective to see a multitude of the old dustbins asking the Doctor to save them. (As Steven mentions, the Dalek Paradigm seem to have forgotten their desire to wipe out all impure Daleks, as they happily mill around in the background.) The Doctor says quite an odd thing to Amy during their time in the Parliament of the Daleks when she asks him what they should do – "Make them remember you". Possibly this is a reference to Amy's first meeting with these monsters in *Victory of the Daleks* (2010) when she had no memory of them, despite humanity's previous conflicts with the Daleks, due to the influence of the Silence. However, as we know from the end of this episode, the Doctor will be dancing deliriously around the TARDIS console when he realizes that Oswin has deleted him from the memory of all the Daleks, via their hive mind, the path web. Now that she has done so, it appears that Oswin has finally realized the Doctor's dream of happy anonymity… (One little detail that I have to point out is that when the Doctor encounters the Dalek eyestalk in the snow, the eye matter has a 'fleshy' appearance that the production team intended to be an integral part of the design of the 'Dalek Paradigm' in *Victory of the Daleks*. However, the production team discarded this design aspect at the time due it being a little too disturbing, so it is great to see that it finally makes an appearance here, although in the form of a disembodied eyestalk. It would seem that Oswin has hacked some of the Daleks' stand-alone organic technology here, as this is obviously not the eyestalk of her own Dalek.)

Writing of Oswin, I must say that her introduction must be the most fantastic of any of the Doctor's companions. Steven Moffat's realisation of her (along with Jenna-Louise Coleman's note-perfect portrayal) is highly ingenious. Indeed, Moffat's writing in this episode is some of the best that he has ever done for the show, and *Asylum of the Daleks* is a very fitting opening to *Doctor Who*'s 50th Anniversary celebrations, especially with all the Classic Series Daleks spinning around on the set. (Although the Daleks from "Spiridon, Kembel, Aridius, Vulcan, Exxilon" all seem to have morphed into the form of the modern brass Daleks.) I was taken aback by Jenna-Louise Coleman's introduction, as I would have thought that it would be impossible for the production team to successfully keep such a dramatic revelation so secret, so I must pay homage to Steven Moffat and co. for pulling this off. I guess I was also a bit disappointed as it became more evident that Coleman was not portraying a resurrected Susan (the Doctor's granddaughter from the beginning of the Classic Series). Readers of our previous book will know that I was anticipating Susan's return, as there have been several hints about the Doctor's family since the beginnings of Moffat's tenure as showrunner.

However, Oswin sparkles so brightly here that I was not too disappointed at the non-appearance of Susan during the 50th Anniversary celebrations (except for a brief glimpse of the Doctor ushering the 'teenage' Susan into the 'wrong' TARDIS at the beginning of *The Name of the Doctor*). Although Oswin was very flirty (much like all the Doctor's other female companions now), the fact that she was flirting with Rory (and not just the Doctor), could have made her a bit different from Rose et al. Not that Oswin appears to be much of a threat to Rory's relationship with Amy, despite its troubles in this episode (even more so since most fans knew that Amy and Rory's departure was imminent). Moffat's fitting use of Bizet's *Carmen* would also seem to signify that Oswin's flirty gypsy persona was not destined to survive the episode.

The ultimate shocker that Oswin is a Dalek is very well played out here, along with her demise, which would have left most fans scratching their heads, wondering how Jenna-Louise Coleman's character was ever going to return. This is especially given that Moffat makes it clear that Oswin has never encountered the Doctor before, so she could only have become the Doctor's companion earlier on in her lifespan if she had forgotten all memories of him (not impossible, as Oswin achieves this very feat by removing all the Daleks' knowledge of the Doctor). Another mystery is how an apparently ordinary human is such a genius, which Moffat later resolves during the introduction of the 'real' Clara Oswald in *The Bells of Saint John*. Of course, the end of this episode harks back to the original mystery of the show (which will again have due prominence throughout this 50th Anniversary year, and during the demise of the Eleventh Doctor), as the Daleks repeatedly and fittingly bark "Doctor Who?!!!" as the TARDIS disappears…

2: Dinosaurs on a Spaceship

Writer: Chris Chibnall
Director: Saul Metzstein
Originally Broadcast: 8 September 2012

Cast

The Doctor: Matt Smith
Amy Pond: Karen Gillan
Rory Williams: Arthur Darvill
Queen Nefertiti: Riann Steele
Indira: Sunetra Sarker
Riddell: Rupert Graves
Brian Williams: Mark Williams
Solomon: David Bradley
Robot 1: Noel Byrne
Robot 1 (voice): David Mitchell
Robot 2: Richard Garaghty
Robot 2 (voice): Robert Webb
Bleytal: Richard Hope
ISA Worker: Rudi Dharmalingam

***Steven's Review*:** In one of the more blatant cases of *Doctor Who* using a B-movie style episode title to pull in the viewers, *Dinosaurs on a Spaceship* lets us know up front that this is going to be a "romp" – big, loud, and hopefully fun. Writer Chris Chibnall, starting from that bare four-word premise given to him by showrunner Steven Moffat, has come up with a very enjoyable stand-alone adventure that lumbers a bit in the set-up (as is usual with Chibnall) but ultimately delivers some excellent tension and excitement, making good use of previously established *Who* continuity along the way.

The start, though, is frankly unpromising, as we find ourselves in ancient Egypt, with the Doctor having apparently just saved its people from disaster, burbling something about a plague of alien locusts. Queen Nefertiti intercepts him as he returns to the TARDIS and comes on to him in exactly the same way Amy did at the end of 2010's *Flesh and Stone*. When he receives a sudden temporal newsflash on his psychic paper, she forces her way into the TARDIS to accompany him. Her appearance is striking (and faithfully recreated from the famous limestone bust currently in a Berlin museum), and she is certainly not badly acted, but her dialogue conveys no sense of another time or place – she comes across as just a standard present-day "feisty" female character who happens to be wearing a blue wastebasket on her head. Later, the story does find a way to use her that justifies her inclusion, but at the beginning, "Neffy" (as the Doctor calls her) feels like a bizarre, fan fiction-style indulgence.

We next see them in 2367 A.D., where an enormous unknown spaceship ("the size of Canada") is on course for Earth. The necessary ticking clock for the story is set up right away – in six hours, the ship will be close enough to Earth that missiles will have to be launched to destroy it. I liked the nicely unexplained touch that the organisation handling the planet's defences is the ISA – which turns out to stand for not the International but the *Indian* Space Agency. It doesn't make any difference to the actual plot of the story, but it helps make the futuristic environment a little more distinctive than usual, with the understated but effective Indian influence in the background set architecture and graphics.

Despite the Doctor saying he's "not really had a gang before," the rest of the teaser rather unwisely invites comparison to the first part of 2011's *A Good Man Goes to War*, with the Doctor collecting people from various times and places to accompany him. He arbitrarily stops off in 1902 to pick up John Riddell, an English big-game hunter who is evidently a prior acquaintance, and then pays a surprise visit to the home of his friends Amy and Rory. Not bothering to explain what's going on, and presuming that Amy and Rory will be happy to drop whatever they're doing to go along with him (as Rory later says, "Why can't you just phone ahead, like any normal person?"), he simply materialises the TARDIS around them, meaning that Rory's father Brian gets dragged along for the ride as they all arrive on the mysterious spaceship. Almost immediately, they discover what sort of life forms are on board this ship – dinosaurs!

As Chibnall has noted in various interviews, while the "dinosaurs on a spaceship" premise forms a great hook to bring in the audience, it's not enough on its own to sustain a 45-minute episode. So the main thrust of the story is the mystery of who built the ship, why it's heading to Earth, and how it can be saved from the threatened destruction by missiles. In the course of investigating, the group is split up, with the Doctor, Rory and Brian being unexpectedly teleported to a beach that is actually just another part of the huge ship.

One of the things that quickly distinguished the new *Doctor Who* from the Classic Series was its approach to the emotional life of companions, outside their relationship with the Doctor. The original series took almost no interest in companions' family lives, but already by *Aliens of London* in 2005, Russell T Davies was building major plot arcs around Jackie Tyler finding out about her daughter Rose's involvement in the bizarre world of the Doctor. As succeeding companions came and went, various permutations of the same dramatic idea were used. Since Steven Moffat took over as showrunner, the companions have become more like those of the Classic Series, with Amy's parents having appeared only very briefly (in the 2010 season finale *The Big Bang*) and Rory's being absent altogether. It was time for the idea to be revisited, although here it's mostly presented in a comic manner – after the requisite boggling at the inside of the TARDIS and the idea of time/space travel, Brian very quickly settles down to become a useful member of the Doctor's team.

Mark Williams presents a very likeable, warm character, and he and Arthur Darvill make a very believable father and son. The episode gets a lot of fun out of the traits Brian and Rory have in common, notably their efforts to be ready for all eventualities. When Rory notices that the beach seems to be humming, Brian produces a handy trowel he happened to have with him ("What sort of a man doesn't carry a trowel? Put it on your Christmas list!") so he can dig down and find there is a metal floor under the sand. Later, Brian gets injured, and it's Rory's turn to show his preparedness when he pulls out some medical supplies he has picked up in his travels – a nice character touch that makes good use of Rory's nursing background.

Meanwhile, Amy and the others manage to find the ship's data records and discover its true nature. Unfortunately, this section in particular exposes Chibnall's weaknesses with dialogue and characterisation. As I mentioned above, Nefertiti gives practically no sense of being a person from the remote past – in fact, she is more modern in outlook than Riddell is, leading to a great deal of tedious "battle of the sexes" bantering between them. As they wander through the ship with Amy, all three are exchanging quips as if they were in an episode of *Buffy the Vampire Slayer*. I did get a laugh from Amy's reaction when she realises that Nefertiti and Riddell are (cliché alert) starting to become attracted to each other ("No, no, no – *I* will not have flirting companions!"), but on the whole Amy is a more superficial character here than at any time since the last time Chibnall wrote for her.

At least, unlike in that 2010 two-parter (*The Hungry Earth* and *Cold Blood*), Amy manages to actually contribute to the story and uncover what's really going on. And here I have to give praise to Chibnall – the revelation that this ship was a creation of the Silurians, a space-going ark containing samples of Earth animals in search of a colony planet, perfectly explains the dinosaurs' presence aboard and is a lovely usage of the previously established reptilian species. It was a nice touch to bring back Richard Hope, one of the main Silurian actors seen previously, to play the recorded Silurian who delivers the necessary information (he's credited as "Bleytal," but I don't think the name is actually mentioned on screen). Even better, Amy then gets to use her brain and perform some detective work with the ship's sensors that reveals another, much smaller ship attached to this one.

The occupant of this intruding ship has been following all the action thus far on his monitors, and overhears Rory calling to the Doctor. Being in need of medical help, he sends his pet robots to fetch them. These hulking, nine-foot-tall creations, with their oversized upper bodies and tiny heads, recall the Mondoshawan aliens from *The Fifth Element* (1997), but their menace is hilariously undermined when their first words to the Doctor are "We're *very* cross with you..." in a deliberately camp voice. Even as they are escorting their prisoners, they are tossing insults back and forth, providing a very funny element which heightens the contrast with some of the darker moments to come.

The robots' master, Solomon, is an extremely unsubtle caricature of a profit-at-all-costs trader, whose attitude to everything he encounters is determined by his value-measuring software. The Doctor (who is half-pleased to be able to describe himself as "worthless" when Solomon's software can't identify him) finds him immobilised in his ship with badly injured legs – the result, he says, of an encounter with some of the dinosaurs. At first the Doctor is enjoying good-naturedly sparring with him, but there's a sudden shocking change of tone as Solomon reveals he is a much more dangerous man than was first apparent. David Bradley expertly conveys the moment, when the Doctor tells Solomon he'll fix his legs "if you tell me how you came by so many dinosaurs" – at this slight hint of opposition, his face slowly hardens, he harshly orders the robots, "Injure the older one," and then he calmly threatens to kill Brian unless the Doctor does as he says.

With all the characters and pieces of the plot now set up, the remainder of the episode is very well worked out and was a pleasure to watch. This is where Chris Chibnall shines – whatever his shortcomings in other areas, he is very good at structuring a story and building a plot to a climax. The driving force of this plot, of course, is the battle of wills between Solomon and the Doctor. Smith and Bradley have a string of excellent scenes, in many of which Solomon seems to have the upper hand – such as when he smugly describes how he disposed of the Silurians he found on board the ship ("We ejected them. The robots woke them from cryo-sleep a handful at a time and jettisoned them from the airlocks. We must have left a trail of dust and bone…"). The Doctor's disgust is palpable, but he can only bide his time.

Director Saul Metzstein, new to the show, does well at creating an expansive feel for the huge spaceship; the unusually large sets give an appropriate sense of scale, and the exterior is a lovely computer-generated creation, looking like an enormous seed cluster floating in space. He also has a high-quality and high-profile ensemble cast to work with – Rupert Graves is easily recognisable as Lestrade from Steven Moffat's *Sherlock*, and both Mark Williams and David Bradley are playing characters not dissimilar to those they portrayed in the *Harry Potter* films. As a final touch (and one that was not announced before the episode's broadcast), Solomon's bickering robots are voiced by the British comedy duo David Mitchell and Robert Webb.

As for the dinosaurs themselves, they are effective creations – perhaps not up to the latest blockbuster movie state-of-the-art, but very well done given the resources of a TV series – not to mention being several orders of magnitude more impressive than those in the Classic Series' most notorious attempt at portraying the giant lizards. 1974's *Invasion of the Dinosaurs* remains one of *Doctor Who*'s most embarrassing visual effects failures, with the creatures represented via small-scale, slow-moving rod puppets, unconvincingly green-screened into the action. Nevertheless, this story shares with *Invasion* the feature that the titular monsters are actually only a small part of the plot. The story reserves them for set pieces, ranging from their opening appearance which allows the Doctor to name-drop the story's title, a flock of pterodactyls on the beach menacing the Doctor, Rory and Brian, a sleeping T-Rex, and a group of velociraptors which Riddell and Amy have to hold at bay with stun-guns.

The major featured dinosaur is a triceratops, beautifully rendered with a seamless mixture of prosthetics and CGI. It's the only one that the characters interact with to any real extent, and it is amusingly given the personality of an over-affectionate puppy, slobbering over Brian and happily chasing after thrown golf balls. After the Doctor, Rory and Brian escape from Solomon, the story's biggest set piece occurs as they ride the triceratops to get away from the robots chasing them. If you ignore the fact that they could quite obviously have got away more effectively just by walking briskly, it's a delightfully fun moment.

The levity soon evaporates as the Doctor confronts Solomon again. He realises that Solomon hasn't been able to change the course of the ship – it's heading back to Earth automatically, and when the ISA launch their missiles as planned, it looks like Solomon will have to leave empty-handed. But now he has a new target; he has discovered Nefertiti's presence on board and wants to take her with him. In another escalation of menace, he casually has his robots kill the triceratops. David Bradley resolutely refuses to indulge in any pantomime-villain histrionics, instead keeping Solomon's voice level and low, letting his actions speak for him, and thereby makes the man genuinely threatening.

Solomon: "I like my possessions to have spirit. Means I can have fun breaking them."

In actual history, Nefertiti's fate is undocumented – she disappears from the historical record around 1330 B.C. This of course provides an irresistible opportunity for a *Doctor Who* episode to play with, as with the similar case of the pirate captain Henry Avery in 2011's *The Curse of the Black Spot*. As I alluded to earlier, it's a clever piece of scripting to have Solomon spot her unique value, and thereby justify her presence in the story – for a moment, it looks as if he will be the one responsible for her disappearance.

The Doctor manages to stop Solomon's ship from leaving, but the missiles are still coming. In a final twist, it emerges that the reason Solomon couldn't change the ship's course is that it requires two pilots from the same "gene chain" (a nice use of previously established Silurian terminology) to control it – and the plot reaches a neat resolution as Brian and Rory, who have exactly the kind of connection needed, take control and turn the ship away from Earth. The Doctor, meanwhile, manages to rescue Nefertiti and plant the signal emitter that the missiles are locked onto on Solomon's ship. He then releases it, sending the trader off to meet his richly deserved doom.

A brief epilogue shows that Nefertiti has decided to stay with Riddell, while we see Brian sitting in the doorway of the TARDIS in space, sipping tea, looking at the Earth suspended below. It's a nice, upbeat ending to a cheerful adventure. Despite my various complaints noted above, I ended up enjoying *Dinosaurs on a Spaceship* – it fulfils the promise of the title with admirable efficiency and a certain amount of cleverness in the plotting. There's only one thread with an obvious connection to wider events, and that's the moments the Doctor has with Amy.

Early in the episode, she tells him it's been ten months since she and Rory last saw him, and wonders if the presence of other people travelling with the Doctor means that she and Rory have been replaced. The Doctor replies, "No, they're just people, they're not Ponds." They are separated for most of the episode, but in the lead-up to the climax they finally have a chance to discuss things. I may be doing Chris Chibnall a disservice here, but I strongly suspect that this conversation was inserted by Steven Moffat to lay the groundwork for upcoming events. It's clearly Karen Gillan's best moment of the episode, as Amy confesses she gave up the modelling job we saw her doing last week:

Amy: "I can't settle. Every minute, I'm listening out for that stupid TARDIS sound."
The Doctor: "Right, so it's my fault now, is it?"
Amy: "I can't not wait for you – even now. And they're getting longer, you know, the gaps between your visits… I think you're weaning us off you."

When Amy tells of her fear that one day he'll simply stop showing up and she'll be left waiting forever, he promises her, "Come on, Pond. You'll be there till the end of me." Amy cheerfully replies, "Or vice versa," and then there's an odd, rather horrible pause until the Doctor finally says softly, "Done…" He immediately pretends that he just meant he had finished what he was working on, but it's obvious that something important has been set in motion. An ominous portent for the future, and a signal that the time for carefree adventuring is over.

Steven's Classic Who DVD Recommendation: As mentioned above, see 1974's *Invasion of the Dinosaurs*, starring Jon Pertwee and Elisabeth Sladen, for some considerably less convincing giant reptiles. Even by the standards of the time, the creature effects are excruciatingly bad, but the story itself is actually quite good – a conspiracy-based eco-thriller that not even ridiculous puppet dinosaurs can quite spoil.

Kevin's Review: *Dinosaurs on a Spaceship* is an action-filled romp, and my favourite addition to the series by scriptwriter Chris Chibnall. This is saying a great deal, as I usually approach Chibnall's stories with a sense of dread. I do not like to disparage a fellow *Doctor Who* fan, especially not one that has achieved the dream of becoming a writer for the show, but I have to say that he has written a few dud scripts in his time. However, since I am writing this review in 2014, I have to mention that Chibnall had a spectacular success in 2013 with his ITV drama series *Broadchurch* (which starred Tenth Doctor David Tennant, along with Arthur Darvill). However, I have to compare this success with Chibnall's rendition of Arthurian myth, *Camelot*, which was a real stinker.

Having watched several of Chibnall's *Life on Mars* episodes, it would appear that he is best at writing for series that feature an ensemble of 'larger than life' characters (such as *Doctor Who* spinoff *Torchwood*, whose first two series he co-produced) which is probably why he opted for more of the same here via John Riddell and Nefertiti. I have often thought that it must be difficult for a TV scriptwriter to write successfully for a character that they have only previously encountered via a script, rather than a finished performance, so this could explain why Chibnall's 2010 *Doctor Who* two-parter was not that successful, as it featured a new Doctor as well as new companions. Steven highlights the Doctor saying that he has "not really had a gang before", so it is possible that Moffat suggested this kind of ensemble to Chibnall as a forerunner of the Paternoster gang. (We will later encounter again the Doctor's group of friends from *A Good Man Goes to War* in the 2012 Christmas Special, *The Snowmen*, along with 2013's *The Crimson Horror* and series finale *The Name of the Doctor*.) Although his 2010 episodes (*The Hungry Earth* and *Cold Blood*) were not that successful, it is pleasing to see that Chibnall was not afraid to revisit his earlier story despite its lacklustre reception by making the Silurians an integral part of the plot of this episode. Indeed, who else but Homo Reptilia could have filled this ark full of dinosaurs? (Although, I must point out that the reason for the Silurians' construction of the ark – their fear that the Earth faced destruction from the planetary object that became our moon – is just one of the many historical inaccuracies that afflicted their original appearance in the Classic Series.)

Dinosaurs on a Spaceship would appear to be one of the few successors to 2011's *Let's Kill Hitler* as an episode title designed to provoke chatter and online speculation prior to its broadcast, just like that which preceded the 2006 Samuel L. Jackson movie *Snakes on a Plane*. (*Journey to the Centre of the TARDIS* has a similar B movie ring to it, while *The Wedding of River Song* provoked plot speculation that was more specific to *Doctor Who*.) However, there are elements of this episode that the production team have definitely recycled from previous episodes. I am writing here of the ark's engine room, which recognisably uses the same beach as 2010's *The Time of Angels/Flesh and Stone*. Southerndown Beach also featured as Bad Wolf Bay in 2006's *Army of Ghosts/Doomsday*, and *Journey's End* in 2008. Just as the Classic Series always seemed to be filmed in the same quarry, so it may be time for the production team to find a new beach, as it is getting as recognisable as the Vasquez Rocks (first made famous by the 1967 *Star Trek* episode *Arena*, which the movie *Bill and Ted's Bogus Journey* later paid homage to).

Amy's humorous remark – "I will not have flirting companions" – is especially resonant for me, as I think that one problem with Clara's character development as this series developed was that she became less flirty and therefore less fun. You may well read this as a sexist sentiment. However, I think the same rings true whether the character involved happens to be male or female. In this instance, both Riddell and Nefertiti give as good as they get during their flirtatious banter. Perhaps the best example of this is Captain Jack Harkness, who famously flirts with anything that has a pulse. Such flirtatious banter has become an integral part of *Doctor Who* since its revival in 2005, which Moffat happily embraced in the form of the Doctor's wife, River Song. However, it does become a problem if the age gap between the Doctor and his companion becomes too big, as a twenty-something female fancying a fifty-odd male is not appropriate in a prime time family programme. (One could argue that not much has changed in the programme's fifty-year history, as the reason why the character of Susan became the Doctor's granddaughter during the development of the Classic Series was because the production team thought that it would be inappropriate for a teenage girl to be travelling with an unrelated older male.) I think that when Moffat was writing *The Bells of Saint John* (the opening episode of the second part of Series 7) he knew for sure that Matt Smith would be leaving the show. Moffat must have had in mind that he would replace him with an older actor, which meant that he felt compelled to make the modern Clara gradually less flirty than she had previously been.

In a book about the show's 50th Anniversary, one must mention that David Bradley (cast as the Doctor's adversary Solomon here) went on to play William Hartnell (the actor who portrayed the First Doctor) in Mark Gatiss's 2013 dramatic recreation of *Doctor Who*'s early years, *An Adventure in Space and Time*. Solomon is a thoroughly nasty piece of work, especially his massacre of the Silurians on the ship, and his implicit threat of sexual violence to Nefertiti. Yet, no matter how loathsome he is, the fact that the Doctor effectively murders Solomon by allowing the ISA missiles to home in on his ship disturbed many fans of the show. Although there is an acknowledgement in this episode that the Doctor disapproves of homicidal violence when Riddell chooses anaesthetic stun guns to ward off the dinosaurs, the Doctor contradicts this by murdering Solomon. Yes, Solomon is a psychopathic killer, rather than an 'innocent' beast (like the triceratops that he needlessly slays, or even the velociraptors that later attack the gang), but the Doctor could have imprisoned Solomon rather than let him die on his ship. The disquiet among fans at the Doctor's out-of-character murder of Solomon was so considerable that it led to Moffat referencing it in the series finale, *The Name of the Doctor*. Since Chibnall is such a big fan of *Doctor Who*, it is surprising that he makes the Doctor act out of character in this way. Then again, the Doctor does tend to make such bad decisions when he has not had enough contact with humans, as Amy points out in the following episode, *A Town Called Mercy*.

As Steven notes, the Doctor and Amy's pact that they will be there for each other at the "end" of either one of them is an implicit nod to Amy and Rory's imminent departure. It is also a subtle reference to Matt Smith's probable leaving of the show too. (As readers will recall from the previous book, I predicted that Matt Smith would leave *Doctor Who* during 2013 – although this was practically my only prediction that did come true!) However, as we now know, this scene is a bit of a misdirection on the production team's part with regards to Amy's eventual fate, as we later learn in *The Angels Take Manhattan* that the Doctor can never visit Amy during her final hours, and Amy is only present at the Eleventh Doctor's 'death' in the form of a flashback.

Overall, *Dinosaurs on a Spaceship* is an enjoyable episode that features Chibnall's writing at his best. I very much liked *The Hitchhiker's Guide to the Galaxy*-type sparring between the robots, which was very much enhanced by David Mitchell and Robert Webb's vocal performances. Although I must point out that David Mitchell's robot has all the best lines, and that his passive/aggressive character is quite similar to that of Mark Corrigan, the role that Mitchell plays in the uncomfortably funny British comedy *Peep Show*. Mark Williams is as likeable as ever in the role of Rory's dad, although during the watching of this episode, you do wonder how he is ever going to react to his son's imminent disappearance. The image of Brian eating sandwiches and drinking his tea in the TARDIS doorway above the Earth is a powerful one that I suspect will stay in the mind of many a younger viewer for a long time. Like Steven, I thought that the inclusion of the Indian Space Agency was a great and intriguing addition to this episode, and it would be good if ISA could reappear in a future adventure. I thought Nefertiti was great too (and it is interesting to note that in real life she played a considerable role in her husband Akhenaten's decision to focus Egypt's religion on one god, Aten, rather than the many that they had worshipped previously, so there's a possible influence from the godlike Doctor there). Perhaps I could have done without the friendly triceratops, and the reference to Brian's golf "balls" was perhaps an innuendo too far. The triceratops licking Brian's face was a bit off-putting, and I thought that his explanation about the grass fragrance on them being too irresistible for it was a bit far-fetched. Or maybe not, if this was the triceratops' only encounter with real grass. No doubt many children would have been entertained by the triceratops' gross slobbering though.

It is good that there is a continuation here of this series' theme of the Doctor's anonymity, as Solomon's computer does not recognise the Doctor. Chibnall also touches upon this theme by conveying that Solomon apparently recognises the Doctor; yet, this turns out to be a bit of a tease, as Solomon's anticipation at meeting the Doctor turns out to be nothing more than his need for the medical attention of an actual doctor. Indeed, it is something of a surprise that Solomon focuses his attention on Nefertiti, as his database obviously has no knowledge of the TARDIS either. It seems that Oswin's wiping of the

Dalek Path Web could have affected many other computer systems. Then again, this tease of an ominous mention of the Doctor's name in reference to an actual doctor is something that is recycled in the next episode, *A Town Called Mercy*, which acts (whether deliberately or not) as a very appropriate companion piece to this episode.

3: A Town Called Mercy

Writer: Toby Whithouse
Director: Saul Metzstein
Originally Broadcast: 15 September 2012

Cast

The Doctor: Matt Smith
Amy Pond: Karen Gillan
Rory Williams: Arthur Darvill
Isaac: Ben Browder
Kahler-Jex: Adrian Scarborough
Kahler-Mas: Dominic Kemp
Walter: Rob Cavazos
Sadie: Joanne McQuinn
The Gunslinger: Andrew Brooke
Abraham: Garrick Hagon
The Preacher: Byrd Wilkins
Dockery: Sean Benedict

***Steven's Review*:** Once upon a time, stories of the Old West were the epitome of straightforward, uncomplicated adventure storytelling. Then, in the last two decades or so, the long out of fashion genre was revived, demythologised, and put to use to tell deeper stories in movies like Clint Eastwood's magnificent *Unforgiven*, or the more recent television series *Deadwood*. In the science fiction arena, Joss Whedon's ill-fated *Firefly* constructed its background universe using an intriguing mix of Western and SF elements. Now *Doctor Who* has taken its turn to use a Western backdrop to present a story with some moral complexity. It's not quite as compelling as it could have been, with the ultimate resolution being taken out of the Doctor's hands, but *A Town Called Mercy* is still a beautifully produced and well told tale.

This is an episode that is, first and foremost, a pure pleasure to look at. The story is given an expansive canvas thanks to an extended location shoot in Almería, Spain. The little frontier town of Mercy (population 81) in the year 1870 looks totally authentic – if not to what the Old West was *really* like, then at least to our shared cultural impression of it, due to the *Who* team being able to make use of many of the locations and sets used in classic Westerns like *The Good, the*

Bad and the Ugly. This production is full of wide open, sunny vistas that are even more striking coming after the dark interiors that dominated the previous two episodes.

The Doctor, Amy, and Rory have arrived outside the town by accident – apparently, they had intended to visit Mexico for the Day of the Dead festival. Oddly, Amy and Rory's relationship with the Doctor in this episode doesn't really feel like it's following up on the recent hints that the Doctor is gradually disengaging himself from their lives ("weaning us off you," as Amy said to him last week). Instead, it's as if we've gone back to when they were permanent travellers aboard the TARDIS, before 2011's *The God Complex*. On the other hand, the Doctor does let slip the fact that he's now 1200 years old – considerably older than the age he claimed to be at the time of his "death" last season – which may or may not become significant later. It's still an open question exactly where these last few adventures for Amy and Rory take place along their and the Doctor's timeline – or even what order they are taking place in. Hopefully the next two episodes will make that clear.

Writer Toby Whithouse's previous *Doctor Who* episodes (*School Reunion* in 2006, *The Vampires of Venice* in 2010, and the aforementioned *The God Complex*) have all been heavily concerned with Doctor/companion relationships, but this one is different. Apart from one scene between Amy and the Doctor, she and (especially) Rory are very much in the background here.

Their initial entry into the town gives director Saul Metzstein the first of several chances to riff on classic Western tropes – the slow tracking shots following them down the empty main street, the suspicious stares of the townsfolk watching them, and so on. Naturally, when they enter the saloon, the honky-tonk piano immediately stops and everyone turns to look at the strangers in the sudden silence. Matt Smith's skill at physical comedy makes for a wonderfully hilarious moment as he saunters over to the bar and growls to the barmaid, "Tea, but the strong stuff. Leave the bag in" – and then gets the toothpick he had been chewing stuck with his mouth wide open. (Incidentally, it was interesting to hear him being called "Son" a couple of times in this episode – one of the relatively few occasions when the youthful appearance of Smith's Doctor has actually been commented on. As usual, when the story turns serious, Smith has no difficulty in being a dominating presence even opposite much older actors.)

It becomes apparent that this is not going to be just a historical tourist visit to the Wild West when the Doctor's announcement of his title brings an immediate reaction from the townsfolk, and one of them asks him straight out, "Are you an alien?" When the Doctor admits he is, they grab him, carry him to the edge of the town and throw him across the line of sticks and rocks marking the town's boundary. Prevented at gunpoint from coming back in, he can only watch as a menacing figure – the Gunslinger – comes out of the desert towards him. This creature is a hugely effective piece of costume and make-up design, with the silhouette of a classic Western gunfighter augmented by technological components such as a bionic eye reminiscent of the Borg from *Star Trek*. We had already seen him in the teaser at the top of the episode, at the end of a battle in some other place, killing a man with the futuristic weapon built into his right arm. When his victim asked if he was "the last one," the Gunslinger replied, "There's one more – the Doctor."

The Doctor is saved by the town's marshall, Isaac, who allows him back inside the boundary. The episode's most high-profile guest star, Ben Browder (of *Farscape* and *Stargate SG-1* fame), is surprisingly underused in this role – his main function, at least initially, is to deliver some necessary exposition. Isaac explains that the Gunslinger has kept the town isolated for three weeks – he put up the boundary line around the town and has been preventing anyone from going in or out. Everyone will die of starvation unless they hand over the "alien Doctor" the Gunslinger is demanding.

There's a moment of humour from Amy ("Why would he want to kill you? Unless he's met you…"), but the confusion is soon resolved as Isaac introduces a man named Kahler-Jex. He is indeed an alien, the last survivor of a group targeted by the Gunslinger, who crashed here and has become accepted as a valued member of the town, thanks to his medical skills which saved the people during a cholera outbreak, and the lighting and heating he has provided for the town using the power from his ship. The episode will end up exploring Jex in depth, and Adrian Scarborough gives a brilliant performance throughout, bringing out all the many facets of this complex, contradictory man.

To start with, though, it looks like a simple rescue operation is in order, and with Rory and Isaac distracting the Gunslinger, the Doctor borrows a horse (whose name is a clever riff on the Johnny Cash hit *A Boy Named Sue*) to ride back to the TARDIS. Meanwhile, Jex and Amy share a moment, as he tells her why he is happy to stay here rather than return home. "Here I could start afresh – could remember myself and help people. That's all I ever wanted to do, end suffering."

Ironically, Jex's own compassion for the town ends up being the seed of his downfall, as the Doctor stumbles across the cable running from his ship to the town, follows it back to the crashed ship, and manages to access Jex's personal files. He rushes back to confront Jex with the truth – Kahler-Jex's people were involved in a years-long war, and Jex was a member of a weapons development team conducting experiments on people in order to develop cyborgs like the Gunslinger. At a horrific cost, they won their war, after which the cyborgs were decommissioned – except for one which went rogue, hunting down and killing its creators.

The Doctor: "What I don't understand is why you haven't just walked into town and killed him."
The Gunslinger: "People will get in the way."
The Doctor: "Look, you want justice, you deserve justice. But this isn't the way. We can put him on trial…"
The Gunslinger: "When he starts killing your people, you can use your justice."

And so the scene is set for the central conflict of the story – a debate on whether Jex's undoubtedly good acts since he arrived in the town can balance his deeds of the past, and what, if anything, should be done to punish him – and indeed, who has the right to make that judgment. The varied ethics of all the characters (including the Gunslinger, who deliberately refrains from attacking Jex while there is a chance that innocents might be caught in the crossfire) are examined. Isaac sticks to his contention that "America's the land of second chances," showing no interest in making judgments about Jex's past deeds. Rory is quite willing to hand Jex over to the Gunslinger for execution, to Amy's dismay – but one can imagine him, as a medical man himself, being particularly revolted by Jex's actions. Amy demands another solution be found, and turns to the Doctor – but he's brooding in silence, having already figured out that there are no good options.

As for Jex himself, he first expresses an "ends justify the means" attitude, telling how the cyborgs' creation actually saved lives by bringing a quick end to the war (an obvious parallel to the arguments over the atomic bombing of Japan in 1945). But when the Doctor angrily yells at him ("How many died screaming on the operating table before you had found your advantage?"), he fires back, showing a perceptive insight into the similarities between them:

Jex: "Looking at you, Doctor, is like looking into a mirror – almost. There's rage there, like me. Guilt, like me. Solitude. Everything but the nerve to do what needs to be done. Thank the gods my people weren't relying on you to save them."
The Doctor: "No, but *these* people are!"

It's an excellent piece of scripting that turns the Gunslinger's search for an "alien Doctor" from a bit of clever plotting sleight-of-hand (designed to mislead the audience into thinking at first that he's after *our* Doctor) into a central thematic strand of the episode. The Doctor's harshness toward Jex is driven partly by his consciousness of his own questionable past actions – in particular, of course, the destruction of his own people in the Time War, which has hung over him since the beginning of the revived series in 2005. Matt Smith does a fine job of showing the Doctor's disturbance at the parallels between himself and Jex; after Jex's taunt he erupts into anger, dragging Jex to the town boundary and throwing him across it.

In her best scene of the episode, Amy grabs a gun and orders the Doctor to let Jex back inside. The Doctor explodes at her, yelling about all the people who have died because he showed mercy to villains like the Daleks or the Master, who have killed again after he has let them go. I got the impression that the Doctor knew he was not being entirely reasonable here, since Jex is clearly not like those unrepentant enemies at all – and indeed, Amy manages to snap him out of it with an unwitting callback to the dangerous psychological places David Tennant's Doctor went to at the end of his tenure (*The Waters of Mars*):

Amy: "See, this is why you shouldn't travel alone."

At this point events spiral out of control, as Jex is confronted by the Gunslinger, and Isaac is accidentally killed protecting him. Before he dies, Isaac makes the Doctor promise to protect Jex – even as the Gunslinger threatens to kill everyone unless Jex is surrendered to him by noon tomorrow. Now the acting marshall of the town, the Doctor orders Jex placed in a cell, as the townsfolk become nervous and a lynch mob forms. In a nice reversal of the confrontation with Amy, the

Doctor manages to talk them down from violence – so much so that the young man who is (somewhat implausibly) their spokesman becomes an active ally. On the whole, though, the townspeople are very much in the background during the second half of the episode – although there is a nice touch for Classic Series fans as the town's undertaker (with his running gag of measuring the Doctor for a coffin) is played by Garrick Hagon, looking considerably different from when he was a fresh-faced rebel leader in the 1972 story *The Mutants*.

The debate between the Doctor and Jex continues, in an extended scene where both Smith and Scarborough are brilliant. Toby Whithouse is excellent at distilling the essence of his story down to a one-on-one confrontation between the Doctor and his opponent (there are similar scenes in *School Reunion* and *The Vampires of Venice*). After his outburst of anger earlier, Scarborough keeps Jex carefully restrained, needling the Doctor (though not really maliciously), until a crucial moment:

Jex: "It would be so much simpler if I was just one thing, wouldn't it? The mad scientist who made that killing machine, or the physician who's dedicated his life to serving this town. The fact that I'm both bewilders you."
The Doctor: "Oh, I know exactly what you are, and I see this reformation for what it really is. You committed an atrocity and chose this as your punishment."

The Doctor's passionate climax ("Justice doesn't work like that. *You* don't get to decide when and how your debt is paid!") seems to impress Jex enough that he opens up about his true fears. Scarborough is particularly moving as Jex tells how his culture believes that the soul after death must climb a mountain carrying the souls of all the people it has wronged: "Imagine the weight I will have to lift."

By the end of the scene, they have both come to an understanding that the Doctor is not going to give Jex up to the Gunslinger. Jex tells him, "We all carry our prisons with us. Mine is my past, yours is your morality." It's a slightly forced moment, but this gives the Doctor an idea for how to get Jex past the cyborg – a creature whose "prison" is its reluctance to risk harm to innocents. In another excellent usage of a standard Western trope, we have a high noon showdown between the Doctor and the Gunslinger in the centre of town. Except that instead of him using a gun, the Doctor's sonic screwdriver disorientates the creature, and the Doctor and his friends provide a distraction that allows Jex to flee back to his ship.

As I suggested at the top of this piece, the conclusion of the story is a slight let-down after the excellence of what has preceded it. The Doctor doesn't manage to come up with a real conclusion for the story; the best he can do is ensure that Jex escapes, drawing the Gunslinger after him to continue their fight elsewhere. The town and its people are saved, but the issues between the Doctor and Jex that loomed so large earlier are basically left unresolved, thereby allowing the story to avoid making a specific commitment about who is right and who is wrong. Instead, a definite ending is provided by having Jex decide to activate his ship's self-destruct sequence. Scarborough sells the moment very well, but it makes nonsense of the whole elaborate showdown scene – if he was willing to take that way out, Jex could simply have walked up to the Gunslinger and given himself up.

The framing sequence enclosing the whole tale, where a woman's voice tells us how over the succeeding decades the Gunslinger became an almost mythological figure – the outsider perpetually protecting the town of Mercy – seemed like an unnecessarily sentimental finishing touch. But on the whole, *A Town Called Mercy* is a very enjoyable episode, with a great guest cast and an excellent production. Despite the Western background, it's not action-packed – quite a talky episode, in fact. But then, it's an episode with a lot to say.

Steven's Classic Who DVD Recommendation: Doctor Who's previous foray into the Western genre came way back in 1966, during the Classic Series' very eclectic (and, alas, now mostly lost) third season. *The Gunfighters*, starring William Hartnell, with Peter Purves and Jackie Lane, places the Doctor and his friends among the events of the famous 1881 gunfight at the O.K. Corral. It's also a deliberate comedy, which for a long time had the reputation in *Who* fandom as the worst *Doctor Who* story ever made – but once it actually became available again on video (and later DVD), it was rapidly rehabilitated as its wit and charm were recognised. It's not without its goofy aspects (the American accents, in particular, range from hilarious to painfully bad), but I think it's great fun and well worth watching.

Kevin's Review: *A Town Called Mercy* is certainly very sunny and cinematic, but like the similarly themed *Dinosaurs on a Spaceship*, it has a very unsavoury twist in the tail. Like the 2011 series opener, *The*

Impossible Astronaut, this episode celebrates *Doctor Who*'s current success in America by doing a homage to the Western. In *The Impossible Astronaut*, the Western theme was touched upon lightly, consisting mainly of the Utah setting, the Doctor wearing a Stetson, and River Song's similar adoption of gunslinger fashion. River Song, like the Gunslinger in this episode, shoots a hole in a Stetson, but this was mainly a continuation of her destructive approach to the Doctor's headgear that first started in the 2010 series finale, *The Big Bang*. These Western touches were pleasing and humorous additions to the visually stunning 2011 series opener. In the case of *A Town Called Mercy*, it appears that Toby Whithouse has borrowed Brian Williams' trowel to dig up and scatter every Western cliché in the book at his script. There is the overzealous undertaker that takes every opportunity to measure up our hero (Garrick Hagon also played the short-lived Biggs in *Star Wars Episode IV: A New Hope*), the 'gunfight' at high noon, the lynch mob, the saloon madame, the weary sheriff, etc. Yes, this adventure may be sunny, but any estate agent will tell you that you can make any dump look pretty if the sun shines on it. (For a more vivid postmodern British television stab at the Western, one could look at the 1967 episode of *The Prisoner* called *Living in Harmony*, which, according to Wikipedia, has been mistakenly claimed to be the first Western to be shot (ahem) for British TV. Which it wasn't, since the Classic Series *Doctor Who* adventure *The Gunfighters* was aired in 1966. Ironically, *Living in Harmony* was not aired as part of *The Prisoner*'s first run in America, since CBS is thought to have believed (incorrectly) that its anti-violence stance was a critique of the Vietnam War.)

Admittedly, the Doctor chews on a cocktail stick instead of a cheroot, but this is seemingly the only innovation that *Doctor Who* has to offer the Western. (The Doctor gave up smoking in his first televised adventure in 1963's *An Unearthly Child*, after a caveman hit him on the head while he was lighting a pipe.) So boring are all these clichés that I'm beginning to wonder if the Doctor's cocktail stick is as anachronistic as the phone charger that Rory left in Henry VIII's en suite. Wikipedia is mysteriously silent as to the origins of the cocktail stick. Of course, there will be another nod to the Doctor's great and deserved US audience in two episodes' time (*The Angels Take Manhattan*), which is a far more pivotal part of our heroes' narrative than this pompous adventure. The Stetson is a great example of this dull-wittedness, as Whithouse has the Doctor pointlessly repeat "I wear a Stetson now" from *The Impossible Astronaut*, which has none of the resonance of "Bow ties are cool". (Although, if the Doctor had met Susan the horse before in a previous adventure, then the above statement about him wearing Stetsons *now* would make more sense. As well as speaking horse, one of the revelations in this episode is that the Doctor really does have a Christmas list, as he first mentioned in *Dinosaurs on a Spaceship*!)

Even the science fiction element of this story is highly derivative. Don't get me wrong – I am not saying here that 'borrowing' tropes from other narratives is wrong, as some of *Doctor Who* at its very best is highly derivative. For instance, a very apt comparison off the top of my head is 1975's *Genesis of the Daleks*, which many fans (like myself) believe to be the best ever *Doctor Who* story (where, appropriately enough, the Time War that is the source of the Doctor's angst here first began). I have often thought that *Genesis* was Terry Nation's riff on the spaghetti Western *A Fistful of Dollars*, as the Doctor acts as a kind of lone warrior caught up between two warring factions, the Thals and the Kaleds. Dalek creator Terry Nation did like to 'borrow' elements from popular film, such as his first *Doctor Who* script, *The Daleks*, which 'fluidly links' to George Pal's 1960 movie of H. G. Wells' *The Time Machine*. Of course, *A Fistful of Dollars* is famously a remake of the 1961 Japanese Samurai movie, *Yojimbo*. This film's director, Akira Kurosawa, said the 1942 film noir *The Glass Key* was an inspiration for his movie. Whichever way you look at it, these are all successful dramatizations of the same classic narrative. (The Doctor, of course, was a man with no name a whole year before Clint Eastwood's 'man with no name' hit cinema screens in 1964's *A Fistful of Dollars*. This episode, like the previous one, plays with the Doctor's desire for anonymity, which led to him stage his own death in the previous season. At the beginning of *A Town Called Mercy*, it would appear that the Doctor has failed dismally, as his enemies are still apparently hunting him down. As in *Dinosaurs on a Spaceship*, it turns out that the protagonists are just looking for a physician, instead of 'the' Doctor.) Of course, *A Town Called Mercy* was filmed in Almería, Spain, on the set where a certain movie called *A Fistful of Dollars* was also filmed…

As well as stealing wholesale from the Western, Whithouse also purloins liberally from *The Terminator* franchise, as he has obviously based the Gunslinger on Arnold Schwarzenegger's cyborg (albeit the more likeable and friendly version from *Terminator II*.) Whithouse has stated that his intention here was to do a revamp of Mary Shelley's *Frankenstein*; this would be fine, if it the *Doctor Who* production team had not already done this theme to death and brought it back to life again a dozen times before. For instance, *Genesis of the Daleks* is probably the most prominent retelling of *Frankenstein* in *Doctor Who*, with Davros playing the role of the mad scientist that creates a monster that later turns on him (i.e. the Daleks). (Admittedly, Davros is perhaps the most severely crippled of the stereotypical presentation of mad scientists onscreen with disabilities that started with Rotwang in Fritz Lang's *Metropolis*.) Unusually, Whithouse does not present Jex as a mad scientist with a disability (possibly because we now live in a more progressive era), although he does have a blue streak on his face that closely resembles the lazy kind of facial prosthetics that *Star Trek: The Next Generation* preferred for almost every kind of alien race. Isaac, Mercy's town marshal, seems like a decent enough fellow, but I suspect that even he would probably have shot Jex dead when he crash landed if he had looked like a bug-eyed monster. Then again, Whithouse is merely being faithful to Mary Shelley's original in his revitalisation of a stitched up corpse as the monster, instead of paying homage to Lang's twist of creating a disabled and mentally unstable scientist.

No, Whithouse's creation of Jex is more akin to the Nazi doctors that the US put on trial at Nuremberg following the Second World War. If we are looking for historical examples of how such villains were punished, then Nuremberg's record is that of the 23 Nazi doctors on trial, seven were executed, seven were acquitted, while the rest were sentenced to life imprisonment. However, like Davros, Jex does claim that his main motivation was to shorten a war that had gone on for far too long by creating a devastating weapon (although Davros is lying when he says this, as he is actually intent on creating a superior species). The Nazi doctors committed unethical and cruel surgical procedures on innocents that were mostly unrelated to the war effort. In comparison, the United States granted Nazi rocket scientists anonymity and protection to prevent their knowledge from falling into the hands of the Soviet Union during the Cold War. So, as Steven points out, America's atom bomb scientists who invented an impersonal weapon that could kill thousands at a stroke, were treated far more favourably than their colleagues in the medical field who also killed people; the difference being that they got their own hands dirty by personally carrying out loathsome surgical procedures at the Nazis' vile concentration camps. If Jex's case were held today in a British court of law where the death penalty is no longer an option, then he would face life imprisonment if found guilty, which is presumably the approach that Amy would go for and most other people in the viewing audience.

Despite all the moral debate in this episode about what to do with Jex, no one pays any attention to what punishment the Gunslinger should face. This may be due to the Gunslinger appearing to be so impregnable and powerful that punishing him is not a realistic option. Or it could be due to Whithouse's presentation of the Gunslinger as being so sympathetic that this is not an option. Of course, in the original *Frankenstein*, Mary Shelley did give the monster a voice, so that readers could identify with his desperate plight, despite his many crimes. Obviously, the Doctor should not put the Gunslinger on trial for what he did during the Kahler war, as he was not in control of his own actions. However, the Gunslinger is guilty of the crimes that he commits after he had developed sentience and a conscience. Of course, when we first encounter the Gunslinger, he shoots Kahler-Mas before Mas can shoot him, but the Gunslinger's intention was always to murder the Kahler who had participated in his creation, like Jex. (Whithouse gives all the Kahler characters three-letter names, which gives the impression that the Kahler are improbably small in number!) Beyond this, the Gunslinger also shoots and kills Isaac. This incident is obviously an accident, yet it is still manslaughter. The Gunslinger's motive for his rampage – bloody revenge – is no different from that of Sharez Jek's in the Fifth Doctor's final adventure (*The Caves of Androzani* in 1984). While Jek restricted humanity's access to spectrox (a drug that could greatly expand lifespan) in his bid to force them to hand over the man responsible for his debilitating injuries, the Gunslinger goes even further by denying the people of Mercy access to food and water to force them into handing over Jex. Having written that, it is clear that the Gunslinger's threats against 'innocent' people are empty, as he never shoots any of the townspeople in anger despite having many opportunities to do so, and, as mentioned above, his killing of Isaac is quite clearly an accident.

In my review of the previous series finale (2011's *The Wedding of River Song*), I wrote how Moffat's vision of *Doctor Who* had seemingly morphed from "dark fairytale" to "comic book fantasy". In this light, I must write that I could easily see the Gunslinger featuring within the pages of British comic book *2000 AD*. Indeed, the

Gunslinger reminded me of a similar character from *Doctor Who*'s own comic book history, Abslom Daak, a 26th Century thug that the courts found guilty of "twenty-three charges of murder, pillage, piracy, massacre and other crimes too horrible to bring to the public attention". Upon sentencing, the judges give Daak the choice of execution or becoming a Dalek Killer. Daak obviously chooses the latter and takes to his task with aplomb, and ever more diligently after the Daleks kill the only woman he has ever loved (and more importantly, probably the only woman who has ever loved him). With his favourite chainsword in hand, Daak is not unlike the Gunslinger, although thankfully he is a little more charismatic.

The Doctor offers the Gunslinger a similar chance of redemption by protecting the peace of Mercy. Unlike Steven, I thought that there was some poignancy in the voiceover describing this solitary figure as "their very own angel who fell from the stars", as this is obviously meant as an analogy to the Doctor. (This is a rather more successful one than the very forced analogy that Whithouse made between the Doctor and the minotaur at the end of *The God Complex* in 2011.) Indeed, as the voiceover that starts the episode states, "When I was a child, my favourite story was about a man who lived forever, but whose eyes were heavy with the weight of all he'd seen. A man who fell from the stars." Of course, a year after *A Town Called Mercy*, in the 50th Anniversary episode *The Day of the Doctor*, we learn that the Doctor does finally find a way to end the Time War without committing the genocide of all Time Lords apart from himself. This revelation does reduce the power of the Doctor's confrontations with Jex that allude to this genocidal act, which is still very real to the Doctor (especially as he has not prevented it yet). Unlike Solomon, the Doctor believes that he has committed genocide from afar. (Although Solomon got the robots to eject the Silurians, you can imagine him standing there witnessing it, rubbing his hands with glee, unlike the torture that afflicts the Doctor after the monstrous act that he commits to bring the universal suffering of the Time War to an end.) Perhaps this is why the Doctor shows no mercy to Solomon, because he feels that this is how the universe should have punished him for his act of genocide, which went very much against his true nature. In the previously mentioned *Genesis of the Daleks*, the Doctor ignored the Time Lords' command to destroy the Daleks at their birth, choosing only to delay their development for a while. This was because the Doctor knew that out of their evil much good would come, such as peoples that had previously been at war with one another uniting to fight off the Daleks.

The resolution of this episode's moral dilemma is rather unsavoury, as Jex chooses to commit suicide rather than to bring his battle with the Gunslinger to the innocent peoples of another planet. However, I suppose Whithouse is being faithful to the original *Frankenstein* here, as the monster in Mary Shelley's novel decides to commit suicide, wracked in the grief that it has hounded its creator to death. Fortunately, as above, Whithouse offers an alternative to the Gunslinger making the same choice. Which is just as well, as the Gunslinger's self-destruction would have been a cop-out (and besides, we have already had at least one tortured monster commit suicide in the revived series – *Dalek* – in 2005). Unlike Steven though, I can understand why Jex chose to do this rather than submit to his fate, as Jex does make it clear that he does not want to cause the Gunslinger any more suffering by providing him with an opportunity to kill again. (However, the ending of this episode did confuse me at first, as I thought that Amy and Rory had bizarrely decided to stay in Mercy without any way of getting home to 2012. It was only when I watched the episode again that I heard the sound of them getting into the TARDIS!)

In the previous book, I had a bit of a moan about why Moffat had chosen to specify the sexual orientation of the Fat Thin Anglican marines in the 2011 mid-season finale *A Good Man Goes to War*. My objection was mainly due to "hanky panky" (as 1980's series producer John Nathan-Turner put it) being banned from the TARDIS and the programme in general during the Classic Series. However, I have now changed my mind on this, especially as Moffat presented the Fat Thin Anglican marines as being married, so revealing that the Church of the 50th Century no longer has a hang-up about homosexuality or same sex attraction. Having recently done a lot of research in this area, I have to say that I truly hope that it does not take the Church of England until the 50th Century to recognise and permit same sex marriages. Russell T Davies, in a recent interview with *Attitude* magazine, pointed out that there are still incredibly no gay characters in the *Star Wars*, *Star Trek*, and Disney franchises. While the Doctor's remark to the pastor in this episode that his male horse is actually "called Susan, and he wants you to respect his life choices" is rather a throwaway remark at first glance, it is important that the Doctor does say it to a priest. This is because much of the persecution that gay people have unjustly suffered at the hands of the law throughout the centuries has ultimately derived from the Bible. While this, and Oswin's mention that the first person she fancied was a girl called Nina, are throwaway lines, it would be great if they contributed to the chipping away of the historical injustice and persecution that gay people have faced throughout the centuries.

4: The Power of Three

Writer: Chris Chibnall
Director: Douglas Mackinnon
Originally Broadcast: 22 September 2012

Cast

The Doctor: Matt Smith
Amy Pond: Karen Gillan
Rory Williams: Arthur Darvill
Brian Williams: Mark Williams
Shakri: Steven Berkoff
Kate Stewart: Jemma Redgrave
Ranjit: Selva Rasalingam
Laura: Alice O'Connell
Arnold Underwood: Peter Cartwright
Orderly 1: David Beck
Orderly 2: Daniel Beck
UNIT Researcher: David Hartley

Steven's Review: Two weeks ago, writer Chris Chibnall presented *Dinosaurs on a Spaceship,* an episode which I felt started poorly but became steadily more interesting and enjoyable as it went along. Regrettably, the reverse is the case with his second episode of the season, *The Power of Three*. The first half is captivating, full of intriguing mysteries and great character moments, but when it comes time to resolve the plot, the story simply falls to pieces.

The most important aspect of this episode is its focus on the relationship between the Doctor and his friends Amy and Rory. Having travelled with him in the TARDIS for nearly two years, at the end of 2011's *The God Complex*, the Doctor deposited them back on Earth, giving them a chance to make their own lives apart from him. But he still turns up on their doorstep every so often to whisk them away on an adventure, and this episode opens with Amy and Rory realising that they will need to make a choice between "real life" and "Doctor life." The catalyst for this choice will be what Amy's opening voiceover calls "the year of the slow invasion – when the Doctor came to stay."

As I have remarked before, Chris Chibnall is clearly a fan of the Jon

Pertwee era of the Classic Series. His previous stories have drawn heavily on the Silurian tales of that time, and here he creates a story with a similar feel to many in Pertwee's first three years (1970 to 1972), when the Doctor was mostly on present-day Earth, assisting the UNIT military organisation in fighting off a succession of alien invasions of the planet (or at least, southern England). The form that this particular invasion takes is wholly original, however – overnight, millions of small, identical, featureless cubes materialise all over the world. No one has any idea where they came from, or what they are for. They are a complete mystery, and defy all attempts at analysis. As months pass in which the cubes do absolutely nothing, they simply become an accepted part of everyone's lives – people start sticking Post-It notes on them, using them as paperweights, and so on.

In a throwback to the style of the Earth invasion stories seen in the era of former showrunner Russell T Davies, we see montages of newsreader footage to show the worldwide scale of the phenomenon, interspersed with amusing celebrity cameos – in this case, from Professor Brian Cox and Sir Alan Sugar (Britain's version of Donald Trump). One of those earlier invasion stories – the rather straightforward two-parter *The Sontaran Stratagem* and *The Poison Sky* – was helmed by director Douglas Mackinnon back in 2008. Here, he gets the chance to be more visually tricky, in keeping with the heightened directorial style of the show under current showrunner Steven Moffat – this episode contains several slickly edited montages, lots of swooping, speeded up camera moves around people, and inventive touches such as indicating the passing of time by inserting month names quirkily into the scene rather than as straightforward captions.

The Doctor soon turns up, and uses Amy and Rory's house as a base while he investigates the cubes. The first hint of tension between them comes as Rory goes off to his job at a local hospital, much to the Doctor's surprise ("Of course I've got a job. What do you think we do when we're not with you?" "I'd imagined mostly kissing…"). Further discussion is forestalled by the arrival of UNIT troops (whose code names like "Trap One" are a nice callback to the Classic Series), who have detected the Doctor's presence. They are led by a capable, no-nonsense woman named Kate Stewart, who quickly enlists the Doctor's help. In a lovely touch for long-time fans, she turns out to be the daughter of the Doctor's old friend Brigadier Lethbridge-Stewart, played by the late Nicholas Courtney (whose death in early 2011 prompted a touching reference to his character in *The Wedding of River Song*).

Another welcome return in this story is for Mark Williams as Rory's father Brian. Now well acquainted with the Doctor after the events of *Dinosaurs on a Spaceship*, he enthusiastically joins in the adventure, happily reeling off a string of possibilities for what the purpose of the cubes might be. His patient, methodical approach to investigating the cubes ("Brian's log, day 67") forms a hilarious counterpoint to the Doctor slowly being driven mad by his failure to crack the problem within a few days. We saw in 2010's *Vincent and the Doctor* how the Doctor lacks patience with the ordinary passing of time, and here there's a great comedy sequence as the Doctor tries anything to keep himself busy – and manages it for all of one hour.

The Doctor decides he has to get away for a while ("Quick jaunt, restore sanity"), and the first real conflict occurs as Rory declines to leave what the Doctor disparages as his "little job." ("It's not little, it's important to me. Look, what you do isn't all there is.") The acting from all the principals is excellent throughout the episode, and especially here; Karen Gillan is superb at showing Amy's real discomfort at the argument, looking resolutely away from both of them and not wanting to get involved. But their trajectory away from the Doctor continues – Amy commits to being a bridesmaid at a friend's wedding, while Rory agrees to work full-time at the hospital.

Rory: "So, the Doctor's God knows where, the cubes aren't doing anything at all… Did real life just get started?"
Amy: "I like it."
Rory: "So do I."

Meanwhile, the mystery of the cubes deepens as various seemingly random plot elements crop up – a spooky child observing events in the hospital, and patients being abducted by a pair of nurses who are actually monsters in human form, with surgical masks that conceal a cube-shaped hole in place of a mouth. Unfortunately, neither of these will ever be properly explained, which is surprising given that there was certainly time to do so; at just over forty minutes long (not counting the end credits and "Next Time" trailer), this episode is the shortest stand-alone story of the entire new series. (In fact, given that all of the stories in the Classic Series were told over multiple episodes, it's fair to say that *The Power of Three* is the briefest story *Doctor*

Who has ever told.)

Really, the story of the strange cubes simply provides a thread that ties together several independent scenes (or short stories) charting the changes in the relationship of the Doctor to Amy and Rory. Another inserted story begins as the Doctor interrupts Amy and Rory's party to celebrate their wedding anniversary and spirits them away. In another quick burst of "Doctor life", they get to celebrate their anniversary at the Savoy hotel in 1890, get caught up in a Zygon invasion, and then Amy somehow accidentally marries Henry VIII. It's also possible that the events of *A Town Called Mercy* take place during this period of traveling, given the Doctor's remark in that episode about Rory leaving his phone charger in Henry VIII's en suite, and Amy saying at the end about wanting to get back before their friends start noticing them aging. When they do finally get back to their party (having been away for seven weeks), Brian notices their changed clothes, and presses the Doctor on what happens to the people who travel with him.

The Doctor: "Some left me, some got left behind, and some – not many, but… some died. Not them, Brian. Never them."

This rather sombre confession seems to signal that the Doctor has recognised he can't drag Amy and Rory around the universe with him anymore. He surprises Amy by asking if he can stay with her and Rory, admitting frankly that "I miss you."

Suddenly the cubes start activating, examining and probing the capabilities and defences of the humans near them. With many people injured, Rory is called in to work, and takes Brian with him to the hospital. Meanwhile, the Doctor and Amy are summoned to meet with Kate Stewart at UNIT's base beneath the Tower of London (as seen in David Tennant's first story *The Christmas Invasion*). He discovers that there are several locations around the world that appear to be controlling the cubes, but before any action can be taken against them, the cubes all shut down again.

The emotional high point of the episode comes as Amy and the Doctor find a quiet place to have a heartfelt discussion about her and Rory's growing desire to stop their adventuring with him. Karen Gillan and Matt Smith make the most of the great material they are given here, as the show once again throws a spotlight onto the Doctor's relationship with his companions. When Amy tells the Doctor about how she and Rory have been making a life for themselves here and that "the travelling is starting to feel like running away," the Doctor lets his guard down with a speech (beautifully delivered by Smith) that is reminiscent of the first really memorable moment in the revived series back in 2005 – Christopher Eccleston's "turn of the Earth" speech in the opening episode, *Rose*.

The Doctor: "I'm not running away… This is one corner, of one country, in one continent, on one planet that's a corner of a galaxy that's a corner of a universe that is forever growing and shrinking and creating and destroying and never remaining the same for a single millisecond, and there is so much, so much to see, Amy. Because it *goes*, so fast. I'm not running away from things, I'm running *to* them – before they flare and fade forever."

Possibly the best work Chris Chibnall ever did during his stint as head writer on *Torchwood* was the episode *Fragments*, the penultimate episode of that show's second season. He took the various scraps of backstory for the main characters that had been floating around over the previous two years and wove them into a compelling collection of vignettes that deepened the characters considerably. So too here, he combines the speech above with the observation, first expressed by David Tennant's Doctor in *School Reunion*, that the Doctor's friendships with his human companions must always be transitory ("You can spend the rest of your life with me, but I can't spend the rest of mine with you"). It's clear that the Doctor is very aware that the Ponds' time with him will soon end. When Amy, in a slightly brittle manner, asks him why then he keeps coming back for them, his reply shows the new angle that Chibnall has come up with:

The Doctor: "Because you were the first. The first face this face saw. You're seared onto my hearts, Amelia Pond… I'm running to you, and Rory, before you… fade from me."

The idea that the Doctor would imprint on the first person he encounters after the trauma of regeneration, and find it hard to let that person go, is so fitting that I'm amazed in retrospect that no one seems to have thought of it before. (For one thing, it also provides a neat explanation for why David Tennant's Doctor found it so hard to move on from the loss of Rose Tyler.) The scene comes to an end on a lovely moment of calm, with Amy resting her head on the Doctor's shoulder.

Cleverly, the Doctor's line to Amy – "You always get what you want" – leads us back into the main story, as it triggers a sudden realisation about why the cubes shut down again. Unfortunately, at this point we're only a little over halfway through the episode, and it's mostly downhill from here.

Having gained the information they needed to launch an assault, the cubes reactivate, stealing electrical power and using it to cause a wave of heart failures around the world. The Doctor is attacked, but manages to stay on his feet thanks to his non-human nature (i.e. his two hearts). Meanwhile, more arbitrary elements are introduced to keep the story moving forwards, as Brian gets abducted by the "nurses" and taken through a dimensional portal which – by a coincidence which is incredibly convenient for the plot – just happens to be disguised as a goods lift in the very hospital Rory works in. Rory manages to follow after them, and finds himself in a spaceship in orbit.

The Doctor and Amy arrive at the hospital, trying to track down the portal. In an "action" sequence that is all but incoherent, the Doctor discovers and deactivates the android child in passing (meaning it had no real effect on the plot whatever), and Amy restores his failing heart with a spot of defibrillation only slightly more convincing than her CPR in 2011's *The Curse of the Black Spot*. The contrast with the earlier, deeply felt scenes is extreme, as Amy falls back into generic companion mode and Matt Smith has nothing but his Doctor's trademark surface wackiness to work with.

Amy and the Doctor soon find their way onto the spaceship – one of seven connected to Earth through dimensional wormholes – and the explanations start coming as the Doctor confronts the occupant, a member of "the Shakri". These are apparently some powerful race that the Doctor's people think of as semi-mythical bogeymen – "the pest controllers of the universe," as the Doctor describes them. They speak of themselves as in service to something called "the Tally", and they have decided that the human species must be wiped out before it can expand into space. But given that we have never heard so much as a hint of their existence before, the effect is rather like that in the 1987 story *The Greatest Show in the Galaxy*, which sprang equally unexplained and unforeshadowed super-beings (the "Gods of Ragnarok") on the audience at a late stage in order to raise the stakes.

It's a great pity that the originality of the "invasion of the very small cubes" (to use the Doctor's phrase) turns out to have such an uninspiring reason behind it. It reminded me of the way the Patrick

Troughton story *The Mind Robber* presented a fantastically imaginative scenario involving a land where fictional characters come to life, before revealing that it was the cover for just another boring invasion of Earth. The most interesting thing about the confrontation scenes is watching Steven Berkoff – an actor of stature in every sense – generate effortless menace in such an underwritten role. The script gives him almost nothing, but thanks to good costume and make-up design, and his own deep-voiced, very controlled performance, Berkoff somehow conjures up an air of danger about the Shakri.

After a few rather facile assertions from the Doctor about the good qualities of humanity, the Shakri simply disappears – it was only an automated holographic interface ("like a talking propaganda poster"), and the Doctor is left to deal with the cubes unhindered. In a frankly lazy plot resolution, it takes literally no more than a few waves of the Doctor's sonic screwdriver to end the invasion. All those cardiac arrests that loomed so large earlier are somehow reversed with no further ill effects. I was particularly annoyed by the blatantly recycled music cue played over the sequences of the world returning to normal. This piece has been used several times over the past two seasons, always associated with emotional moments in Amy's personal story; it seemed very inappropriate to press it into use as generic "happy ending" music.

Fortunately, after that low point, the episode recovers to end well, first with an enjoyable farewell scene between the Doctor and Kate (and I hope we get to see her again someday), and then with a quiet dinner scene with the Ponds. When he goes to leave, the Doctor no longer urges Amy and Rory to come with him, but it's Brian who points out that *they* are finding it difficult to give him up, and pushes them to go with the Doctor one more time. In a lovely touch, the Doctor offers to take him as well, but Brian refuses in his understated way ("Someone's got to water the plants").

And so Amy and Rory take off with the Doctor again, although Amy's final voiceover line about "cubed" meaning "the power of three" seemed like a very forced *non sequitur*, an attempt to justify the surging music over the shot of the three of them entering the TARDIS together for the last time. I actually did appreciate that moment, but it was because of behind-the-scenes knowledge – this episode was in fact recorded after the next one, and that final shot was Karen Gillan and Arthur Darvill's last work on *Doctor Who*. It's a pity that it comes at the end of an episode that has many good points, but (to use the

Doctor's phrase) flared, and then faded.

Steven's Classic Who DVD Recommendation: For a look at how the Classic Series handled the present-day alien invasion scenario, try *The Claws of Axos*, starring Jon Pertwee and Katy Manning, along with Nicholas Courtney as Brigadier Lethbridge-Stewart.

***Kevin's Review*:** *The Power of Three* is an action-packed thrill-a-minute episode that also contains a considerable degree of poignancy. Its premise is similar to that of penultimate episode of the 2006 series, *Army of Ghosts*, which featured mysterious alien figures appearing on Earth, which humanity gradually begins to accept and incorporate into their lives. Russell T Davies, of course, followed *Army of Ghosts* with *Doomsday*, which famously tells of how the Doctor lost his beloved Rose to a parallel universe. It is probably not an accident on the part of the production team that a similar fate lies in wait for the Ponds… This episode is not only important in prefiguring Amy and Rory's fate, it also lays the foundations for the 50th Anniversary adventure, *The Day of the Doctor*, which will again feature the Brigadier's daughter, Kate Stewart, and a resurgence of the Zygon threat.

Chris Chibnall should probably stick to writing upbeat and comedic episodes like this and *Dinosaurs on a Spaceship*, as they are much more enjoyable than his more serious *Doctor Who* adventures. Of course, there are some sombre notes here, such as when the Doctor admits to Rory's father, Brian, that some of his companions have died due to travelling with him. There is also a hint of this when the Doctor and Amy discuss his lifestyle outside the Tower of London, where the Doctor effectively says that he is running to Amy and Rory before they flare and fade… Unlike Steven, I do not mind too much that this episode is wrapped up quite quickly, as Chibnall achieves the task that Moffat set him – to make us cherish the Doctor's relationship with the Ponds far more so that their departure in the next episode will be even more gut wrenching for us. The production team also cheekily play with our emotions by suggesting that the Ponds are going to die. As the old saying goes, "pride comes before a fall", so it's clear that Amy's belief in 'the power of three' at the end of this episode is somewhat misguided. However, I think that it's more than a little cruel that it's the affable Brian who makes Rory and Amy's mind up about travelling with the Doctor again, and thence to their doom. Perhaps one day the Doctor will get an opportunity to tell Brian what happened to Rory and Amy while he patiently waters their plants for them. (There were plans for Brian to learn of Rory and Amy's fate via a DVD extra that the production team ran out of time to film. This extra, written by Chibnall, would have involved Brian being given the news via a letter from Rory, passed on a week after he and Amy left by the son they adopted in 1946.)

There are some excellent comedic scenes in this episode. *The Apprentice*'s Lord Sugar is quite an unremitting taskmaster in his demand that his acolytes go out and sell an object that is freely lying about everywhere. Professor Brian Cox has a splendid cameo in which he ponders about whether the cubes could be extraterrestrial, and somehow manages to avoid saying his favourite word ("universe"). It is amusing that the Doctor can do five million keepy-uppies, given Matt Smith's former footballing prowess (although Rory must surely be fibbing when he says that this has only taken the Doctor an hour, along with all the vacuuming, creosoting, and mowing). In what might almost be a prefiguring of Andy Murray's winning of Wimbledon in 2013, it's funny to hear that the Doctor still has a pair of Fred Perry's shorts that he hasn't given back. It's also quite funny that Amy seriously latches onto the idea of being a bridesmaid, even though bride-to-be Laura is quite evidently trying to break it gently to her that she hasn't chosen Amy. (Chris Chibnall is possibly echoing the very popular 2011 movie *Bridesmaids* here that features two women's fight to become their best friend's maid of honour. I take my hat off to Chibnall here for making this a same sex wedding a year before the UK government legalized such ceremonies.)

It's clear that Chibnall does take a great deal of care in crafting his scripts, and that he evidently does do quite a bit of research. This is given away by the Doctor saluting one of the Savoy's staff as "Auguste", for French chef Auguste Escoffier was indeed an integral part of the hotel's early success. It is also true that the exact derivation of the Yorkshire Pudding is unknown, so the Doctor could have invented it. There's also some lovely nostalgia in this episode, with clips of the Doctor's previous adventures with the Ponds (which are again designed to make us miss them even more). It's lovely to see the Doctor and the Ponds sitting on the sofa tucking into fish fingers and custard, the culinary dish that this Doctor famously served up during his first encounter with the young Amelia Pond.

Steven Berkoff is brilliantly understated (but still menacing) in his role as the Shakri. His cameo appearance struck me as being akin to one of several mysterious aliens that appeared on *Space: 1999* in the 1970's, albeit with better make-up and costuming here (Berkoff made an early appearance in Gerry Anderson's preceding show *UFO*). However, the best guest appearance in this episode is that of Jemma Redgrave as Kate Stewart, who does a brilliant job of bringing the Brigadier's daughter to life. I don't know how much research she did for the role, but some of her mannerisms were spookily like Nicholas Courtney's, the actor who portrayed the Doctor's long-time friend, Brigadier Lethbridge-Stewart. Consequently, it was brilliant to see her play Kate again so soon afterwards in *The Day of the Doctor*, in what I hope very much will be a recurring role.

One of the running themes in this first part of the seventh series has been the Doctor's desire for anonymity. However, no matter how many computer records containing his name are erased, it doesn't matter a jot as long as there are people out there who love and cherish him, and who tell tales about him, such as the Brigadier has done with regards to his daughter. As a result, it does not take long for UNIT to track him down at the Ponds' house. Yet there is a suggestion that Kate Stewart does respect the Doctor's privacy, as she only lets the troops out to hunt him down in the event of an emergency.

This episode also touches on the other theme of this half-series: genocide, as the Shakri are intent on killing all humans on Earth. This explains their use of the cubes, as humans are the only species on Earth with a great enough intelligence to make them philosophise about these mysterious objects, and to bring them into their own homes. Due to the cubes' intense scrutiny of humanity, the Shakri are able to devise a way of killing them that will not affect any other creatures on Earth. The Shakri's justification for this act of mass murder (that it is necessary to prevent humanity wreaking great destruction when they become capable of intergalactic travel) is similar to my pessimistic view of humanity's future that I portrayed in the *Doctor Who* scripts that I wrote as a teenager in the late 80's. So I can sympathise with a narrative which presents humanity as the monsters that must be stopped rather than aliens beings. In a similar way, the Doctor I created (in the wake of Sylvester McCoy's later dark performance) was a rather haunted figure, much like Christopher Eccleston's Ninth Doctor. However, the Eleventh Doctor has a much more optimistic view of humanity as "creatures of hope", and so finds a way to reverse the Shakri's genocidal plan. In the same way, there is perhaps some early hope here that the Doctor can reverse his own genocide of the Time Lords, which he achieved from afar, especially as this went against his nature. "Remotely isn't my style," the Doctor says here, perhaps unconsciously referencing his uncharacteristic activation of the Moment, the weapon that wiped out the Daleks and the Time Lords. Just as the Doctor will later find a way of preventing his act of genocide, there is perhaps some hope that the Doctor will one day find a way of resolving another seemingly intractable problem: that of getting Amy and Rory home again…

There are a few duff moments in this episode, especially during its conclusion, as Steven comments. First off, the Doctor appears to steal Rory's idea of using mass defibrillation to revive the people who had already suffered cardiac arrest in what appears to be a rare bit of clumsy dialogue. As Steven writes, it is more than a little convenient for the plot that the hospital in which Rory works has a portal to a Shakri ship. There's no particular explanation for the physical appearance of the alien hospital orderlies, apart from it being creepy. (By contrast, Steven Moffat provided a good narrative explanation for why people's faces horrifyingly morphed into gas masks during 2005's *The Empty Child/The Doctor Dances* adventure.) Twin actors David and Daniel Beck insert a great deal of menace during the fleeting glimpses of these two orderlies. It was also unclear whether Amy and the Rory were able to rescue the other patients that the alien orderlies had kidnapped before the Shakri ship exploded. In addition to this, although there is an international alert to remove all the cubes from buildings, no one thinks to remove the cube that the girl outlier droid clutches, and so discover her true nature sooner. If the resolution is more than a little magical, involving not much more than the Doctor waving his magic wand (i.e. sonic screwdriver), then this is possibly due to a reference by Chibnall to the American drama series *Charmed*, which featured a family of witches who wielded the "power of three". (Then again, the Shakri possibly were not expecting a presence of a technologically advanced higher intelligence like the Doctor on Earth, due perhaps to the Doctor's partial success in his bid for anonymity. Although it's telling that one cube that observes him closely responds by shooting at him with a laser.) Although the Doctor tells Brian that he took Rory and Amy away for seven weeks during the party, the aftermath of the Zygon infiltration of the Savoy looks to be set in winter, i.e. about six months after they had arrived at the hotel. Then again, the snow that falls on our heroes in this scene could be ash from the destroyed Zygon ship, in the same way that debris from the

Sycorax ship fell on London as snow in 2005's *The Christmas Invasion*. Despite these quibbles, Chris Chibnall very successfully plays with our emotions in this episode by reliving the Ponds' greatest triumphs with some laughs, while also paving the way to their doom…

5: The Angels Take Manhattan

Writer: Steven Moffat
Director: Nick Hurran
Originally broadcast: 29 September 2012

Cast

The Doctor: Matt Smith
Amy Pond: Karen Gillan
Rory Williams: Arthur Darvill
River Song: Alex Kingston
Julius Grayle: Mike McShane
Sam Garner: Rob David
Hood: Bentley Kalu
Foreman: Ozzie Yue
Old Garner: Burnell Tucker

Steven's Review: Over the course of its original run, *Doctor Who* seldom used to make a big deal of the times when one or more of the Doctor's companions departed the series. There were exceptions, of course, but the majority of companions would receive no more than a brief, bittersweet moment at the end of an otherwise unrelated story. Sometimes even less – Liz Shaw, the first companion to Jon Pertwee's Doctor, simply vanished from the show after the 1970 season, with only a brief mention in the first story of the following year to cover her absence. Such a thing would be unthinkable in the new series, where the increased complexity of characterisation and the centrality of the Doctor's companions within the arc of the stories has meant that all of the episodes where a companion departs have been special, emotional high points. In *The Angels Take Manhattan*, the finale for Series 7's first stretch of five episodes, showrunner Steven Moffat takes on the responsibility of providing a fitting and satisfying payoff for two and a half years of adventuring for Amy and her husband Rory, and succeeds brilliantly.

As often with Moffat's scripts, even just recapping what happens in the episode can be quite a challenge because he is amazingly adept at making plot elements serve multiple purposes simultaneously, at linking lines of dialogue across the episode so that they contrast or reflect each other, and at introducing new twists that throw an entirely new light on what has gone before. The pre-credits teaser, a lovely *noir* pastiche from director Nick Hurran, provides a good example. We are in 1938 New York, where a private detective, Sam Garner, is hired by a Mr. Grayle to investigate what he says are statues that move by themselves – but only when you're not looking at them. Directed to an apartment block "where the statues live," Garner finds something even more disturbing – a room containing a bedridden, dying old version of himself. Then the statues start coming after him, and pursue him up to the roof, where he is confronted by a Statue of Liberty whose face is disturbingly different from the version familiar to us…

The moving statues might be a mystery to Garner, but they certainly aren't to any *Doctor Who* viewer of the past five years. The Weeping Angels, probably the greatest new monster created so far in the new series, have been a fan favourite ever since their sensational debut in Moffat's 2007 episode *Blink.* With their combination of a brilliantly convincing design and (far more unusual) a wonderfully original concept, they are clearly one of Moffat's greatest contributions to the show. I did think he mishandled them slightly when they were brought back for 2010's two-parter *The Time of Angels* and *Flesh and Stone*, when they gained the ability to speak (at least, using others' voices), and the clever idea that even the audience never sees them move was abandoned in favour of more conventional attempts at creepiness. Thankfully, no such lapses occur in this episode – the angels are back to their inscrutable, menacing best, with a few new developments thrown in for good measure.

But to return to Moffat's multi-layered plotting – after the opening titles, we get a whole new perspective on what we just saw as we join the Doctor, Amy, and Rory in the present day, enjoying a picnic in Central Park. The Doctor is happily reciting to them from a book, a hardboiled detective yarn called *Melody Malone* ("A Private Detective in Old New York Town") – and it becomes obvious that we have been watching a dramatization of the fiction he has just been reading. A second viewing of the episode reveals that the director has signposted this in retrospect, so to speak – a great many of the shots and camera moves in the teaser are replicated later in the episode, in the "real" part of the story. That even includes the striking final moment, when Garner is framed so as to appear within the fanged mouth of the Statue of Liberty angel (an idea, incidentally, which Moffat has said people have been suggesting to him about twice a week ever since *Blink* aired) – the exact same sequence will later occur with Rory.

The early picnic scenes have some lovely, relaxed banter between the three leads. Beneath the surface, though, Moffat is busy establishing elements that will be significant later, such as the fact that Amy now uses reading glasses, or the Doctor ripping out the last page of the book because "I hate endings." Hilariously, Amy and Rory start kissing and then riff on the fact that (as of the end of last season) the Doctor is actually their son-in-law ("We have company" "I'll get a babysitter"). While Rory goes off to get coffee, the Doctor continues reading to Amy, but the line between fiction and reality starts blurring as the realisation gradually strikes first the audience, then the Doctor and Amy, that the book isn't just paralleling events on screen, but actually narrating them.

The Doctor: (*reading*) "He said, 'I just went to get coffees for the Doctor and Amy. Hello, River.'"

Rory has been transported back to 1938, where he encounters River Song, who is investigating the angels infesting New York, under the alias of Melody Malone. The first shot of River meeting Rory ("Hello, dad") is the point where the fictional recounting gives way to real events. She and Rory are captured and taken to Mr. Grayle, who is now revealed to be a wealthy collector who thinks his house is under siege by the statues – with good reason, since he has a basement full of cherub-like baby angels and keeps another, full-sized one chained up and badly damaged ("I wanted to know if it could feel pain"). Grayle momentarily turns off the lights, and his prisoner angel grabs River's wrist. Meanwhile, Rory is thrown into the basement, with only a box of matches for illumination. Moffat shows he hasn't lost the ability to come up with scary new concepts – the cherubs, with their high-pitched giggling in the dark, are unnerving, and the moment when one is suddenly right there beside Rory, blowing out his lighted match, is memorable. Another clever idea is that the angels no longer just send people back in time as in *Blink*; they have taken over an entire apartment block where they can feed off the "time energy" from their victims, keeping them imprisoned until they die.

Back in 2012, the Doctor is still reading from the book (which, as is now obvious, River will eventually write), providing a real-time narration of events in 1938. River manages to use this slender thread of communication to provide the Doctor with a signal to home in on. The ingenious "conversation" via an inanimate object recalls the DVD

Easter egg recording in *Blink*, while the Doctor's method of sending a message across time using Grayle's Qing dynasty vases is reminiscent of River's message to him at the start of *The Time of Angels*. (Unfortunately, I have to point out some faulty research on Moffat's part here. We see a brief flash of the Doctor visiting ancient China, and the on-screen date of 221 B.C. is indeed the start of the *Qin* dynasty – but the *Qing* dynasty, the one associated with the vases, actually dates from nearly two thousand years later.)

The TARDIS arrives (knocking out Grayle in the process), and while Amy goes off in search of her husband, the Doctor greets his own spouse, as he and River immediately fall back into the comfortable teasing relationship that has developed over the past two and a half years. The Doctor's new determination to keep a low profile in the universe has affected River as well, resulting in her pardon and release from prison:

River: "Apparently the man I killed no longer exists… It's almost as if someone's gone around deleting himself from every database in the universe."
The Doctor: "You said I got too big."
River: "And now no one's heard of you. Didn't you used to be somebody?"
The Doctor: "Weren't you the woman who killed the Doctor?"
River: "Doctor who?"

Now that Grayle has served his purpose of bringing everyone together in 1938, the plot quickly disposes of him via the angels, and the rest of the episode is devoted exclusively to the four principals. Just as in previous Moffat season finales *The Big Bang* and (to an extent) *The Wedding of River Song*, the outside universe barely impinges upon the story; there are periodic portentous warnings about New York or even the whole planet potentially being ripped apart, and so on, but the focus is very much on our four central characters negotiating Moffat's maze of plot twists. The real enemy is not so much the angels as Time itself – or rather, predestination and foreknowledge. The idea that once you know any aspect of your personal future it's locked in, unable to be avoided, has been used by Moffat for poignant effect as long ago as the end of *The Girl in the Fireplace* in 2006. Here it's driven home several times in succession, as characters gain insight into their future and wish they hadn't. As the

Doctor says, “Once we know what’s coming, it’s written in stone” – with the camera ironically lingering on a shot of a gravestone with Rory’s name on it, foreshadowing his final fate.

When he finds Grayle’s angel is holding River’s arm in an unbreakable grip, the Doctor is upset because earlier Amy had read a couple of lines from the *Melody Malone* book before he could stop her, hinting that he would have to break something – which it’s now obvious refers to freeing River’s arm from the angel. Since they can’t simply read ahead in the book without spoilers, Amy cleverly suggests using the list of chapter titles as hints to find Rory. Unfortunately, they find that Rory has already been transported by the angels to their “battery farm” apartment block (which, amusingly, the script earlier noted is located in Battery Park). Far worse, the Doctor accidentally catches sight of the last chapter title – “Amelia’s Last Farewell”. Faced with evidence that he is about to lose Amy, he angrily tells River she has to change the future by getting her wrist away from the angel without breaking it, and leaves her to it. When he comes back with Amy from the basement, he is delighted to see that River has managed to free herself, but (somewhat implausibly) fails to notice the stiff way she is holding her arm, and when he grabs it she yelps with pain.

The Doctor: “Why did you lie to me?”
River: “When one’s in love with an ageless god, who insists on the face of a twelve-year-old, one does one’s best to hide the damage.”
The Doctor: (*gently taking her arm*) “It must hurt… Come here.”
River: “Yes. The wrist is pretty bad, too.”

It’s always great to watch Matt Smith and Alex Kingston playing these two characters, especially with the material Moffat has given them here. Smith’s ability to convey a maturity that belies his youthful appearance (which it’s easy to take for granted, now that he’s demonstrated it so many times) makes the relationship entirely convincing as one between equals – two characters that have come to thoroughly understand and respect each other. That, in turn, means the twenty-year age difference between the actors does not need to be downplayed or obscured in any way; indeed, it’s deliberately used here to emphasize River’s pain at the inevitability of her aging while the Doctor does not.

Not that she’s looking for pity – when the Doctor gives up some of his regeneration energy to heal her arm, she berates him for being a sentimental fool, and storms out in embarrassment. Amy follows her, and we have a rare moment between these two – who are, after all, mother and daughter. It's a pity that the relationship between River and her parents has ended up receiving little emphasis compared to that between her and the Doctor. (In this episode, even the Doctor is startled, after Amy and Rory are gone, to recollect that River has just seen her parents disappear.) I suppose there would always have been the temptation to exploit the age-reversal for comedy, but scenes like River's quiet confession of her fears to Rory in *The Impossible Astronaut* worked very well (admittedly, though, he wasn't aware of the relationship at that point). Here, too, Alex Kingston is touching as River passes on to Amy a piece of heartfelt advice: "Never let him see the damage, and never, ever let him see you age. He doesn't like endings."

Eventually, they track down Rory to the angel-controlled apartment block and catch up with him, but just a little too late. The Doctor is unable to prevent disaster when Rory encounters the aged, dying version of himself, a helpless victim of the angels. It's a moving moment when the Doctor instantly understands that old Rory was so delighted to see Amy because he had been kept apart from her for so long. To Rory, it's a fate literally worse than death, and so it's totally believable when, after trying to escape the angels, he and Amy end up on the roof of the building facing the Statue of Liberty angel, and Rory realises he can create a paradox by jumping from the roof, which will erase this entire timeline and wipe out the creatures.

Gillan and Darvill rise to the occasion with the unrestrained emotion of this intense scene, as Rory begs Amy to help him, and she eventually climbs up onto the ledge with him and decides they should jump together. I suppose some could see their all-encompassing devotion to each other ("If it was me, could you do it?" "To save you, I could do anything") as being hopelessly sentimental or corny, but it felt fully sincere to me, earned and justified by the way we have seen these two come together over the last two and a half years. There's also an unexpected shaft of humour as Rory makes a joking reference to his repeated resurrections in previous stories. Set within what is actually a very dark scene, the line is all the more effective. (In fact, with the mutual suicide idea here, and the wrist-breaking earlier, this story has some unusually grim material for *Doctor Who*.)

Again, the Doctor arrives too late; he can only watch as Amy and Rory fall. Indeed, from the point where he realised Amy's fate, he has been unusually passive, carried along by events. His only contribution to Rory's plan to create a paradox by escaping the angels was to say how unlikely it was to work. However, despite his fears, everything seems to work out – the paradox is created, the timeline is reset, and they all end up in the same 2012 graveyard we saw earlier, with Amy and Rory still alive. It would be a happy ending – except for our memory of that gravestone shot from earlier. The twist in the tale comes when Rory catches sight of his own grave; his fate is sealed, as a solitary weak, surviving angel touches him and he vanishes into the past.

After all the twists of predestination, it's ironic that Amy is left free to choose her own fate – and yet there is of course no choice to be made at all. The Doctor's desperate exhortation, "Come along, Pond!" no longer works, as Amy Williams gives up her childhood friend for good and lets the angel take her to her husband. Karen Gillan sells this hugely emotional climax magnificently, culminating in a final heartfelt farewell to her "raggedy man" as Amy disappears forever. Her name appears on the gravestone below Rory's, signalling that she too is now part of an unavoidably fixed timeline.

Matt Smith shows the Doctor bereft and grieving, in much the same way David Tennant's Doctor was after Rose Tyler was lost to a parallel universe in *Doomsday*. It did somewhat surprise me that the Doctor seemed so unprepared, though – it doesn't seem to square with the hints dropped in previous episodes (especially *The Power of Three* last week) that the Doctor was aware of Amy and Rory's upcoming fate. The story also insists that Amy and Rory are now as inaccessible to the Doctor as Rose was – the timelines are apparently too scrambled now in that place and time period for the TARDIS to handle. (I suppose that could be seen as a justification for the New York setting, which otherwise played remarkably little part in the story. If the Doctor can never go there again, it couldn't be a city that the show uses regularly, like London.) Considered in the cold light of day, it seems implausible that the Doctor can never even pay a visit to them – River's vortex manipulator seemed to be able to cope with the time distortions, and even if that is ruled out now due to the creation of the paradox, surely he could always land in New Jersey and take a bus. In the final analysis, though, while Amy and Rory's separation from the Doctor may not be completely watertight plotwise, emotionally it's absolutely the right ending.

It's a real wrench to see two major characters depart with such finality. They've been a huge part of the show over the past two and a half years – the longest-serving companions of the new *Who* series; even over the entire fifty-year run of the show, only a handful of characters have been around for longer. They were given a wider range of material to work with than any previous companion, as Steven Moffat wove the companions' lives into the structure of the stories to a greater extent even than Russell T Davies before him. My favourite Karen Gillan performance is probably her *tour de force* double role in 2011's *The Girl Who Waited*, while Arthur Darvill deserves particular praise for the way in which he handled Rory's steadily increasing importance in the stories, starting as a definitely subsidiary character and progressing to the point where Amy and Rory were fully convincing as a couple. After the work they've put in on *Doctor Who*, I hope both of them go on to even greater successes.

Meanwhile, the Doctor, as always, has to carry on even after the irrevocable loss of his two close friends. He still has River, who promises to travel with him "wherever and whenever you like," but immediately qualifies that to mean not on a permanent basis ("One psychopath per TARDIS, don't you think?"). She helps him to start moving on, matter-of-factly talking about the *Melody Malone* book which she now has to write, and promising to send it to Amy to be published – and to get her to write an afterword for him. I think this story shows that River still works well as a character even now that all the mysteries of her identity and origin have been revealed, but she is definitely more suited to being someone the Doctor's life occasionally intersects than a constant companion.

As she says, though, the Doctor shouldn't travel alone. Fortunately, we've already had a taste of how well Matt Smith works with Jenna-Louise Coleman, who will be introduced as his new companion this Christmas, which makes the wait of three months until then one of pleasant anticipation. For now, Moffat brings the story of The Girl Who Waited and The Boy Who Waited For Her gracefully to a close, as the Doctor races back to their picnic spot in Central Park to find the last page he tore out from the book earlier. Matt Smith is superb in his non-verbal reactions as Amy's last message sounds in voiceover (and it becomes an even more impressive feat if you watch the behind-the-scenes footage, which revealed that this intimate moment was actually recorded on location with several hundred fans nearby watching him).

Amy's message asks the Doctor to do one last thing for her. In a perfect coda, Moffat brilliantly links the end of Amy's story to the beginning, as he ties up a loose end from *The Eleventh Hour*, left hanging for two and a half years. A flashback to that episode reminds us of how the seven-year-old Amelia packed her suitcase and waited in her backyard for her magic Doctor to return from a promised five-minute trip – only to end up waiting for twelve years. But the odd, isolated shot inserted into the climactic sequence, of the young girl suddenly looking up and smiling as she hears the TARDIS arriving, could only previously be explained as a dream premonition of the now grown-up Amy, who was about to be awakened by the return of the Doctor into her life and the chance to finally join him. Now the truth is revealed – it was *not* a dream; at her future self's urging, the Doctor did return to give the little girl hope during her long wait, telling her stories of the adventures to come.

Regardless of whether you believe that Moffat really did have all this planned from the start, it's beautifully consistent with the theme of fairytale and storytelling that has permeated his entire era. "We're all stories in the end," the Doctor tells the sleeping Amelia in *The Big Bang* – and at the end of that episode Amy is able to bring him back from nonexistence by remembering the story he planted in her mind. Even in this, her last episode, she wanted the Doctor to read to her from the book that would soon blend into the story of her life. The freeze-frame ending (for long-time fans, a flawless evocation of our last sight of Sarah Jane Smith in 1976's *The Hand of Fear*) is the perfect way to finish – the little girl smiling into the sky, waiting for her adventures to start. As the last line of the episode tells us: "This is the story of Amelia Pond. And this is how it ends…" – and ends well.

Steven's Classic Who DVD Recommendation: The one occasion when the Classic Series did take the time to weave the departure of a companion through her entire final story was with 1973's *The Green Death*, starring Jon Pertwee and Katy Manning. It was the culmination of a three-year stint on *Doctor Who* for Manning and her character Jo Grant, whose gradual turning away from the Doctor and embrace of a new direction in her life was marvellously written and played. The final scene is an emotional high point of Classic *Who*, well able to stand comparison with the similar moments in the new series.

***Kevin's Review*:** This is a very emotional episode of *Doctor Who* that certainly had me weeping at the end; proof, if any be needed, that I ain't no stone angel. Having written that though, I must admit that I did detect a few chinks in Steven Moffat's storyline here, which he usually plots far more intricately.

Then again, as showrunner, Moffat's already played a huge role in the plotting of the five episodes that make up the first half of Series 7. For instance, we get to see here the reading glasses that were first mentioned via a voicemail from Amy's opticians at the beginning of *The Power of Three*. In this previous episode, Amy told the Doctor that she thought that she and Rory had been travelling in the TARDIS for ten years of their lives (which would probably make them the Doctor's most constant companions, apart from possibly his granddaughter, Susan.) The Doctor dipped in and out of the Brigadier and Sarah Jane Smith's lives on and off as they aged, but even Sarah Jane didn't travel with him for a decade. This is possibly why the Doctor's companions usually tend to young adults, before they "flare and fade", as the Doctor himself put it in *The Power of Three*. This seems a rather an ageist policy on the Doctor's behalf that especially distresses the aging River Song. Then again, it could be that this Doctor, very aware of his own imminent death in his last regeneration, is more fearful of mortality than most, especially as this will mean the extinction of his own species.

Another running theme that Moffat picks up in this episode is the revelation that the Doctor has been actively deleting his name from every known database in his bid to achieve anonymity. So successful has he been in this that it has led to the authorities to release and pardon River Song, as it appears that there is no longer any record of the person that she is supposed to have killed. This is an apt occasion for Steven Moffat to provide a gentle reminder for the "oldest question in the universe" by getting River to playfully ask, "Doctor who?" As we know from 2011's *Let's Kill Hitler* and *The Wedding of River Song*, this question is prophetically linked to the Eleventh Doctor's demise, which comes into fruition during Matt Smith's final outing, *The Time of the Doctor*. Names are very important here, as from River's revelation that she is a Professor, we know that she is now closer to her death, as seen in 2008's *Forest of the Dead*. However, as I write this, we are just over a month away from the airing of Peter Capaldi's first *Doctor Who* adventure. I wonder how River Song will react to seeing the Doctor looking a tad more aged than her? Of course, since the Doctor will have a new life cycle, he will be both potentially older and younger than her! (I'll stop here, as my previous predictions for future *Doctor Who* dramas rarely come true. Although it's fun to keep a record of these speculations.) When you intricately plot stories over many seasons, as Moffat does here, then it's inevitable than a few mistakes will creep in here and there, as I think occur in this episode.

Of course, one character who does come eye to eye with a memento mori in this episode is Rory, who witnesses his death of old age. Although the aged Rory's room is quite nondescript, this scene did remind me of astronaut David Bowman's witnessing of his bedridden old age in a rather more stylish and neoclassical setting at the end of *2001: A Space Odyssey*. Although the monolith in Stanley Kubrick's movie appears to be made of stone, just like the Weeping Angels, it seems to have more benign (if enigmatic) intentions than they have. Moffat does have a tendency to recycle ideas, and so here, just as in their original appearance in 2007's *Blink*, the Weeping Angels feed on the energy they create by sending hapless humans back in time. (During 2010's *The Time of Angels/Flesh and Stones*, the Angels displayed a tendency to creep up on people and kill them mainly by snapping their necks. This is perhaps a tactic the Angels adopt when weak and hungry, like the Angel that captures River by the wrist in this episode.) Not only does Moffat display a subtle allusion to Kubrick, he also shows a more obvious reference to Russell T Davies' *Doctor Who*, by presenting a wounded Angel, bound in chains, much like the Doctor's nemesis in *Dalek*. Only four episodes ago, we saw Moffat's previous nod to this 2005 adventure, since he also showed a Dalek bound in chains in *Asylum of the Daleks*. Grayle, the villainous Angel collector in this episode, is a rather less well-developed version of Henry van Statten from *Dalek*, who was also American. Moffat has stated while he was in the process of writing this episode, he debated over whether he should feature the Daleks or the Weeping Angels, so it is possible that Grayle originally kept a Dalek left over from 2007's *Daleks in Manhattan* bound in chains, which Moffat then changed to a Weeping Angel.

Grayle's name seems to suggest that this is going to be a narrative about a knight-errant's doomed quest for immortality, so it's fitting that he's dispatched halfway through by the source of his fascination. Moffat doesn't explain how Grayle came to capture this Angel in the first place, or how he was able to injure it, which could be quite a big hole in the plot of *The Angels Take Manhattan*. It is possible though that this injured Angel is just bait to lure in our heroes, for what could provide a better meal for the Angels than an experienced time traveller like Rory Williams? It may be that the Angels, so well-fed from their battery farm at Winter Quay, have gotten a little bit cocky and a bit too big for their stone boots by trying to procure such a massive feast. Indeed, it is noticeable that the Angels don't kill Grayle until he has achieved their purpose. For, if they can turn any statue into an Angel, why do the Angels not use a statue from Grayle's own collection inside his mansion to kill him? He has at least one golden statue of a feminine figure that would be ideal Angel material. The suggestion that Grayle keeps the Angels at bay using mere locks and bolts appears to diminish them in this episode otherwise. It is also a bit odd that Grayle correctly guesses that River is an archaeologist, rather than just an antiques lover, when she correctly identifies a Qing vase. (Although this is probably due to Moffat getting his Qin and Qing dynasties mixed up, as Steven points out.) Grayle is not the only collector of bits and bobs in this episode, as before the Doctor leaves the TARDIS to meet River again, he pauses to inspect that his appearance is suitable via a shiny sign that seemingly comes from a NATO vessel built by Rolls Royce. Since the demise of the Time Lords, the Doctor has evidently replaced parts of the TARDIS with human bric-a-brac! However, when we next see the TARDIS console in *The Snowmen*, the Doctor has removed all this junk, perhaps because he does not want to be reminded of humanity in the wake of Amy and Rory's departure.

There is a 'blink-and-you'll miss it' echo of the Angels' first adventure *Blink* in this episode (when the Doctor and Amy hurry through the giant video screens in Times Square), as one of the screens shows an eye blinking. On the whole though, I think the Angels in this episode are shadows of their former selves. For instance, their pursuit of Rory (their main meal) is ponderously slow. Indeed, for much of this episode, the Angels are far too static. For instance, River doesn't keep her eyes constantly on the Angel that holds her, often turning her head away to talk to someone. Likewise, during the very compelling scene where Rory and Amy decide to commit suicide in order to bring about the time paradox that will poison the Angels' food supply, they quite often forget to look at the massive Angel Statue of Liberty, so allowing it ample time to bring the Angels' plan to fruition if it had wanted to. Despite the Doctor's assertion that 'the city that never sleeps' is a brilliant place for the Angels, I would have thought that this was a logical non sequitur. For surely, if there's always someone awake in New York, how can the Angel Statue of Liberty ever move without being seen? This is especially so when you consider how noisy it is when it moves through the city, despite its short journey to Battery Park. (It would appear that the Angels only have this effect on their sentient prey, as it would be a bit of a bore for them if they had to interrupt their hunt of a hapless human due to a squirrel observing them.)

Indeed, I wasn't very convinced by the Angel Statue of Liberty. Perhaps it would have been better for the production team to use some CGI to animate the Angel's growl, or maybe a way could have been found to show Liberty stomping through the streets of Manhattan much as the Cyberking did through London in *The Next Doctor*. No doubt this was an additional expense that the production team could not afford, or maybe it was because this scene in the 2008 Christmas Special was so heavily criticised by fans due to it being so unrealistic for humanity to forget the Cyberking's attack on what was then considered to be the capital of the world. Just like in the wake of the Cyberking's assault, the Silents must be very busy erasing the memory of anyone that sees the Statue of Liberty's awesome journey! (Incidentally, I must point here that the real Statue has shattered chains around its feet as part of its representation of 'Liberty' and the celebration of the defeat of slavery during the American Civil War. Perhaps Moffat could have utilised this feature to suggest that someone had previously tried to immobilise this errant statue?)

River's having to break her wrist to escape from the Angel appeared quite arbitrary. Although here, of course, it's written in stone. Then again, it would appear that the Doctor has changed the future by not breaking her wrist personally (unless the 'something' that the Doctor broke was always going to be River's heart by being so callous in this scene when he abandons her to free herself). Since River has the vortex manipulator, one would have thought that she could have freed herself by merely teleporting away from the Angel. However, it's possible that River fears that the timelines will be too scrambled if she does this. As Steven points out, the Doctor could get past the fixed point in time merely by going to New Jersey in 1938 by TARDIS, and thence to Manhattan by public transport, but I guess this is not how the Doctor rolls. Besides, even if the Doctor could visit the Ponds, it appears that he cannot take them home to their own time.

For much of this episode, Moffat conveys River's vortex manipulator as unsatisfyingly superior to the Doctor's TARDIS in its ability to nick in and out of congested time traffic. Since the Doctor's TARDIS is dimensionally transcendental, it doesn't matter how big its outer shell appears to be visually. Indeed, there is the suggestion that once River has written the Melody Malone novel, she will somehow send it to Amy to get it published, despite the imminent risk of New York exploding if she crosses the timelines again… Although, having written that, this is possibly allowed, as *The Angel's Kiss* is an integral part of the events in Manhattan in 1938. Since Amy then appears to switch from writing travel articles to fiction (as evidenced by the book called *Summer Falls* in 2013's *The Bells of Saint John*), it's possible that Amy could have written all of *The Angel's Kiss*, not just the afterword addressed to the Doctor. River Song is the most likely candidate to have slipped the book in the Doctor's jacket pocket in the first place, or perhaps some kind Angel put it there as part of their cunning plan? The Angels do, after all, kick off the action by sending Rory back to 1938.

As Steven notes, this episode does have some quite dark notes, such as Rory's suggestion that he may need Amy's help to commit suicide, and his putting of her hand upon his chest… As well as the jokey reference to Rory's several returns from the death, in his anxiety, Rory again expresses his belief that Amy lies about her feelings for him. (Rory shouldn't ever have any more doubts in this department after Amy sacrifices herself to the last Angel, so that she will be with him throughout his exile in the past.) The scene where Rory died of old age was very convincing and brilliantly acted by Darvill. (Although I thought the similar scene of Garner confronting his aged self was less convincing, since Burnell Tucker doesn't look like an aged Rob David, and the older Garner has to say "I'm you. I'm you," to make what is happening concrete. On a side note, I was wondering if Moffat had named this doomed detective after actor James Garner, who played detective Jim Rockford in *The Rockford Files* during the 70's.)

Despite his success at deleting himself from databases throughout the universe, the Doctor can never erase himself from the hearts and minds of his beloved companions, and they live on in his, as we will see in Matt Smith's final episode, *The Time of the Doctor*. Although I have been quite critical of some plot holes in this episode, Moffat does hit exactly the right notes when it comes down to the emotional drama. I did feel quite tearful when it came to Amy's demise, and especially during her emotional and heartfelt afterword, which was pitch-perfect. (By the way, if Amy did age ten years while travelling with the Doctor, then this would make her 33 when the Angel sends her back to 1938; so Amy probably dies in 1992.) Although Amy and Rory do not die, they are effectively dead to the Doctor, as he can never see them again, except through his memories. In this way, *The Angels Take Manhattan* is a very fitting way for the Ponds to end their association with the Doctor.

2012 Christmas Special: The Snowmen

Writer: Steven Moffat
Director: Saul Metzstein
Originally broadcast: 25 December 2012

Cast

The Doctor: Matt Smith
Clara: Jenna-Louise Coleman
Captain Latimer: Tom Ward
Dr Simeon: Richard E. Grant
Jenny: Catrin Stewart
Madame Vastra: Neve McIntosh
Strax: Dan Starkey
Uncle Josh: Jim Conway
Walter: Cameron Strefford
Digby: Joseph Darcey-Alden
Francesca: Ellie Darcey-Alden
Alice: Liz White
Walter's Mother: Annabelle Dowler
Bob Chilcott: Ben Addis
Lead Workman: Daniel Hyde
Clara's Friend: Sophie Miller-Sheen
Voice of the Great Intelligence: Ian McKellen
Voice of the Ice Governess: Juliet Cadzow

***Steven's Review*:** Jenna-Louise Coleman, playing the Doctor's new companion Clara, has certainly received the most protracted and complex introduction into the series of any regular cast member ever. She made a surprise appearance in the opening episode of this season, *Asylum of the Daleks*, portraying not Clara but a different character named Oswin Oswald, a crew member of a far-future spaceship who died after having been captured by the Daleks. This year's Christmas special (like *Asylum*, written by showrunner Steven Moffat), was expected to be the episode that would see Clara introduced and begin her travelling with the Doctor. But Moffat, the master of unexpected plot twists, has faked us out again – apart from one brief glimpse, the Clara we see in this episode is not the companion-to-be. After the events of *The Snowmen*, while we can definitely welcome Jenna-

Louise Coleman aboard *Doctor Who*, Clara remains, for both us and the Doctor, an enigma.

Coleman showed in *Asylum* – where she spent the whole story isolated from the rest of the cast – that she has a mesmerising screen presence, even confined to sitting in a chair, communicating with other characters only over monitor screens. Given far more scope in this episode, she is even more impressive, right from Clara's first appearance. A barmaid working in a London tavern of 1892, her attention is caught by an odd snowman that seems to have appeared instantaneously, just as her back was turned. The Doctor, happening to pass by, takes a brief interest in the snowman, and there is an immediate spark between him and Clara. However, the Doctor has changed – he is no longer interested in solving mysteries, or in making new friends, and simply walks off. Intrigued, Clara impulsively pursues him, leaps onto his carriage, and an amusing shot of her upside-down face saying "Doctor *who*?" launches us into the titles.

The feeling of the show entering a new era is only increased by the unveiling of a new title sequence and theme music. During the five previous episodes, the production team experimented a little with the titles, fiddling with the colours and the texture of the logo, but now we have an entirely new sequence. On the whole I like the changes, particularly the toning down of the bombast of the previous titles – no thunderclaps or lightning flashes, and the blaring fanfares are also now not so prominent. The last part of the sequence (also utilised for the closing credits) is particularly effective, strongly evoking the vortex used in the title sequences of the 1970's. But the first half is a bit of a mess – it seems to be just a random assortment of images swirling around without much rhyme or reason. It is nice, though, to have a brief glimpse of the Doctor's face in the titles for the first time since the show was brought back (something that was a fixture of the Classic Series for all the Doctors apart from the very first one). On the other hand, I could have done without the final gimmick, in which the TARDIS flies towards the camera and the doors open to reveal the opening shot of the first Act in exactly the same way the menus appear for the DVD releases of the Classic Series.

Later in the episode, we will discover that the interior of the TARDIS has also been completely revamped. Michael Pickwoad, the vastly talented production designer largely responsible for *Doctor Who* being one of the best-looking shows on television over the last two years, finally gets the chance to put his stamp on the show's only standing set. In keeping with the changes in the Doctor's character shown in this episode, the whimsy of the previous interior has been dialled back to something much more austere and streamlined. The feeling is once again of being at the control centre of a machine, a vehicle, rather than entering a wizard's home. The only part of the new interior I don't like is the set of counter-rotating rings of lights at the top of the time rotor – an unnecessary embellishment that would be more at home on a game show. Hopefully, directors of future episodes will not feel the need to show these things spinning around madly every time the TARDIS takes off. Other than that minor complaint, though, I have nothing but praise for Saul Metzstein's direction of this episode.

As I wrote in connection with 2011's *Closing Time*, the idea of the Doctor going into retirement – becoming fed up with his unending life of travel, exploration and (usually) doing good deeds throughout the universe – dates back as far as Douglas Adams' tenure as *Doctor Who* script editor in the late 1970's. Adams, advancing the idea in his characteristic comic manner, had the Doctor retiring more or less on a whim. Moffat, however, makes it a logical development of recent events. In the wake of the loss of his close friends Amy and Rory in *The Angels Take Manhattan* – a loss at least partly attributable to his inability to keep himself from dropping into their lives and dragging them into his adventures – it's not at all surprising that the Doctor has become disillusioned and withdrawn.

The Doctor: "Over a thousand years of saving the universe… Do you know the one thing I learned? The universe doesn't care."

It seems very appropriate that the Doctor creates a retreat for himself in the London of 1892. The Victorian era is a period that the show has always had an affinity for, with the Classic Series setting stories there several times – *The Evil of the Daleks* (1967), *The Talons of Weng-Chiang* (1977), and *Ghost Light* (1989) are all high points in *Doctor Who*'s run. In 2005, Victorian-era Cardiff provided the backdrop for the revived series' first historical episode, *The Unquiet Dead*. The period is also the source of a lot of our standard Christmas imagery, making it particularly fitting for a Christmas Special (as seen in 2008's *The Next Doctor*, and even the ersatz Victoriana of 2010's *A Christmas Carol*).

But the significance of the Victorian milieu goes beyond providing the opportunity for the show to present a sumptuously realised period background for the story (something at which the BBC costume and production design departments have always excelled). The Doctor himself has always borne the influence of this period in his manner of dress, especially the original Doctor, William Hartnell. His successors in the Classic Series tended to tone down or caricature the Victorian element in their costumes, but it returned in full force with Paul McGann's short-lived Eighth Doctor in the telemovie that failed to lead to a revival of the series in 1996. When the show actually returned nine years later, it made a deliberate break with the past by putting Christopher Eccleston's Doctor into a simple leather jacket. Only in the last year or so, with Matt Smith sporting a long green coat in some of the later episodes of the 2011 series, has the Victorian element slowly crept back into the Doctor's silhouette.

In this episode, though, the Doctor is presented as fully Victorian, a rather grumpy figure in a dark frock coat and a tall hat that recalls one occasionally worn by Patrick Troughton. Sometimes in *Doctor Who*, it's necessary to suspend one's disbelief at how the people the Doctor encounters generally seem to cope with his odd outfits without comment, but not here. It's disconcerting to see the Doctor, whose clothes usually set him apart from the times and places he finds himself in, fitting in so well. No better method could have been found to visually indicate how the Doctor is trying to suppress his usual nature. And, of course, there's a lovely payoff later when he finally takes an active part in the story, and discovers he has unconsciously put on his normal bow tie before doing so. As he turns back towards the Doctor we know, so too does his outward appearance.

With the Doctor initially refusing to get involved, Moffat needed someone else to take over his usual role of getting mixed up in strange events and setting the story into motion. For this purpose, he makes great use of three characters that he created for 2011's mid-season finale *A Good Man Goes to War*. The pairing of the Silurian investigator Madame Vastra and her maid/lover, Jenny Flint, had made a great impression on their first appearance and were a natural choice to bring back for this story, since they were already based in the correct time period. Adding the Sontaran warrior Strax to serve as their butler was an inspired touch. Together, the three make a kind of steampunk Scooby Gang, no doubt already inspiring plenty of fan-fiction writers. It's certainly easy to imagine a spinoff series being developed around these characters.

Vastra, in a very Doctor-like manner, confronts the villain of the piece, Dr. Walter Simeon, who she has determined has some connection with the strange snowmen that have been appearing. The concept of snow (or rather, an alien intelligence distributed among snow-like flakes) that can mirror the thoughts and feelings of those near it is another neat idea of Moffat's, and he develops it well. The snowmen, with their wide, grinning mouths full of shark-like teeth, are a quirky and memorable monster design, no doubt appropriately scary for *Doctor Who*'s younger viewers. It's probably fortunate, though, that we never see them actually move – like many other *Who* monsters, they are at their best when looming menacingly, rather than lumbering slowly in pursuit of some luckless victim. In fact, apart from the implied massacre of a few nameless workers in the teaser, the snowmen have a fairly minor role in the story. The main focus is a contest of wills between the mysterious intelligence, Simeon, and the Doctor.

Richard E. Grant has had two previous, rather tangential brushes with *Doctor Who* – although both of them, oddly, involved playing the Doctor. Back in 1999, in Steven Moffat's hilarious spoof of the show written for Comic Relief, *The Curse of Fatal Death*, he was one of a whole line of well-known actors playing later regenerations of the Doctor, being given about a minute of screen time. Then, in 2003, he created a putative Ninth Doctor for a web-based animation, *Scream of the Shalka* by Paul Cornell, which would have led to further adventures had the whole project not been derailed by the announcement of *Doctor Who*'s return to television under Russell T Davies, and relegated to a footnote in *Who* history. He certainly makes more of an impact playing a villain, giving Simeon an appropriately frozen intensity at all times that suggests this man hasn't so much as smiled in decades. The flashback scene at the top of the show makes it clear that as a boy, the painfully shy, introverted Simeon avoided all other company, making him an easy target for the manipulations of the intelligence behind the snow. (Incidentally, while it's great that the show managed to get such a high-profile actor as the wonderful Ian McKellen to provide the voice of the intelligence, hearing Gandalf's distinctive tones emanating from a giant snowglobe wanting to rule the world was possibly the most unsettling aspect of the whole episode.)

Meanwhile, the Doctor tries to deal with Clara, in a laugh-out-loud sequence involving Strax and a "memory worm" – a not very convincing alien which looks like an escapee from the late, lamented *Sarah Jane Adventures*. The scene is particularly admirable not only for the comedy, which Dan Starkey and Matt Smith execute with impeccable timing, but also because of the way that (in retrospect) Moffat uses it to hide in plain sight the method by which the Doctor will deal with Simeon. As always with Moffat episodes, the script is packed full of plot elements and lines of dialogue with multiple purposes.

The interaction between Smith and Coleman fizzes along, and they already feel like a well-practised team as the Doctor and Clara face their first shared danger: the snow starts picking up thoughts from Clara and creates a horde of the menacing snowmen around them. After they escape, the Doctor still wants nothing to do with any possibility of companionship, but Clara easily evades Strax and follows the Doctor back to his hidden TARDIS. There's some lovely imagery as she finds herself climbing a ladder and a huge, invisible spiral staircase leading to a cloud-like platform, and knocking on the door of the police box. At this point it's easy to imagine this girl as the Doctor's new companion, but Moffat has something more complex in mind. And so she reconsiders, and heads back down the staircase before the Doctor can find her.

The next day, we discover that Clara is leading a double life – in the course of a carriage ride, she transforms herself from *Oliver Twist*'s Nancy into a prim Mary Poppins. Both the character and the actress playing her get to show off their versatility as, with sculpted enunciation worthy of Julie Andrews, Clara resumes her role of governess to the two children of Captain Latimer, a widower who is clearly smitten with her – when his house is later invaded by all manner of weirdness, the thing that most arrests his attention is the Doctor trying to pass himself off as Clara's "gentleman friend".

Clara learns that one of her young charges, Francesca, has been having nightmares about their previous governess, who drowned some weeks ago in the ornamental pond in front of their house. When she notices that the pond is still frozen over even though the snow everywhere around it has thawed, Clara realises she needs the Doctor's help. But attempting to find the TARDIS again soon brings her to the notice of Jenny, who takes her to see Vastra. The Silurian tells Clara that she, Jenny and Strax act as the Doctor's gatekeepers: "We assist him in his isolation, but that does not mean we approve of it."

The scene between Vastra and Clara is an excellent one that gives Coleman her first chance to portray Clara as something deeper than cute and perky. Vastra demands that she restrict herself to one-word answers to her questions ("Truth is singular; lies are words, words, words"), and Coleman adroitly shows Clara carefully thinking through each response. She even sometimes gains the upper hand; when she suggests that the Doctor should help her out of kindness, Vastra is goaded into expressing her own disappointment with the Doctor's inactivity ("The Doctor is not kind… He stands above this world and doesn't interfere in the affairs of its inhabitants. He is not your salvation nor your protector. Do you understand what I am saying to you?"). Clara's retort is simply: "Words."

This powerful scene is a great example of Moffat's talent for adding depth to his plotting by seizing the chance to create resonances with earlier stories – resonances that can't possibly have been planned in advance. Here, he must surely have started from the realisation of the coincidence that Amy's surname could also signify one of the crucial elements of this story. From there, the whole one-word-only thing must have been built up, so that the scene could reach its climax with Clara – tasked by Vastra to come up with a message for the Doctor – producing the only word that could break through the Doctor's isolation: "Pond." A costuming choice adds the final touch: up to this point we have seen the Doctor using the glasses he took from Amy in the previous episode – his only physical memento of her. After he hears the magic word, the glasses come off, and are not seen again.

With the turning point reached, the Doctor leaps into action, and almost immediately penetrates to the heart of Simeon's scheme, running rings around the man with the sort of hyperactive wackiness ("Big globe-y thing!") which normally sets my teeth on edge. Here, though, it works well, feeling like a release after the Doctor's previous glum disposition. It's also helped along by a very funny nod to Moffat's other hit series, *Sherlock*. Accompanied by a music cue very reminiscent of that show, the Doctor enters dressed as the classic Sherlock Holmes, deerstalker and all, and starts throwing out deductions – all of them comically wrong – to keep Simeon off-balance. (Amusingly, earlier Simeon had told Vastra that Conan Doyle was "almost certainly" basing his Sherlock Holmes stories on her exploits.)

Finding a clue that leads him to the Latimer estate, the Doctor quickly works out that the drowned governess in the pond was being used by the alien intelligence to gain an understanding of the human form, so that it could create an army of minions more capable than the clumsy snowmen. Sure enough, Clara and the children are soon being menaced by a living ice sculpture in the shape of the woman (a beautiful effect, although unfortunately its movement can't help betraying its CGI nature). The Doctor manages to temporarily disable it, but the house is surrounded by snowmen as Simeon arrives and demands that the creature be surrendered to him.

Another wonderful, extended two-hander scene between Smith and Coleman follows as the Doctor, followed by Clara, leads the ice creature up to the roof of the house to keep it isolated. Clara impresses the Doctor greatly with her quick-fire deduction that he has moved the cloud platform holding his TARDIS to hover over the house, and they escape up the ladder and staircase, drawing the creature after them. At the top, the Doctor quickly immobilises the creature, and Clara finally gets to see inside the TARDIS. (And I must compliment director Metzstein here on showing the Doctor walking into the console room from outside the box, right up to the console and operating the controls, all in one seamless shot. I don't remember that ever being achieved on the show before.)

The scene where someone gets introduced to the TARDIS is one of those fundamental *Doctor Who* sense-of-wonder moments that never gets old, and Smith and Coleman play this one perfectly. When the Doctor gives her a TARDIS key ("I never know why; I only know who"), the reappearance of the sweet, wistful theme we have already heard a couple of times in this episode (and also in *Asylum of the Daleks*) – clearly destined to be Clara's personal theme – makes it a magic moment.

It's a real moment of triumph for both of them, and it seems that *now* the Doctor has definitely acquired his new companion. But again, Moffat has something else in mind. In the most shockingly unexpected plot turn of the episode, the ice creature, having escaped its confinement, grabs Clara and drags the two of them off the cloud platform, falling to the ground far below. The creature is smashed, but Clara is also fatally injured. The Doctor uses the TARDIS to retrieve her and bring her back inside the house.

With the story we were expecting suddenly twisting into something darker and more tragic, a guilt-ridden Doctor coaxes Clara into agreeing to come away with him if he saves the world, the way "the green lady" told her he used to do. Vastra points out that he is trying to make a bargain with the uncaring universe – he'll save the world if it lets Clara live – and "I don't think the universe makes bargains." The Doctor reacts angrily, but that's at least partly because he knows that she is right, and they head off in the TARDIS to confront Simeon in his office. It has to be said that Simeon is probably not the most challenging role Richard E. Grant has ever had to play, but he makes the most of his final scene, when he shows the man almost visibly collapsing into himself as the Doctor reveals how the intelligence has been manipulating him since childhood.

It would be thematically appropriate for the controlling intelligence to be finally vanquished at this point. The Doctor has been prodded into action, breaking him out of his apathy; he has penetrated the lair of the villain and revealed its true nature; and he has found a way to defeat it by breaking its link with Simeon. It would take only a few trivial changes to the script to end the snowy menace once and for all here, leaving the remaining events of the episode unaltered. But Moffat has one more clever twist he wants to show off.

In late 1967, in the fifth season of the Classic Series, Patrick Troughton's Doctor paid a visit to Tibet in the 1930s, where he faced a threat from monstrous Yeti controlled by a mysterious "Great Intelligence" – a strange, bodiless force that had the ability to mentally dominate its human servants, and wanted to generate a physical form for itself to enable it to take over the Earth. (In true *Doctor Who* style, underneath their furry exteriors the Yeti actually turned out to be robots.) *The Abominable Snowmen* was considered such a success by the production team that even before it was broadcast its writers, Mervyn Haisman and Henry Lincoln, were commissioned to produce a sequel. And so, just three months later, Troughton faced the Yeti again in *The Web of Fear*. This time the story took place in London, in what was then the near-future year of 1975, and the Intelligence was using the Yeti and an ever-expanding flood of web-like fungus to attack the city through the tunnels of the London Underground system. *The Web of Fear* turned out to be one of the most memorable and important stories of that era, not least because it introduced a character – Colonel (later Brigadier) Lethbridge-Stewart, played by the late Nicholas Courtney – who would become one of the linchpins of the series in the 1970's.

Haisman and Lincoln left the origin of their "Great Intelligence" as a complete mystery, providing an opening for someone like Steven Moffat to come along and advance his own explanation. As a long-time fan, I loved the ingenious payoff signalled by these knowing lines:

Jenny: "Well, we can't be in much danger from a disembodied intelligence that thinks it can invade the world with snowmen."
Vastra: "Or that the London Underground is a key strategic weakness."
The Doctor: *(examining Simeon's business card)* "The Great Intelligence… rings a bell…"

Regrettably, this payoff does come at a cost. Giving the Intelligence the capacity to survive independently of Simeon – in fact, to take him over and control him, zombie-style, to provide a few moments of further menace – means that the Doctor doesn't actually get to achieve the neutralization of the threat. Instead, we have an unwelcome intrusion from the kind of bathos that doomed last year's Christmas special. Somehow Latimer and his family's reaction to the dying Clara ("a whole family crying on Christmas Eve") creates an emotional force which overwhelms the snow at the house, and somehow this gets fed back into the controlling Intelligence, which somehow leads to all the snow suddenly just melting away into salty rain… Not even Matt Smith's best efforts can make this remotely convincing. Fortunately, unlike with *The Doctor, the Widow, and the Wardrobe*, this bogus fairytale ending does not undo all the consequences of the story. Clara is still dying, and there is nothing the Doctor can do about it.

It's Clara's death that prevents her story being a simple duplication of what Moffat did with River Song. Her full name – revealed to be Clara Oswin Oswald – and her final words to the Doctor ("Run, you clever boy… and remember"), link her beyond doubt with the Oswin who died in *Asylum of the Daleks*. Before this episode aired, speculation was rife about what the connection could be between the two characters, with a favourite theory being that Clara would travel with the Doctor for a time, then eventually, under the name Oswin, join the crew of the starship *Alaska* and – just as with River – meet her end in the encounter which was their first meeting from the Doctor's perspective. But it's clear now that something much stranger is going on:

The Doctor: "Oswin… It was *her*… I never saw her face the first time, with the Daleks, but her voice… it was the same voice. The same woman, twice! And she died, both times. The same woman!"

A shot of Clara's gravestone (which, incidentally, gives her birthdate as November 23rd – the same as *Doctor Who* itself) dissolves to the same shot of it, now overgrown and weathered, in the present day. Another Clara – finally, the *real* companion-to-be – pauses next to it, oblivious, as she is telling a friend, "I don't believe in ghosts." Meanwhile, the Doctor is back in his TARDIS, setting off on his mission to find Clara – no longer avoiding his future, but running toward it.

The trailer which aired after this episode for the second half of Series 7 makes it clear that the mystery of "the woman twice dead" will be an important component in the next story arc. It's exactly the kind of puzzle that was needed to bring the Doctor back to himself, and in the final analysis that is the main accomplishment of this episode. Taken as a stand-alone story, *The Snowmen* would be well-made and entertaining but nothing more – a traditional 'romp' of a Christmas special no more significant than, say, 2007's *Voyage of the Damned*. It's the connections to the past and the inescapable set-up for the future that are the real meat of the episode – as well as the demonstration that with the pairing of Matt Smith and Jenna-Louise Coleman, the *Doctor Who* producers have come up with another winning team.

Steven's Classic Who DVD Recommendation: Unfortunately, the Yeti stories of the 1960's mentioned above were victims of the BBC archive purges of decades ago – in both cases, just one episode out of six is all that remains. So instead I'm going to recommend another icy story with a (literally) cold-hearted villain – check out 1987's *Dragonfire* starring Sylvester McCoy, with Bonnie Langford and Sophie Aldred. (*Editor's note*: Since Steven wrote the above recommendation, all episodes of 1968's *The Web of Fear* apart from one have, of course, famously been rediscovered, and are now available via download and DVD.)

Kevin's Review: *The Snowmen* is the best Christmas Special that Steven Moffat has written so far. Not only does it contain elements that please long-time fans of the show, but there is also much to entertain the casual viewer, along with important plot developments that will be integral to the second half of Series 7 and beyond.

At first glance, it would appear impossible to make snowmen abominable, but the *Doctor Who* production team accomplishes this with some aplomb, by providing them with shark's teeth instead of the usual, more impotent carrot nose. Even the snowflakes snarl and gnash their teeth in this episode. Richard E. Grant exudes disinterested menace in the form of Simeon, while Sir Ian McKellen superbly voices the Great Intelligence. "Simeon", appropriately enough, means "he has heard", as our opening shows him as a little boy startled by his snowman as it begins to reflect his anxieties back at him. No doubt such a boy would have otherwise buried his head in books to escape from his peers, but the Great Intelligence has a more malign need for Simeon's Victorian imagination and values.

However, the star billing belongs to Jenna-Louise Coleman's Clara, who sparkles with real energy in this episode. As Steven writes, Clara's introduction has to be the most intricately plotted of any companion in the series. Most viewers will have remembered her from the series opener, *Asylum of the Daleks*, but it's a mystery as to how she has ended up in Victorian London without having been transported there by the Doctor in the TARDIS, if indeed this is the first time that she has met our hero. As Steven has also noted, it is a very nice touch on Moffat's part to reinforce the mourning the Doctor has for the recently departed Ponds via the device of the Doctor wearing Amy's reading glasses. I thought that they were perhaps a bit large and obtrusive while Amy was wearing them, which Moffat jokingly played upon in *The Angels in Manhattan* when the Doctor struggles to discern what is different about her face. (Although, tellingly in the context of that story, it's the lines about Amy's eyes that the Doctor notices for the first time, which signify her aging, instead of her spectacles.)

Matt Smith brilliantly conveys the Doctor's mourning for the Ponds here, as the wretched Time Lord (along with Amy's reading glasses) does indeed very much fit his Victorian surroundings. Even the Doctor's stovepipe hat, ridiculous in any other context, does not look out of place here. Still, despite the Doctor's world-weariness, Clara does get him to smile. Yet the Doctor still resists her advances. The importance of this "dangerous question" – "Doctor who?" for the resolution of this series and beyond is highlighted by it leading into the opening titles. As for these new titles, I thought that they were okay, not quite as dramatic and classic as when the series was revived in 2005, but not bad. Contrary to Steven, I think that the opening of the TARDIS doors to signal the start of a new adventure is an excellent device. It was also nice to spot the Doctor's face in the opening titles once more, although Matt Smith's facial features are scarcely visible, no doubt due to the production team's inkling that their lead actor would be making his departure in a year's time.

It's brilliant to see Strax back from the dead in *A Good Man Goes to War*. Indeed, it's hard to believe that the Paternoster gang are still a relatively new addition to *Doctor Who*, because they seem (somehow) to have always been there. This is probably down to them being such a classic ensemble, with all the right elements to create some truly wonderful chemistry. Strax is still as belligerent as ever, with his comic love for grenades; yet he also retains his nursing skills, which come in handy later on in the episode, when he ministers to the prone Clara. (It would appear that this Doctor always needs a first aider on hand, like the late lamented Rory Williams.) However, as the Doctor observes, not all of Strax's brains have made the return trip, so the Sontaran is more bungling this time around. In this way, Strax is akin to Blackadder's legendary sidekick Baldrick, who appeared to be quite intelligent in Plantagenet times, but who evidently lost most of his brain cells by the time of his next appearance in the Elizabethan era. Fortunately for us and the Paternoster gang, Strax, unlike Baldrick, is very disciplined about his appearance, and treats his butler suit and his personal hygiene with due reverence.

Another humorous moment (of many) occurs when Jenny and Vastra confront the villain of the piece. Simeon cuttingly observes that the readers of *The Strand* would have difficulty believing that Conan Doyle's Sherlock Holmes was actually modelled on a woman, and so overlooks the more obvious detail that Vastra is a centuries-old Homo Reptilia with green skin! Then again, Simeon has been communing with the Great Intelligence, so encounters with exotic species are not so alien to him. Indeed, it would appear at first sight, that we have moved a long way from the patriarchal culture of the Victorians, who saw women as the 'angel of the house' at best, and 'fallen women' at worst. (It's interesting here that Moffat gets Clara to embody both these caricatures in this episode, for she's the 'angel of the house' while acting as the governess of Captain Latimer's children, while Victorian society had a dim view of women who worked in say, the theatre or public houses.) Then again, we as a society haven't progressed that much, as the Church of England only approved the creation of women bishops yesterday, and today (as I am writing this review) the British Prime Minister has undertaken a cabinet reshuffle to promote more women, although they will still be very much a minority in his government. I know that some critics of Moffat do argue that he is sexist. This is not something that I would agree with myself, although it is a bit unfortunate that Moffat seemingly has the Doctor refer to Clara as "some bird" at one point. In addition to this, there is the titillating scene in the carriage where Clara changes clothes, which appears to hark back to the production team's desire in the 70's and 80's to hook the dads in the audience by getting the Doctor's female companions to show off some flesh. Yet, this is very much a tease at most – we are a long way away from the depiction of the Doctor's female companions in bikinis, which sometimes happened in the 80's. This is perhaps Moffat playing with the Victorian notion that women's bodies had to be covered up at all times, with the result that even the flash of a lady's ankle could bring a man to blush. No doubt the revelation that Jenny and Vastra are married could cause many a bigot to hyperventilate even today, so we still have a long way to go in the equality stakes.

Steven Moffat, just like in *Asylum of the Daleks*, presents the Doctor as being almost akin to a godlike figure here, as Vastra says:

> "The Doctor doesn't help people. Not anyone, not ever. He stands above this world and doesn't interfere in the affairs of its inhabitants. He is not your salvation, nor your protector."

The name of the Paternoster gang almost seems to suggest that Vastra, Jenny, and Strax worship the Doctor. "Pater noster", of course, are the first two words of the Lord's Prayer in Latin. However, as we know from *The Great Detective* minisode of *Doctor Who* (the prequel for this episode, first shown by the BBC during Children in Need 2012), the gang acquired this name because Vastra lives in Paternoster Row, so-called because in medieval times, priests would chant the Lord's Prayer while in procession to the nearby St. Paul's cathedral. During the time that Vastra lives there, Paternoster Row was the centre of the British publishing industry, and so contained many bookshops before the Blitz wiped them out. In Clara's brilliant 'one word' conversation with Vastra, one of her responses puzzled me. However, when Clara states "Man", I think she does it to dispute the divine reverence in which Vastra speaks of the Doctor. As Steven writes, it is especially brilliant when we learn that Clara has unconsciously spoken the one word that can shake the Doctor out of his apathy: "Pond". For, of course, Clara can know nothing of Amy and Rory, can she?

In this episode, Moffat presents the Doctor and Clara as almost courting each other, checking each other out as potential soul mates, instead of the flirting that accompanied their first encounter in *Asylum of the Daleks*. For instance, when the Doctor inspects Captain Latimer's pond outside of Clara's bedroom window, the Doctor is determined not to engage with her, but somehow manages to signal that he'll pop up to see her in five minutes. Also, when Captain Latimer confronts the Doctor's intrusion in his house, the Doctor inappropriately declares that he is Clara's "gentleman friend", and that they've just been upstairs kissing, which is exactly the one thing that your average Victorian patriarch would not want to hear. Of course, Clara will later get to kiss the Doctor (which appears to be something of a traditional interaction between our hero and a female guest star in a *Doctor Who* Christmas Special).

Of course, the rapid bond that the Doctor has developed with Clara is rather shattered when the ice governess pulls both herself and Clara to their doom. The ice governess, for her part, seems to be the epitome of the 'madwoman in the attic' (as Susan Gubar and Sandra Gilbert put it in their brilliant book of feminist literary criticism, of which this is the title). As Gilbert and Gubar argue, many Victorian novels presented women as either being the 'angel in the house' or the 'madwoman in the attic', with the most famous example of these being Jane Eyre (like Clara, a governess) and Mr Rochester's insane first wife, who he keeps locked in the attic. Daphne Du Maurier's later novel *Rebecca* shares similar themes of a house haunted by the mysterious death of its master's first wife, while Latimer's household has the mystery of the previous governess's death hanging over it. (The fate of Captain Latimer's wife isn't mentioned; she probably just died, as people were wont to do due to the high mortality rates in Victorian Britain.) The Doctor, of course, hilariously interrupts any romantic intentions that Captain Latimer may have with regards to his own would-be Jane Eyre.

Long-time viewers of the show since 2005 will have become accustomed to the Doctor's having a 'romantic' relationship with his female lead, so no doubt many of them were expecting Clara to pull through at the end, especially as the Doctor presses the engagement ring of the TARDIS key into her hand more than once. Of course, one way to heighten the stakes in a drama is to have one of the heroes die, which is something that Steven Moffat has deployed often (which led Rory to jokingly talk about the many times that he has come back from the dead in the last episode). However, with Clara, Moffat has found a legitimate way to kill her off more than once. For, as we know from the series' finale, the Oswalds that featured in *Asylum of the Daleks* and here are merely essences of the real Clara Oswald (who we will see at the end of this episode for the first time) that have splintered throughout the Doctor's lifecycle. Unlike Steven, I thought the ending was rather fitting. Usually, I am a bit disparaging of the more sentimental moments of the revived series of *Doctor Who*, whose emotional drama the production team seem to have borrowed wholesale from *Star Trek: The Next Generation*. However, I think it really does work here, as throughout the episode, Clara is shown to be loved by everyone who encounters her, especially within the Latimer household, the epicentre of the grief for her. It could be that I'm just a sucker for a good death scene (or of the high death count of a Victorian Christmas ghost story such as this). Throughout this episode, Moffat highlights how the snow reflects the emotions of the people around it, so I thought that it was true to the drama that it would be overwhelmed by such a downpour of grief. Again, death scenes such as this, like that of Little Nell in Dickens' *The Old Curiosity Shop*, are a staple of Victorian drama, and could be so powerful that they could affect the mood of a nation.

However, the narrative of *Doctor Who* must go on, and the Doctor is offered some hope by Clara's final words, which spookily resemble those of Oswin's from *Asylum of the Daleks* (along with her fondness for making soufflés). And so the quest is on to find out where all these Oswalds are coming from… Overall, *The Snowmen* is a brilliantly entertaining adventure. I particularly enjoyed the in-joke references to Steven Moffat's other hit, *Sherlock*, and the fanboy nod to the Great Intelligence. (Although I thought the joke about "key strategic weakness" of the London Underground in 1967 to be a bit too forced, and one that didn't really work in the circumstances.) Along with tunnels, the Doctor must hate Victorian graveyards; fortunately, there are uncharacteristically no statues of weeping angels in sight at Clara's grave. It's interesting that Moffat chooses "November 23 1866" as the date of Clara's birth, as "November 23 1863" would have been exactly a century before the first broadcast of *Doctor Who*. Then again, Moffat was effectively tied to setting the story in 1892 to include all the references to Sherlock Holmes in *The Strand*, so seems to have chosen to convey that Clara was the same age as the actress playing her, because showing Clara as being so much closer to 30 would not have fitted her character. So, it's not long before we see the real Clara standing next to this gravestone when it has become more decrepit in modern times. As this cameo (and the preview of the rest of the series) reveals, the Doctor will definitely meet Clara again (if not her friend who features briefly in the cameo and who we never see again). Moffat's introduction of Clara was as big as they come; it wouldn't be too long before viewers would find out if the real Clara lived up to the hype....

6: The Bells of Saint John

Writer: Steven Moffat
Director: Colm McCarthy
Originally broadcast: 30 March 2013

Cast

The Doctor: Matt Smith
Clara: Jenna-Louise Coleman
Nabile: Manpreet Bachu
Paul: Sean Knopp
The Abbot: James Greene
Angie: Eve De Leon Allen
Artie: Kassius Carey Johnson
George: Geff Francis
Miss Kizlet: Celia Imrie
Mahler: Robert Whitelock
Alexei: Dan Li
Little Girl: Daniella Eames
Pilot: Antony Edridge
Barista: Fred Pearson
Waitress: Jade Anouka
Newsreader: Olivia Hill
Man with Chips: Matthew Earley
Child reading Comic: Isabella Blake-Thomas
The Great Intelligence: Richard E. Grant

Steven's Review: It's been a while since the last episode, but with *The Bells of Saint John*, the second half of *Doctor Who*'s seventh season follows on smoothly from last year's Christmas Special just as if several months hadn't gone by in the interim. With the Doctor finally meeting his new traveling companion Clara, showrunner Steven Moffat presents an episode that efficiently sets several plot-arc threads in motion, but whose actual story is fairly thin, and relies rather too much on devices he has used before to be totally satisfying.

For one thing, the rather evocative title of the episode turns out to be a red herring – just a throwaway gag. We find ourselves rejoining the Doctor when he has gone into retreat in a Cumbrian monastery in the year 1207, still contemplating the mystery of Clara, the woman he has encountered twice now. To some extent, this initial section exists as an attempt to provide painless exposition for viewers who didn't see *The Snowmen* and *Asylum of the Daleks* – in particular, to emphasize Clara's status as "the woman twice dead," and her enigmatic last words on both occasions: "Run, you clever boy – and remember." Then one of the monks comes running in with news that "the bells of Saint John are ringing," and the Doctor quickly returns to the TARDIS – which has a prominent St. John Ambulance badge on its door (a detail on the original police box prop from 1963 which disappeared after the series' first few years, but which was restored when Moffat took over as showrunner in 2009 and had a new TARDIS prop constructed for Matt Smith's first season). It's a cute little twist, but it makes this episode surely the most irrelevantly-titled one in the whole history of the show.

One thing I did like about this opening section was its use of another time period, in the sort of casual way that only *Doctor Who* can do. The Doctor, after all, is supposed to be a citizen of all times, belonging to none; he sees absolutely nothing incongruous about being in the 13th century one moment and the 21st the next. In this case, too, it's not a matter of Moffat's usual time-twisting plotting, but rather a pure character touch. There's no real need for us to see the Doctor hanging around in 1207; it makes no difference to the actual story whatever. In the Classic Series, there would occasionally be stories which showed more than one time period – *Day of the Daleks* (1972) and *Mawdryn Undead* (1983) are two prominent examples. But there, the multiple time periods were always strictly a matter of plot necessity – in those days, the show's resources would barely stretch to showing one time and place on screen, never mind more. It was only with the advent of the new series, and particularly since Moffat took over, that the Doctor's trans-temporal nature has been foregrounded like this, and it was pleasing to see.

Unfortunately, to kick off the story, Moffat resorts to recycling one of his more memorable tricks. The idea of the TARDIS's external police box phone actually ringing provided a wonderfully unexpected and spooky moment in the very first episode Moffat wrote for *Doctor Who* (*The Empty Child* back in 2005). Repeating the moment here ("That is not supposed to happen!") can't help but be less effective, particularly as it's reused for more comic effect, as the Doctor finds himself somehow talking to a present-day Clara, who is calling for technical support to help her with a missing internet connection. In this way the Doctor is pulled into the action, not only encountering Clara again, but becoming aware of the menace he will have to defeat in this episode.

As so often with *Doctor Who* (and particularly with Moffat), the threat is an extrapolation from everyday experience. With the now ubiquitous nature of webcams, wireless networking and cloud-based data storage, it's an entirely *Who*-ish thing to do to take the idea of "something lurking in the wi-fi" as the hook for a story. The teaser at the top of the episode lays it all out for us – if your computer's wi-fi detection shows a strange network with a name that looks like alien gibberish, don't click on it… Because if you do, some shadowy organisation will be able to hack into your computer, observe you through your webcam, and may choose to upload your personality into a virtual entity under their control, leaving your body as an inert husk.

The actual uploading is done by the aptly-named "spoonheads". These walking robotic wi-fi base stations are able to camouflage themselves in human form, until they are ready to strike. Then the human head twists around 180 degrees, to reveal that it is just a hollow shell, a housing for a dish antenna. This head-turning trick would be much more macabre and effective if Moffat hadn't used a similar gimmick twice before – with the Nodes in 2008's *Silence in the Library* and the Smilers in 2010's *The Beast Below*. It's also unfortunate that the turning is so slow that their victims should have plenty of time to run away, rather than just cowering in fear in front of them. On the other hand, I did like the way Moffat constructed their dialogue, simply taking the last thing said to them and transforming it to make as realistic a conversation as possible ("I know you, don't I?" "You know me, don't you?"). Not only is it effectively spooky the first time, when Clara encounters one in the form of a small girl, but it provides an excellent moment of delayed realisation when one of them later takes on the Doctor's appearance.

Once the Doctor realises that he has made contact with Clara again, he rushes to meet her. She, on the other hand, is understandably wary of this crazy guy dressed as a monk who claims to know her. When his initial approach fails, the Doctor dashes back to the TARDIS to find his usual clothes, while Clara is attacked by one of the spoonheads. After an annoyingly over-the-top clothes-changing sequence (complete with ridiculous music), the Doctor returns to rescue her by using her computer to override the uploading of her personality. (As an aside, as someone whose work involves computer programming, I can only wish it was as simple as the frantic flailing away at a keyboard seen several times in this episode. But of course, movies and TV shows – especially sci-fi ones – almost never make any concessions to realism when it comes to computers.)

As the Doctor and this version of Clara get to know each other properly, the interaction between Matt Smith and Jenna-Louise Coleman is as delightful as in their two previous episodes. Smith's Doctor can be irritating when he's being deliberately wacky (see the aforementioned clothes-changing scene), but when he's not trying to be funny – telling Clara about the telephone calls she missed, or reeling off a list of things he did around the house while she was sleeping – he is alternately charming and hilarious. ("I found a disassembled quadracycle in the garage." "I don't think you did." "I invented the quadracycle!") For her part, Clara is quickly intrigued by the Doctor, who is repeatedly put off-balance as he tries to avoid hinting that he has met her before. By the end, they are already well on the way to becoming friends, and I'm really looking forward to seeing how this relationship develops over the course of the season.

The episode suddenly switches to action, as the Doctor and Clara come under attack from the mysterious enemy organisation. It's an indication of the level of sheer confidence with which the show is produced these days that the makers can simply insert into a story a couple of minutes aboard a crashing airplane as an action set-piece. Clara gets to make her first quick journey in the TARDIS as the Doctor materialises on board the aircraft, which is about to smash into her house. Almost before she has time to draw breath, the Doctor has pulled the plane out of its dive, revived the unconscious crew, and taken her to the next morning, where he retrieves a motorcycle from the depths of the TARDIS and gives her a ride to a cafe in the heart of London for breakfast. The whole sequence is an excellent change of pace, and (like the rest of the episode) is well directed by newcomer Colm McCarthy. In fact, the only directorial flaw worth noting in the episode is that the various sequences of people's personalities being manipulated via tablet screens really needed some bigger close-ups of those screens to make it clear to the audience exactly what was going on.

The Doctor: "Human souls, trapped like flies in the world-wide web. Stuck forever, crying out for help."
Clara: "Isn't that basically Twitter?"

It remains a mystery both to the Doctor and to us exactly what is the relationship between the various versions of Clara we've seen. For example, Clara in this episode starts out as hopeless with computers, but as part of the partially completed upload which the Doctor interrupted, she receives a package of computer knowledge and skills. In *Asylum of the Daleks*, Oswin was a computer genius. Are they actually the same woman, or is there some trickier connection? We actually see Clara come up with the name Oswin here when she needs a user ID for her hacking ("Clara Oswald for the win… Os-win!") Is this significant, or is Moffat simply having fun with us? The Clara of 1892 (in *The Snowmen*) was a governess; the present-day Clara has effectively been a live-in nanny for the children of a family friend for the last year. The Doctor spots the similarities, but can only speculate for the moment. This is obviously one of the major plot questions we can expect to see resolved by the end of the season.

As I mentioned above, the use of computers in this story lives up (or rather, down) to the usual standard of realism for sci-fi TV, but there is one element of the plot that is thoroughly plausible. Clara finding out the location of the enemy organisation via the employees' social media pages was a clever touch – and exactly the kind of boneheaded security breach that happens in real life, like people keeping their passwords on handwritten notes stuck to their monitors. With the knowledge that the organisation is based in the Shard (a right-up-to-date element of the story – this 95-floor skyscraper, the new tallest building in London, was opened only in February 2013), the Doctor can now take action. In another casually spectacular set-piece, he reveals that his motorcycle is actually an anti-gravity vehicle ("I rode this in the anti-grav Olympics, 2074… I came last"), and enters the building by simply riding up the outside to the top, where he breaks in and faces Miss Kizlet, the head of the organisation.

This episode's main guest star, accomplished actress Celia Imrie, doesn't get a great deal to work with as Miss Kizlet, but her confrontation with the Doctor is well done, as it is revealed that the Doctor is actually still back at the cafe – he reprogrammed a spoonhead double to break into the building for him. Neatly hoist by her own petard, Miss Kizlet is herself uploaded into the cloud – leaving her subordinates with no alternative but to download the entire cloud to restore her and all the other victims, including Clara. At least, all those with bodies still to return to; what might seem like a rather easy victory for the Doctor is complicated by the fact that most of the virtual personalities have nowhere to go back to, and will be lost forever. The Doctor contends that the best that can be done is to release them from a "living hell" – which is rather a contrast to his behaviour in 2008's *Forest of the Dead*, when he took pains to create a virtual afterlife for River Song. The difference here is due to the presence of Miss Kizlet's mysterious "client," which has been feeding on the uploaded minds – indeed, in a striking (albeit slightly strained) metaphor, she compares the situation to a farmer raising livestock for slaughter.

Imrie does a nicely creepy job with her best moment of the story – Miss Kizlet's final scene, as her augmented intelligence is removed and she regresses to a small, frightened girl. For in a surprising reveal, Miss Kizlet's client is revealed to be the Great Intelligence (as seen in *The Snowmen*) – a bodiless entity capable of mentally dominating humans and forcing them to serve its own ends. I certainly hadn't expected such a direct link between the Christmas episode and the second half of the season, particularly in view of Moffat's statement that he would be dialling back on the season-arc plotting after the intricacies of the 2011 season. It remains to be seen just how much of this season (and Clara's story) will be linked to the Intelligence; since the entity appears to be confined to Earth, some of the episodes (next week's, for example) should certainly be stand-alones.

As has become the norm with Moffat's *Doctor Who*, we start a new season (or half-season, in this case), with many questions awaiting answers. Apart from the central mystery of what's going on with Clara herself, several other threads were left dangling after this episode. Some of them will probably turn out to be mere mystification on Moffat's part – like (I hope) the fact that the book which Clara was shown holding early in the episode (the cover of which showed the little girl that the spoonhead attacking her used for its disguise) is called *Summer Falls*, by a certain Amelia Williams. Then there's the whole question of how Clara managed to call the Doctor's TARDIS in the first place. She said there was a "woman in the shop" who gave her the phone number ("It's a help line, isn't it? She said it's the best help line out there. In the universe, she said"). My first thought was that River Song might be making another appearance in the Doctor's life. But recent casting news about the fiftieth anniversary special episode which will be shown in November this year brings other possibilities to mind… There was even a reminder of the big unanswered question

("Doctor who?") which was left hanging over the Doctor at the end of the 2011 season.

Unlike previous episodes which have introduced a new companion, this one ends with Clara still not yet convinced to join the Doctor on his travels. In the delightfully playful final scene, Clara is clearly tempted, but instead walks out of the TARDIS, telling the Doctor to ask her again tomorrow ("Why?" "Because tomorrow I might say yes"). The Doctor, for his part, is both amused at Clara stringing him along and eager to get to work on the other challenge she poses: "Right then, Clara Oswald. Time to find out who you are."

In the final analysis, a judgment on *The Bells of Saint John* can't really be made at this point, except to say that the unfinished business with Clara and (as yet unknown to the Doctor) the Great Intelligence outweighs the relatively slight and straightforward adventure involving Miss Kizlet and her organisation. There was enough to keep me interested (particularly the Smith/Coleman scenes), but like the "bells" of the title, this episode was more a trigger for the story being told over this next stretch of episodes than a memorable story in itself.

Steven's Classic Who DVD Recommendation: For a much, much earlier look at computers in *Doctor Who*, check out 1966's *The War Machines*, starring William Hartnell, with Jackie Lane, and introducing Anneke Wills and Michael Craze. (*Editor's note*: This recommendation is also appropriate because like the Shard in *The Bells of Saint John*, *The War Machines*' main setting was a new arrival on the London horizon, the Post Office Tower.)

***Kevin's Review*:** When you have the luxury of using three episodes to introduce a character to a TV series, there is always a risk that one of them will turn out to be a dud. Unfortunately, it turns out to be this one, the main episode that reveals Clara Oswald for the first time. Not that many showrunners other than Moffat would be daring enough to try and pull something like this off.

While the Oswald we first saw in *Asylum of the Daleks* was very flirty and super-intelligent, and the barmaid/governess in *The Snowmen* was quick-witted and charming, modern-day Clara is a bit dull. As the young Clara says in the prequel minisode to *The Bells of Saint John*, she has most definitely lost her mojo here. As I argued in my review of *Dinosaurs on a Spaceship*, this is most likely due to Moffat knowing that he was going to cast an older actor to play the

Doctor following the departure of Matt Smith. Although there is a bit of flirty banter here when Clara suggests that the TARDIS may be a "snogging booth", most of it is rather awkward and less than convincing. (The casting news for Series 8 suggests that there may soon be a young male companion for Clara to flirt with in the TARDIS, which may help her get her mojo back. Not that she would be restricted to flirting with a male companion, as Oswin Oswald went through a phase of fancying women.) There's still an element of courting in the Doctor/Clara relationship, especially when she tells him to come back tomorrow and ask her again if she will travel with him, but this has none of the charm of their quick-fire relationship in *The Snowmen*. Moffat allowed the Doctor and Clara to get to 'first base' in the previous adventure, probably only because that version of Clara was about to die. Despite modern-day Clara bearing no Victorian baggage about morals, she's a bit less committal in her approach to forming relationships, perhaps as a result of her mother dying young.

This early bereavement has gone a long way to forming Clara's character here, as she has stepped in to look after the Maitland children after their mother similarly died young. Yet it is evident that modern-day Clara isn't as efficient in her approach to nannying as her Victorian alter ego was. As Steven writes, Moffat has repeated several of his favourite devices here, one of which is the Doctor's attempt to find out more about Clara via her baggage. Like Amy, Clara keeps some of her possessions from childhood in her bedroom. Of particular importance is a book called *101 Places to See*, which is so important to Clara that she has taken the unusual step of recording her age in the front of the book well into her adult years. (With the exception of 23, which at some point may have some relevance beyond 23rd November 1963. Curse you Moffat for making us examine everything in such tiny detail!) Of course, we will find out a lot more about the leaf in the book in the next episode, and in this series' finale.

One device that Moffat repeats from *The Angels Take Manhattan* is including a book that will play a part in the plot. Obviously, there are some Victorian profit values at work here (as the Doctor may have put it in *The Snowmen*) since *Summer Falls*, like *The Angel's Kiss*, was released by BBC Books as a spin-off from this episode. From the production team's point of view, this is a good merchandising opportunity if there aren't any aliens that would make a good toy in an episode. While I was not too convinced by the realisation of the girl on the book cover coming to life, I did chuckle when Clara tells Artie that

"[Chapter] Eleven is the best. You'll cry your eyes out." Moffat is clearly referring to the Eleventh Doctor here, and his eventual fate…

Another recycled device that does not work so well is that of the 'disembodied voice crying over a microphone', which Moffat used to much better effect at the end of *The Impossible Astronaut*. Now that I've watched *The Bells of Saint John* several more times, I've come to the conclusion that there is particularly nothing wrong with Jenna-Louise Coleman's performance when she is partially downloaded here, it's just that this device has been used too many times before for it to be truly startling this time. Indeed, Moffat uses this device a great deal at the beginning of the episode to set the scene. It could be that what is wrong here is the inclusion of the webcam footage. This is a good device to emphasise that peoples' souls have somehow been pulled into their computers, but ultimately it doesn't really work. For instance, the opening narrator is able to draw the alien wi-fi symbols on a piece of paper using the black marker pen from his home office… Indeed, I think that it is this exposition of the scenario at the beginning of the episode that is ultimately at fault here, for clearly Nabile must have some idea that he is trapped within a digital simulation of his office, if nothing else. Indeed, a much better representation of disembodied people within the wi-fi cloud would have been to just have their faces set against a blank black background, to make the experience even more disorientating and disembodying for them. There's nothing particularly original about my suggestion, as I have most likely derived it from the 1999 film *The Matrix*. Indeed, Moffat probably drew a great deal of influence from this movie for *The Bells of Saint John*, especially as Mahler appears to be a poor man's Agent Smith. This Keanu Reeves film, in turn, contains echoes of the Time Lords' Matrix, which first featured in the 1976 Classic Series adventure, *The Deadly Assassin*.

It is a big surprise to see the Great Intelligence reappearing so soon after the previous episode, especially as Richard E. Grant's Simeon seemed to be the usual one-off villain for the Christmas Special. As we now know though, Moffat intricately binds up Clara's fate with that of the Great Intelligence in the series finale, *The Name of the Doctor*. Since the title of the Yeti's last adventure in the Classic Series is *The Web of Fear,* it is not a big surprise that Moffat would have the Great Intelligence attacking the world via the Internet. Indeed, in the early years of the World Wide Web (1995), the Great Intelligence made a similar, but more basic assault on humanity via computer in

Downtime. This fan-produced *Doctor Who* spinoff featured Brigadier Lethbridge-Stewart, and introduced his daughter Kate, who would later pop up in this series' *The Power of Three* and *The Day of the Doctor*. I recall this Reeltime Pictures production as being quite fun and well-made at the time, although it has probably aged quite a bit now. Since it was the events of *The Web of Fear* that inspired the formation of UNIT, it's appropriate that they get a cameo appearance at the end of this episode. Unlike Steven, I thought the analogy of the Great Intelligence's care for humanity as being akin to a farmer's cultivation of his cattle to be an appropriate one. However, it is yet another device that Moffat has already used this series, as a mere two episodes ago, the Weeping Angels imprisoned human livestock within their version of a battery farm. Not that this is a particularly original idea on Moffat's part, as I'm sure similar ideas have been expressed before in vampire fictions like the 2009 movie *Daybreakers*.

I think Celia Imrie's performance is excellent in this episode, and I especially liked the way that whenever she takes over another human, they adopt Miss Kizlet's Received Pronunciation. Miss Kizlet's reversion to her childhood, when she first encountered the Great Intelligence (like Simeon in *The Snowmen*), is something that Imrie brilliantly brings off. The way that the spoonheads repeat what their victims say back to them could be a subtle hint on Moffat's part here that the Doctor is dealing with the Great Intelligence again, since it reflected people's unconscious thoughts and anxieties back at them in *The Snowmen*, much as it does here. However, I think that it's a huge leap that having control of the wi-fi enables the Great Intelligence to control the actions of ordinary people, even those that they have not downloaded yet. (I know, I know - uploading people's souls into a wi-fi cloud is just as impossible, but it's more believable, as we have seen this happen before in other narratives like *The Matrix*.)

Having watched the whole series, it's evident that Clara derived her skill at hacking computers from the Great Intelligence, which the other Oswald, Oswin, put to great use in *Asylum of the Daleks*. This tends to suggest that the Clara that we are dealing with here is the original. To put it another way, if Oswin is a genius computer hacker due to the events of this episode, then all the splinters of Clara must be also, for Clara was a genius computer hacker when she entered the Doctor's life cycle in *The Name of the Doctor*. So if the Clara we see here is one of these splinters, then she should have been a genius computer hacker from the start of this episode... Since she is not, then this must be the original Clara. Reviewing Moffat makes my head hurt, since it's all timey-wimey, wibbly-wobbly stuff. The Doctor's huge deductive leap that Clara is now a computer genius because she made an innocuous joke about Twitter was one of several duff moments in this episode. (I found the reference to the real police box outside Earl's Court tube station to be much funnier.) This episode also sees Clara devising the name "Oswin" as a computer password, as it's similar to the memorable phrase "Clara Oswald for the win!" It's likely that Clara half-remembers the first and middle name of her future and Victorian selves that the Doctor mentioned at the beginning of this episode. However, as I previously discussed in my review of *Asylum of the Daleks*, Moffat most probably used the masculine name of Oswin for Clara in her first appearance due to its etymology in Old English, since Clara's surname, Oswald, has similar roots.

When the Doctor exits the TARDIS on his motorbike, the doors appear to shut behind him automatically, something that we've never seen them do before. Another possible mistake is that when the camera zooms out while Clara wakes up in the café, we can see the Doctor's motorcycle helmet and goggles on top of the next table. However, the reason why the spoonhead double of the Doctor is so effective is because it's wearing the Doctor's motorcycle helmet and goggles… I suppose the Doctor could have programmed the spoonhead to copy his helmet and goggles as it did the rest of his clothes, but why not just give it the originals? While I'm writing about the Doctor's clothes, I must point out that it's rather strange that the Doctor now keeps all his clothes at the base of the TARDIS console. I guess the production team did this for budgetary reasons, or because they wanted to save the reveal of the TARDIS interior for *Journey to the Centre of the TARDIS* later on in the series. On a more positive note, there is nice continuity in the Doctor wearing Amy's reading glasses prior to his attempt to entice Clara into becoming his new companion. Indeed, once you get rid of the Doctor's flirtatious banter with a companion, the only motivation any human would have to join the Doctor in his travels would be a death wish, or insatiable wanderlust, so it's just as well that Clara suffers from the latter, especially as the Doctor doesn't kidnap humans any more. As to who gave Clara the TARDIS phone number? Well, since Billie Piper's appearance in *The Day of the Doctor* was as an avatar for the Moment, it cannot have been Rose, so I think that we will have to go with the presumption that it was River Song, unless Moffat ever tells us otherwise. (The suggestion from Peter Capaldi's opening episode, *Deep Breath*, is that it was the previously unseen character Missy who gave Clara the Doctor's phone number.) *The Bells of Saint John* is not a beauteous bounty, but it does keep us ticking over with hints of future plotlines. For now, the emphasis is not on "Doctor who?", rather it is on "Clara who?"

7: The Rings of Akhaten

Writer: Neil Cross
Director: Farren Blackburn
Originally broadcast: 6 April 2013

Cast

The Doctor: Matt Smith
Clara: Jenna-Louise Coleman
Dave: Michael Dixon
Ellie: Nicola Sian
Merry: Emilia Jones
The Chorister: Chris Anderson
The Mummy: Aidan Cook
Dor'een: Karl Greenwood

Steven's Review: It may just be coincidence – although, given showrunner Steven Moffat's fondness for building in connections and references between episodes, I wouldn't bet on it – but the story of the Doctor's new companion Clara is following a very similar trajectory as those of two of his previous fellow travellers. Just as happened with Rose in 2005 (*The End of the World*) and Amy in 2010 (*The Beast Below*), when Clara tells the Doctor that for her first trip into time and space, she wants to see "something awesome," she finds herself being whisked away from present-day Earth to a fantastical adventure in a weird alien environment.

Last week I expressed the expectation that this episode would be a stand-alone story, separate from the ongoing season arc plot. I was partially right – there's certainly no sign of the Great Intelligence, the behind-the-scenes adversary of *The Bells of Saint John*. But the Doctor is now fully engaged with the mystery of Clara, and the teaser shows him digging through the story of her life. He travels back to observe the meeting of her parents, a chance occurrence as a young Ellie Ravenwood saves Dave Oswald from a hit-and-run accident. He checks in at various points as their daughter grows up, culminating with him observing a sixteen-year-old Clara (nice costume and makeup work to turn Coleman back into a convincing teenager for that scene, by the way) standing with her father over Ellie's grave. But to his bafflement, the Doctor can find nothing to connect this girl with the 19th-century Clara he met in *The Snowmen* or with Oswin from *Asylum of the Daleks*.

Eventually, we're going to have to start getting some answers about what's going on with Clara, but as the brooding shot of the Doctor that closes the episode indicates, right now both he and we are still in the dark. We do get some further possible clues in this episode, though. At one point, the TARDIS refuses to open for Clara, and she gets the "feeling" that it doesn't like her. It may also be significant that the language translation feature of the TARDIS doesn't seem to be working for Clara with regard to some of the aliens she meets in this episode. (However, the translation feature of the TARDIS has occasionally failed before, mostly for comic effect; see, for example, the Hath in 2008's *The Doctor's Daughter*.) It seems like Clara will turn out be some kind of temporal paradox or anomaly, and we've seen the TARDIS react badly to such things before – for example, when it encountered the resurrected Captain Jack Harkness in *Utopia* (2007), it travelled to the end of the universe itself in an effort to shake him off.

This season's new addition to *Doctor Who*'s stable of writers is Neil Cross, the creator of the dark psychological crime thriller series *Luther*. After writing the forthcoming episode *Hide* (due to be shown in two weeks' time), he was then commissioned for a second script, and came up with this piece, which would seem to be somewhat outside his normal comfort zone. He brings the Doctor and Clara to the Saturn-like rings of the planet Akhaten, which contain a bustling marketplace (clearly inspired by the Mos Eisley scenes in *Star Wars*) where many different creatures from the seven inhabited planets of the system come together. The tone is light and whimsical, as several minutes are spent on Clara's reactions to the variety of creatures around her, and some silliness involving her and the Doctor barking like a dog to communicate with one of the aliens in order to hire a moped-like vehicle.

Apart from the *Star Wars* influences, there's a vaguely ancient Egyptian feel to this alien environment, ranging from the name Akhaten itself, to the pyramid on one of the rings' asteroids which is the main focus of the story, to the mummy-like creature imprisoned inside it that serves as a decoy villain (although as the Doctor points out, it actually behaves more like a vampire). The use of memories as currency is a nice touch – in order to buy things here, you have to give up an object that is important to you. Pleasingly, this is not just a clever bit of world-building, but actually ties in to the resolution of the story. Not so pleasingly, the plot contrivance that requires Clara to be the one to give something up (a ring that she received from her mother) rather than the Doctor – who should have any number of such memories in his pockets – is jarringly obvious.

There have been quite a few episodes of the new *Who* series that have been a little too fast-paced for their own good, but *The Rings of Akhaten* has the opposite problem: it's not until ten minutes into the episode that the first suggestion of actual plot appears. In a frankly rather clumsy piece of either scripting or direction, the Doctor simply wanders away for no good reason so that Clara is alone when she encounters a young girl who is clearly running from something. *Doctor Who* has showcased quite a number of good child actors in important roles over the last few years, and Emilia Jones is another of them. As Merry, the "Queen of Years" who is apparently a repository of the accumulated songs and stories of her people, she is the central character of the story, the one who is supposed to lead a ritual hymn to the "sleeping god" within the pyramid. Jones is entirely natural and believable as she convincingly conveys Merry's fear of messing up the upcoming performance. She establishes a nice rapport with Coleman, as Clara – in what is no doubt a deliberate echo of the governess version of the character in *The Snowmen*, as well as her own role as nanny to two young charges – reassures the young girl and leads her back to those searching for her.

The direction of this episode is by Farren Blackburn, whose previous work (on *The Doctor, the Widow and the Wardrobe*) I found to be rather lacking. This is a stronger script than that 2011 Christmas special, but he still fails to bring much above and beyond the most workmanlike telling of the story. The marketplace seems very small-scale, with no open spaces, giving no sense of a larger world beyond the few dressed corridors we see. As mentioned above, the episode is very slow-paced (even discounting the singing sequences, where a measured, deliberate tempo is appropriate), and drags at several points. Just compare the space moped scenes here with the motorcycle sequences from last week's episode to see the lack of dynamism in Blackburn's direction. For almost its entire first half, the episode just ambles along, with the only hint of menace coming from the Vigil, a trio of impressively designed black-coated humanoids with metallic skulls for heads. These creatures are also searching for Merry, but (thanks to Clara) the girl gets back to her guardians without Clara or the Doctor even seeing them.

The critical moment of the plot, when Merry's song is disrupted and the sleeping god begins to wake, is quite badly mishandled. It's totally unclear whether it happened by accident (due to Merry making a mistake), or whether the sleeping god somehow caused it (as the Doctor later guesses). Even more annoying, as Merry is seized by some force and dragged through space toward the pyramid, only the Doctor and Clara show any reaction – not one of the hundreds of other creatures taking part in the ceremony seems to want to do anything about it. (There's a half-hearted attempt later to explain this away by saying that they all regard the pyramid as sacred ground; it's not remotely believable.) While the profusion of creature designs in this episode is certainly eye-catching, the fact that they're all effectively nothing more than background local colour is regrettable.

There is, at least, an effective set-piece when the Doctor, Clara, and Merry are trapped inside the pyramid with the awakening "god". The Doctor has to hold off the Vigil, who are trying to force Merry to sacrifice herself to the creature – something which, thanks to her training, she is half-willing to do, and the Doctor and Clara have to talk her out of it. With the focus narrowing back down to just the main characters, the episode briefly becomes tense and exciting. I'm even prepared to forgive the overuse of the Doctor's sonic screwdriver, since unlike other episodes where the device has been treated as a magic wand, the writer took care to ensure that the obstacles here were appropriately sonic in nature (sonic locks on the door, and some kind of sound-based attack from the Vigil).

Although the storytelling is muddled, the episode still contains some interesting thematic ideas, particularly an approach to the idea of a soul that is not conventionally religious. The show has generally tended to be quite antagonistic toward religion (particularly organized religion). Here, though, the Doctor espouses a "live and let live" approach – when he tells Clara about the belief of the people of this system that all life in the universe originated on Akhaten, she asks if it's true, and he simply replies: "Well, it's what they believe… It's a nice story." Later, he expounds on the notion of "soul" as a term for the sum total of memories, experiences, and circumstances that make up a person, with a speech (beautifully delivered by Matt Smith) that sounds like it could have been inspired by Carl Sagan (with an *Alice in Wonderland* reference thrown in for good measure):

The Doctor: “Hey, do you mind if I tell you a story, one you might not have heard? All the elements in your body were forged many many millions of years ago, in the heart of a faraway star that exploded and died. That explosion scattered those elements across the desolations of deep space. After so many millions of years those elements came together to form new stars and new planets. And on and on it went – the elements came together and burst apart, forming shoes and ships and sealing wax, and cabbages and kings. Until, eventually, they came together to make you. You are unique in the universe. There is only one Merry Galell, and there will never be another. Getting rid of that existence isn’t a sacrifice – it is a *waste*.”

Having convinced Merry not to sacrifice herself, the Doctor, Clara and the girl manage to escape from the pyramid through a rather too convenient secret door. But the Doctor then finds himself facing a much bigger problem, as the creature within the pyramid is revealed to be nothing more than an “alarm clock” – a mechanism to wake up the real “sleeping god”. The actual enemy is a voracious mental parasite that covers the entire planet of Akhaten (or perhaps *is* the planet Akhaten – again, the writing and direction leaves it unclear). It’s a nicely unexpected plot turn that escalates the stakes well, although it does have the effect of making all the stuff with the vampire creature threatening to escape from its cage seem rather redundant.

The Doctor attempts to overload the planet-creature by feeding it his own vast lifetime of memories and experiences. The combination of Matt Smith’s performance and the music and singing in the background is very effective, even though we’ve seen the Doctor give this kind of bombastic speech several times before (most memorably, in 2010’s *The Pandorica Opens*). But the creature manages to successfully absorb the Doctor’s memories, with no apparent deleterious effect on the Doctor, which means this part of the ending falls flat – if the Doctor was actually under no threat, why was he so reluctant to face the creature? At least the final twist successfully ties together the previously separate strands of plot, as Clara ends up destroying the planet-creature by utilizing the very leaf which we saw at the top of the episode leading to her parents meeting, and which she has kept ever since her mother died. For her, it signifies an infinity of possible days that her mother might have had.

It’s a poetic idea for an ending – although it seems rather baffling that Clara could affect the creature with her possible future "memories", but the Doctor couldn't. (Unless it's all tied up with the still unexplained mystery of Clara.) Unfortunately, the way the resolution is depicted on screen seems to have misled many people into thinking that Akhaten's star was being destroyed (which would of course instantly doom all life in that system). The confusion is understandable, even though the Doctor explicitly named the object as the *planet* Akhaten early in the episode, thanks to the fiery CGI effects used to depict the creature and its destruction. (I'd also contend that it was a misjudgment to show crude facial features within the swirling flames while the Doctor and Clara were talking to the creature, making it look like they were confronting a gigantic Halloween pumpkin.) But the episode simply forgets about Akhaten in its haste to get back to Earth, leaving the ending unnecessarily incoherent.

At least the final scene is nicely reflective and provides some real character development, as Clara finds her house "looks different" now, even though the Doctor has returned her to the very same day she left. Conveniently, she happens at this moment to realise that the Doctor was watching her years ago at her mother's gravesite, and naturally wants to know why.

The Doctor: "You remind me of someone."
Clara: "Who?"
The Doctor: "Someone who died."
Clara: "Well whoever she was, I'm not her, okay? If you want me to travel with you, that's fine. But as me… I'm not going to compete with a ghost."

But she still isn't joining the Doctor for good yet; she exits the TARDIS to return to her home, leaving the Doctor still pondering her mystery, having reached another dead end.

The Rings of Akhaten had the potential to be an excellent story, an elegant fable about the importance of memories and stories. It's still worth watching for its unusual lyrical feel (I loved the final touch of Clara receiving back the ring she gave up, as a reward for her actions in saving all the people of Akhaten), but with more clarity and focus in the script to reduce the arbitrariness of the plotting, and some more dynamic direction, it would have been considerably more effective.

Steven's Classic Who DVD Recommendation: Actually, the word "recommendation" may not be quite fitting in this context, since it's one of the poorest stories of the Classic Series, but *Time and the Rani*, the story which introduced Sylvester McCoy as the Seventh Doctor, with Bonnie Langford as his companion Melanie, did come to mind when I was watching the gaudy background aliens in *The Rings of Akhaten* – the bat-like Tetraps from *Time and the Rani* would have fit right in.

***Kevin's Review*:** I struggled a bit with *The Rings of Akhaten* at first. I loved the brilliant opening, where we discovered more about Clara's origins. The opening scenes set in the rings of Akhaten were also visually stunning. However, the singing then started, and it seemed that Neil Cross had contrived this episode to be an empty parody of religion. My initial thoughts were that the production team had thrown a lot of money at a very poor episode. There are some Classic Series adventures that look very exciting when you judge them by their promotional photos, which then turn out to be very lacklustre when you see them all the way through, and I thought that *The Rings of Akhaten* had turned out to be one of these. In particular, there are some brilliant examples of costume design that I thought would be wasted on what I initially thought was a weak episode.

However, I think that this one of those *Doctor Who* adventures that you need to watch with the curtains drawn, and all other distractions curtailed. I very much enjoyed Neil Cross's other episode this series, *Hide*, so I decided to give *The Rings of Akhaten* another chance. Steven has previously argued that Chris Chibnall must be a fan of the Pertwee years, and I think that Cross possibly is too. However, it is evident that Cross is a fan of Lucasfilm too. Steven has already mentioned that the Akhaten marketplace looks like Mos Eisley cantina from *Star Wars Episode IV: A New Hope*. Yet it is revealing that the maiden name of Clara's mother is "Ravenwood", which, of course, is also the surname of the heroine in *Raiders of the Lost Ark*. The first Indiana Jones film was released in the summer of 1981, just before Clara's parents meet. The Doctor will later save his sonic screwdriver from being crushed under a falling stone door in this episode, something that Indy was always apt to do with regards to his hat. Having written that, it's possible that Moffat is the Indiana Jones fan rather than Cross, as the *Doctor Who* showrunner has previously paid homage to Indy in the 2010 and 2011 finales.

As Steven mentions, there is a considerable Egyptian feel to this episode. Of course, this is not unusual in movie and TV Sci-Fi, since the original *Battlestar Galatica* and *Stargate* (to name but two) borrowed elements from Egyptology that are so fantastical that it is easy to imagine that they may have extraterrestrial origins. The Classic Series of *Doctor Who* also has two brilliant adventures derived from Egyptology: 1975's *The Pyramids of Mars* and 1979's *City of Death* (a great candidate for the best ever *Doctor Who* story). As soon as I heard of Cross's episode title, I thought that it might have an Egyptian theme, as Akhaten is fairly similar to the name of Pharaoh Akhenaten's capital city, Akhetaten, which means 'horizon of Aten'. Of course, we have already come across Pharaoh Akhenaten's wife, Nefertiti, this series during *Dinosaurs on a Spaceship*. However, Akhenaten is most famous for his changing of Egyptian religious practices from polytheism to monotheism. So profound was this change from the worship of many gods to one god (which many scholars believe that Akhenaten was the first to introduce) that some authorities (such as Sigmund Freud) believe that Akhenaten was a direct influence on Moses' efforts to introduce monotheism. Moses succeeded, where Akhenaten failed, for after the death of his son (the infamous Tutankhamun) succeeding Pharaohs restored the old Egyptian gods and excised references to Akhenaten and his god, Aten. Indeed, in this way, Cross's naming of the Akhaten culture could be his way of subtly referring to the Biblical God with little risk of offending anyone. Aten was a solar god, who manifested his power via our sun. This is probably why Akhaten looks and acts like a sun here, although it is actually a planet. Indeed, as Steven points out, Cross's script hasn't been fully realised on screen, as when Clara and the Doctor first step out on to the rings of Akhaten, there is supposed to be "the light of an alien sun" as well as the planet Akhaten. Part of the confusion is that, as the Doctor says, the pyramid is the "holy site for the Sun Singers of Akhat". Then again, even if Akhaten is a planet, instead of the sun, its constant fluctuations in size must have some gravitational effect on its ring system!

Unlike with Amy, there is a more immediate resolution to some of the mystery concerning Clara, as it does not take long for us to discover the significance of the leaf in Clara's book, *101 Places to See*, as it played an integral part in the meeting of Clara's parents. We also learn that Clara's mother was the original owner of *101 Places to See*. However, it is implicit that Ellie never got to see any of these places, possibly due to her being too busy rearing Clara, and then falling ill while her daughter matured. Indeed, it is this sense of the endless possibilities of a life unlived that is key to the resolution of this episode. Of course, since the BBC revived *Doctor Who* in 2005, it has become something of a tradition for a new companion to prove their worth by saving the day in their first trip in the TARDIS, so there is nothing new here in Clara's achievement. Yet there is an added irony that Clara is the perhaps the only person in the universe who can ever really reach her full potential, as she has many parallel lives.

I got very excited when the Doctor mentioned that he had previously visited the rings of Akhaten with his granddaughter, as when I first watched this episode, I was still hoping (somewhat improbably) that Clara would somehow be a manifestation of Susan. However, there is another possible subtle mention of the Doctor's granddaughter via the sight of the Doctor's cot in *Journey to the Centre of the TARDIS*. (When it first appeared in 2011's *A Good Man Goes to War*, the only reason why I could think the Doctor still had his cot was if he used it to ferry Susan into the TARDIS as a baby in his original escape from Gallifrey. However, we catch a brief glimpse of the teenaged Susan entering the 'wrong' TARDIS at the start of *The Name of the Doctor*, which does really spoil my theory!) Clara's apprehension that the TARDIS doesn't like her is confirmed later in this series; although, another reason why she possibly has trouble getting into the TARDIS is because she doesn't have a key. There is still a very subtle element of courtship about Clara's relationship with the Doctor at this moment, with Clara constantly popping back to the Maitland household, and thereby deferring a decision to 'move in' with the Doctor. Of course, the Doctor gave the TARDIS key to the Victorian Clara, but we haven't seen him hand over a key to modern-day Clara. At the end, Clara makes it clear that she's her own person, and not a stand-in for someone else. When Clara says, "I'm not going to compete with a ghost," she's subconsciously referring to the Victorian Clara that the Doctor lost in *The Snowmen*. However, I believe that Moffat implicitly means us to think that this is also a reference to Amy Pond, for the Doctor still appears to be suffering in the wake of her 'death'. When Clara hands over her dead mother's ring to Dor'een, the Doctor doesn't even think about handing over Amy's reading glasses, a similar memento that we know that he still has, as he uses them at the beginning of this episode. Indeed, I originally thought that that sentiment had passed for the Doctor by this story, and that his use of the reading glasses was perhaps nothing more than a memento mori of the Doctor's own aging, but now I believe that it still a subtle way for

Moffat to show that the Doctor is missing Amy. It is fitting that the Akhaten market uses the psychometric system, as this is what will ultimately save the day, when Clara presents Akhaten with "the most important leaf in human history".

Many commentators think that Clara's inability to converse with Dor'een is an example of the TARDIS's dislike of her by not enabling its automatic translation for her. However, it's only Dor'een's language that Clara is unable to understand. It may be that Dor'een's language is too basic to be translated, as the Doctor only communicates with her by barking. Clara's encounter with a runaway queen at the beginning of this episode is probably another reference to *Star Wars Episode IV*, which famously opens with a princess on the run. At first glance, I thought that Cross had presented a rather Marxist view of religion as the "opium of the people", which would explain why the crowd in the amphitheatre do nothing to help Merry or to save themselves. However, I now think that Cross presents a more sympathetic view of religion, since the singing of hymns does help a little to relieve the catastrophe at the end. Having written that, the Akhaten priests were prepared to sacrifice Merry's soul. (This is the third episode in quick succession that has featured people and/or their souls being bred as food for vampiric alien hosts. You wait fifty years for a soultrain, and then three turn up at once!) (RT Packard has written a very entertaining and insightful post about *The Rings of Akhaten* called *Oh My Stars: Doctor Who and Atheism* on his blog that is very worthwhile checking out – sometimesrhymes.com.)

Although this is Clara's first trip in the TARDIS, she has evidently adopted the Doctor's manner of speaking, especially when she describes the TARDIS as "A space-shippy thing. Timey, spacey." More touching is Clara's adoption of her mother's exclamation "Oh my stars!" – this is very poignant when used in such a cosmologically fascinating place as the rings of Akhaten. At first, I thought the Doctor's speech to Akhaten at the end was just a piece of hot air, with the Doctor pontificating for no good reason. Of course, it's a necessary part of the plot that the Doctor fails here, and now that I have watched this story again, the Doctor's speech is more measured than I initially thought it to be. Beyond that, the Doctor's speech is another opportunity to highlight how important his name is going to be during the resolution of *Doctor Who*'s 50th Anniversary: "And I know things. Secrets that must never be told. Knowledge that must never be spoken." Then again, when Clara tells Merry that she is no longer scared of being lost, I couldn't help recall that Clara sounded pretty frightened in the last episode after she had been uploaded to the Great Intelligence's data cloud, as she didn't know where she was… As Steven writes, Clara does a great job of comforting this young girl who appears to be a kind of Dalai Lama.

Although *The Rings of Akhaten* does have its faults, now that I have watched it a few times, I am much more enthusiastic about it. There are a few parts where the CGI is a bit strained, and where the illusion fails. But for the most part, *The Rings of Akhaten* is visually stunning, so I am sure that its imagery will live long in the memory of many young fans. It is also good to see that the production team are prepared to make such an ambitious episode, so hopefully we will see more of this boldness in Series 8's narrative.

8: Cold War

Writer: Mark Gatiss
Director: Douglas Mackinnon
Originally broadcast: 13 April 2013

Cast

The Doctor: Matt Smith
Clara: Jenna-Louise Coleman
Captain Zhukov: Liam Cunningham
Professor Grisenko: David Warner
Lieutenant Stepashin: Tobias Menzies
Piotr: Josh O'Connor
Onegin: James Norton
Belevich: Charlie Anson
Skaldak: Spencer Wilding
Voice of Skaldak: Nicholas Briggs

Steven's Review: I'm not the greatest fan of Mark Gatiss's writing for *Doctor Who*, which generally hasn't reached the heights of his work elsewhere (for example, on *Sherlock*). Certainly his previous two efforts for Matt Smith's Doctor, *Victory of the Daleks* in 2010 and *Night Terrors* a year later, were unimpressive at best. But *Cold War* is probably his best script yet for the show – a straightforward adrenalin rush of an episode, which very successfully reinvents a well-remembered monster from the Classic Series for the 21st century.

First seen in 1967, back when Patrick Troughton was the Doctor, the Ice Warriors always loomed large in any list of the show's most memorable aliens. Even though they only made four appearances on television (the last one as long ago as 1974), they made such an impression that they've been repeatedly used by the authors of the various *Doctor Who* ancillary media (comics, novels, and audio plays), who have built up quite a complex mythos on the scant back-story the television stories provided, of a militaristic race which evolved millennia ago in the cold, barren climate of Mars. It's somewhat surprising that it's taken this long for them to reappear in the revived series, but by all accounts showrunner Steven Moffat was worried that the creatures' design would be unsuited to the sort of fast-paced storytelling characteristic of the show these days. Indeed, despite their striking physical presence, the classic Ice Warriors are basically the archetype of the lumbering *Doctor Who* monster – stiff-legged green giants that shamble at a snail's pace in pursuit of their victims and talk with slow, hissing, hard to understand voices.

A neat demonstration of the contrast in pace between then and now is provided by the first five minutes of *Cold War*, which cover roughly the same narrative distance as the entire first episode of 1967's *The Ice Warriors*. A strange, alien creature has been found, frozen in ice, and brought back to the isolated location in which the story will take place. One of the humans who found it unwisely decides to melt the ice, resulting in the creature returning to life. The Doctor and company arrive in the middle of an emergency that threatens to destroy the whole place, which the Doctor scrambles to defuse, thereby gaining the respect (though not yet the trust) of the leader of the humans.

In this case, we are on board a Soviet nuclear submarine cruising beneath the North Pole in 1983 – a time when tensions between the United States and the USSR were running dangerously high. The Doctor and Clara start the story at a dead run, dumped straight into the crisis of the submarine being damaged and sinking as a result of a rampage from the reawakened Ice Warrior. Only after the Doctor manages to locate a nearby undersea ridge which can be used to arrest the sub's descent does the story pause for the traditional "who are you and what are you doing here" scenes as everyone finally stops shouting at each other long enough to listen. The period setting is evoked well by costumes and performances that resonate with Cold War-era films like *The Hunt for Red October* – Liam Cunningham as Captain Zhukov certainly seems to be channelling Sean Connery's appearance and performance from that film. The captain turns out to be the most open-minded of the crew, able to accept the Doctor's presence and work with him. On the other hand, his lieutenant Stepashin can only see the intruders as Western spies (which leads to a reiteration, for Clara and any new viewers' benefit, of the ability of the TARDIS to translate any language, when Clara innocently denies being able to speak Russian). The other members of the crew are barely even sketched; their main purpose is to provide a supply of victims for that venerable *Doctor Who* plot staple, the "base under siege", where a small group of trapped humans are picked off one at a time by a lurking alien menace.

The Doctor's confrontation with the captain as he tries to come up with an explanation for their presence that Zhukov can accept is cut short when the Ice Warrior comes upon them. His initial attempt to resolve the situation peacefully is thwarted when one of the crew uses an electrified cattle prod to temporarily stun the creature, which is then quickly chained up before it can recover. The episode's plotting is a little clumsy here, with the Ice Warrior's mere name being enough for the Doctor to know all about him. He spouts a lot of stuff about this "Grand Marshal Skaldak" being "sovereign of the Tharseesian Caste, vanquisher of the Phobos Heresy, the greatest hero the proud Martian race has ever produced," and so on – the gist of which is that Skaldak is a highly honourable foe, and the humans have now made an enemy unnecessarily. The situation deteriorates further as Skaldak, sending out a distress signal, learns he has been entombed for five thousand years, and is now alone.

The idea of the honourable nature of the Ice Warriors has its roots in the 1972 story *The Curse of Peladon* where they were shown as members of a far-future Galactic Federation, in the same way that *Star Trek*'s Klingons evolved from the simplistic adversaries of the original series into a much more complex culture in *The Next Generation* whose interests would sometimes be aligned with those of our heroes. The idea that Zhukov and the Doctor have now defined themselves as warriors opposed to Skaldak leads Clara to volunteer to go in and negotiate with the Ice Warrior. In a tense scene, she discovers that the chained-up Warrior is simply an empty shell – the creature has left its armour and is now lurking in the shadows.

The Doctor: "Skaldak got no answer from his Martian brothers. Now he's given up hope of being rescued. He thinks he's been abandoned. He's got nothing left to lose."

Gatiss here overhauls the Ice Warrior using the same approach to revamping a Classic Series icon that Robert Shearman took in 2005's *Dalek*. The external appearance of the creature is kept as unchanged as possible (although the crude pincers of the original have been sensibly upgraded to rather more flexible hands), and its toughness is emphasized – a shot of the Ice Warrior striding down a corridor, shrugging off a hail of bullets, is an iconic moment. Spencer Wilding brings the same imposing physicality to Skaldak as he did for the minotaur creature in 2011's *The God Complex*. Meanwhile, Nicholas Briggs, provider of all manner of monster voices for 21st Century *Who*, delivers a vocal presence to match. It is perhaps not as immediately distinctive as the halting, hissing sound of the classic Ice Warriors (in fact, it's very reminiscent of the voice he created for the Judoon in 2007's *Smith and Jones*), but the deep, gravelly tone does suit Skaldak's appearance well, while the old hissing voice would have been tedious and impractical given the amount of dialogue and range of characterisation that he has to exhibit in this episode. (This problem was actually recognised back in the days of the Classic Series – in all of their subsequent appearances after the first, the Ice Warriors were led by an "Ice Lord", a much more streamlined figure with a far less restrictive costume which allowed the actor inside to deliver a fully expressive performance, with his attendant Warriors reduced to barely-speaking supporting characters. Gatiss, however, chose not to utilise this option here, concentrating instead on the original Ice Warrior.)

The fact that just one isolated member of the race is shown as being more than a match for all the humans around it makes it a powerful threat. Most importantly, the episode shows off new capabilities which address the idiosyncrasies of the original design while still maintaining continuity with past stories. By revealing that the Ice Warrior is capable of leaving its armoured shell, Gatiss can have both the hulking behemoth and a fast, dangerous creature that lurks in the shadows, suddenly snatching people from above (like the monster in *Alien*) and ripping them apart. Although the Doctor says that Skaldak is doing this to learn about the defences and capabilities of his adversaries, it plays more like sheer brutal savagery – it's difficult to see why it would be necessary to "dismantle" the humans to find out how their submarine works – and rather undercuts the Doctor's constant reiteration that Skaldak must be treated as a civilized, honourable opponent.

David Warner as Professor Grisenko, the episode's main guest star, is very good in a role that is small but crucial, both plot-wise (it's the professor who sets everything off by finding Skaldak entombed in the ice) and in terms of character. With his shabby dress and eccentric obsession with Western pop music, he makes a delightful contrast to the strait-laced crew, and his bonding with Clara across several scenes is very nicely done. Amusingly, when he learns that she is from the future, his overriding concern is to find out whether his favourite band will split up. Unlike the cannon-fodder crew members, it means something when Skaldak suddenly grabs him from above, and when he is eventually released unharmed it's a real relief – even when Skaldak announces that he now has the information he requires "to end this cold war."

The direction, by Douglas Mackinnon, makes the most of the story's enclosed setting. Of course, some artistic license has been employed with the design of the submarine interiors – a real sub is considerably more cramped than is shown here – but Mackinnon maintains the necessary feeling of being in a confined space by using a lot of low-angle shots to keep the ceilings of the sets in view wherever possible. The constant presence of dripping water is also effective, and can't have been easy (or pleasant) to film in. True, there are a couple of ham-handed moments in the storytelling, such as when the Doctor first sees the Ice Warrior, where his reactions are stretched out to pantomime lengths, or the very predictable cut from the Doctor's "No, no… Never!" when Clara suggests herself as negotiator to the next shot of her entering the chamber where Skaldak is chained up. But he successfully generates plenty of pace and tension during the chase scenes by keeping the actual Ice Warrior creature out of sight as much as possible. Unfortunately, in the final face-off the Ice Warrior has to be fully visible, and the CGI rendering of Skaldak's head (the first time *Doctor Who* has ever fully shown the face of the Ice Warrior creature) is just a little too cartoony to be fully convincing.

In order to keep the Doctor and Clara trapped in the story, it's necessary for the writer to remove their access to the TARDIS. It's a rather shocking moment when the time machine suddenly disappears of its own accord early in the episode, but the explanation at the end is something of a let-down. Gatiss chooses to indulge in a fannish in-joke, as the embarrassed Doctor admits that he was tinkering with his ship and accidentally activated the HADS (Hostile Action Displacement System) – whose function is to allow the TARDIS to automatically remove itself from dangerous environments. It's one of the sillier examples in the Classic Series of a writer inventing a capability of the TARDIS for the sake of one story (in this case, 1969's *The Krotons*) which was then conveniently forgotten about in later stories. (The gag at the end of the episode also falls flat, with the Doctor asking the captain to give them a lift back to the TARDIS, which has apparently relocated itself to the South Pole. Unfortunately, that's in the middle of the Antarctic continent – good luck getting a submarine there!)

This episode was shot well before the two previous ones, which perhaps explains why Jenna-Louise Coleman's Clara is much more of a generic companion most of the time here. She does, however, get a telling moment, well played, when Clara sees the bodies of two of the crewmen killed by Skaldak. Shaken, she tells Professor Grisenko, "Seeing those bodies back there, it's all got very… real." Coleman also does well showing Clara screwing up her courage to approach the chained Ice Warrior, and her giddy relief afterwards. Interestingly, the Doctor's reply ("This wasn't a test, Clara") is about the only glancing nod that this stand-alone episode makes toward the ongoing season-arc plot of the Doctor's investigations into the mystery surrounding Clara. Otherwise, with their rapid-fire banter lobbed back and forth, there's no hint that they haven't been adventuring together for years.

Matt Smith gives his usual sure performance as the Doctor. His initial clowning around (when he arrives on the submarine thinking he's taking Clara to Las Vegas) soon gives way to seriousness as the magnitude of the problem becomes clear. In his speeches to the Ice Warrior, Smith shows great intensity as the Doctor tries to make a connection with the creature behind the mask, knowing he has nothing but words at his disposal to stop Skaldak from firing a missile that will trigger a nuclear holocaust. His appeal to the Warrior's sense of honour is suitably passionate, but falls a little flat due to the fact that, as mentioned above, this "honour" has not been much in evidence in Skaldak's actions throughout the story. An even greater problem is the unfortunate fact that the missiles could not have been successfully fired anyway while the submarine was trapped several hundred metres below the ice-covered surface of the sea. With the plausibility of this climax fatally undermined, it's perhaps just as well that the story is actually resolved via a completely unexpected twist. Suddenly it turns out that Skaldak's distress signal was not a failure after all – a Martian spaceship arrives, pulls the submarine back to the surface and simply beams Skaldak away.

This development, simply negating the supposition that had been driving the whole story until now (that Skaldak was alone and had nothing left to live for), imparts an unfortunate glibness to the ending. But on the positive side, it leaves room for Gatiss to finally pay off all the Doctor's (and Clara's) appeals to Skaldak's honour, as the tension remains until Skaldak, after being rescued, remotely aborts the missile launch, indicating that they did ultimately achieve a meeting of minds with the alien. (Although frankly, I'm not as convinced as Gatiss would probably like me to be that if Skaldak had managed to fire the missiles and *then* been rescued a few seconds later, he would have felt any great remorse.) The episode thus ends with a sense of relief that resonates strongly with its Cold War setting – our characters are left waiting, powerless, until forces beyond their control only just pull back from the brink the threatened apocalypse.

Steven's Classic Who DVD Recommendation: The original story featuring the Martian monsters, *The Ice Warriors* starring Patrick Troughton, with Frazer Hines and Deborah Watling, was recently released on DVD, with animation replacing the two episodes (of six) which no longer exist. Alternatively, for another *Doctor Who* inspired by the Cold War, check out a story made at the very time depicted in this episode, *Warriors of the Deep* starring Peter Davison, with Janet Fielding and Mark Strickson.

***Kevin's Review*:** It appears that during the 50th Anniversary year, the *Doctor Who* production team made a decision to increase the horror quota. As a result, this episode features an alien hunting down humans in a confined space. Steven has mentioned the similarity between this scenario and that of *Alien*; however, I think that the design of the unclothed Skaldak, especially with regards to his talon-like hands, is closer to that of the monsters in George Pal's 1953 version of *The War of the Worlds*. Indeed, since the alien invaders in H. G. Wells' novel are Martians, I am convinced that Mark Gatiss is making a deliberate homage to the Pal film. I'm not a great fan of Pal's version of *The War of the Worlds*, especially as all the action was moved from the UK to the USA and other liberties taken with the plot. No, I've a much closer affinity with Pal's more faithful adaptation of Wells' *The Time Machine* (1960), which, as I've discussed elsewhere in this book, I believe was a great influence to Terry Nation in his creation of the Daleks. The special effects and model work in *Cold War* are certainly a lot more polished and convincing than those in *The War of the Worlds*!

As Steven has mentioned, it does appear as though Robert Shearman's *Dalek* in 2005 is the template for introducing Classic Series monsters into 21st Century *Who*. As in Shearman's episode, it's not long before the monster is bound in chains. This is the third monster we've seen bound in chains so far this series – the Doctor really ought to get some better chains from B&Q, because most of the chains used throughout the series are quite clearly not alien proof. Although the Ice Warriors appear to have become more invincible in this episode, I think that Gatiss has also weakened their appeal somewhat by making them yet another cyborg monster, like the

Daleks and the Cybermen. (We'll probably find out in 20 years' time that the Weeping Angels are cyborgs too!) However, Spencer Wilding does a brilliant job of bringing the Martian body armour to life. Obviously, despite the threat that it poses, the Ice Warrior armour is not all that manoeuvrable within the tight confines of a sub, so it is good character development on Skaldak's part to show him 'thinking outside the box' in this way. Apart from the revelation that the Ice Warriors are cyborgs, Mark Gatiss brings very little other innovation to their realisation here. It's probably a wise choice that Gatiss has presented Skaldak as wearing the uniform of an Ice Warrior foot soldier here, as the armour that the Ice Lord Grand Marshals wore in the Classic Series was very effete and not very imposing. Consequently, it appears that Grand Marshals like Skaldak can wear whatever armour they like. (I certainly wouldn't want to argue with him about it!) It's good to hear that Martian women go into battle along with males, as Skaldak relates here, so it appears that Ice Warriors are not misogynist. Yet, as Steven points out, all Skaldak's and the Doctor's guff about Ice Warrior honour is quite hypocritical, given that the Martian attacks the humans first, and especially since the humans have rescued him from the ice. (Quite why Piotr takes it upon himself to release Skaldak from the ice is a bit of a mystery. Obviously, he was expecting to find a bit of frozen mammoth, but he doesn't look like the kind of chap that would get excited about prehistoric remains, especially as keeping the 'mammoth' in ice would be the best means to preserve it on their return to Moscow. Perhaps Piotr just wanted a mammoth burger? He must be one of this series' best candidates for a Darwin award!)

Mark Gatiss is quite traditional by first presenting Skaldak as an Ice Warrior trapped in ice, as that is how they first appeared in 1967's *The Ice Warriors*. It would have been nice if Gatiss had coined a more suitable name for this species, as this nomenclature derives from their first appearance. No doubt one day a Martian will say this in homage to 2010's *The Lodger*: "I'm an Ice Warrior. Well, they call me an Ice Warrior; I don't know why. I call me an Ice Warrior, too. I still don't know why." 'Martian' itself is a bit too generic. Skaldak talks about red snow here, so Ice Warriors evidently love the cold of Mars's polar regions. Indeed, if Ice Warriors do live in Mars's polar ice caps, then I suppose that they could keep this rather rudimentary name. (I guess it was inevitable that there was going to be an Ice Warrior episode called *Cold War* one day. Dan Abnett's 2011 Ice Warrior novel *The Silent*

Stars Go By was also set in a suitably wintry location.) One thing I did like though was Skaldak's use of "Martian Law", instead of the more common human term 'Martial Law'.

It's interesting to hear that Skaldak is famed as the "vanquisher of the Phobos heresy", as Phobos is, of course, one of Mars's moons, which Eton science master Henry Madan named after the Greek god of horror ('phobia' has the same etymology). Gatiss probably named Zhukov's deputy here after Sergei Stepashin, the former Russian prime minister (whose approach to warfare, I must point out, is almost the polar opposite of that of the bloodthirsty lieutenant). The Soviet submarine captain likely gets his name from Georgy Zhukov, the famed Red Army general from the Second World War, whose exploits appear equal to that of Skaldak. Liam Cunningham's performance is excellent – thankfully Zhukov is a much better role for him than the wooden president that he had to play in the BBC's 2011 sci-fi ratings disaster *Outcasts*. Having written that, I must admit that *Cold War* didn't grip me that much. My attention did wander quite a bit while rewatching this episode while preparing to write my review. Perhaps there could have been a literary subplot where Onegin spurns the attentions of a beautiful woman, shoots his best mate in a duel, and then falls for the woman, who rejects him in turn? (*Eugene Onegin*, is, of course, the title of a famous Russian novel by Alexander Pushkin.) David Warner's role as the professor is quite fun, and very much helps with the 80's setting. This is the second episode in a row that has featured 80's music and locations, and I must admit that it's a bit scary seeing years from my childhood being depicted onscreen as 'historical'. 1983 was rather a tense period in the Cold War. In September of that year, the Soviet Union shot down a Korean Air Lines plane that had wandered into Soviet airspace, killing many Americans aboard (an incident that the media has compared to the shooting down of a Malaysian passenger plane over Ukraine while I was writing this book). Also in September 1983, the Soviet Union's early warning system twice reported the launch of American missiles, but fortunately a Soviet military officer correctly recognised these as being false alarms.

Unlike Steven, I do think that there was a rationale for Skaldak's dissection of the submariners, as this was his way of learning about human anatomy; the Shakri kidnapped humans from the hospitals in which Rory worked in *The Power of Three* for much the same reason. Fortunately, Gatiss spares us the sight of dissected humans, but Clara does see them. Jenna-Louise Coleman portrays Clara's shock really well, and it's lucky that the affable Grisenko is on hand to comfort her. Perhaps Peter Capaldi's Doctor will provide a similar grandfatherly shoulder to cry on? This bloodshed really brings it home to Clara that there is a deadly serious side to travelling with the Doctor and saving the world. Kudos must also go to Coleman and all the other actors for putting up with the constant dripping water in this episode. *Cold War* also contains another subtle allusion to the Doctor's role in bringing about an end to the mutually assured destruction of the Time War. As we know from later in the series, the War Doctor was prepared to push the nuclear button of the Moment in order to prevent more peoples suffering from the Time War. In light of his tremendous grief at having taken this action, the Doctor finds an alternative solution to a similar dilemma here, when he becomes prepared to destroy the whole submarine as a way of preventing Skaldak from launching the missiles. The Doctor is prepared to sacrifice himself to stop Skaldak making the same mistake of committing the genocide of billions of innocent people. Zhukov's recognition of the Doctor as a fellow warrior is another subtle allusion to the War Doctor, in a dialogue that is otherwise a pretty pointless way of placing Clara in peril.

Probably the only new thing that we learn about the Doctor here is that he carries a Barbie doll around with him to which he is quite attached. (I'm not quite sure how Dor'een would have reacted if the Doctor had presented it as payment to her during the previous episode!) Admittedly, I'm uncertain what to make of 21st Century *Who*'s practice of constant product placing. Obviously, the *Doctor Who* production team haven't really entered into commercial deals with the likes of Mattel or Nintendo, and I think the inclusion of products like the Wii do add a lovely element of verisimilitude to the programme. If I ever see a Dalek for real, then who knows? Maybe I'll take the Doctor's example, and threaten it with a Jammie Dodger. I'm sure that this would be a more ethical approach than threatening it with a cattle prod (an apparent North American trait that Grisenko has introduced to the Soviets). I'm sure that Ultravox and Duran Duran aren't complaining about the royalty cheques that they'll be getting as a result of this episode. However, I think the one thing that would really would have made this story come alive for me was if Skaldak had been allowed to dispatch the crew one by one with *Hungry Like the Wolf* pounding out of the soundtrack… That really would have made my mouth come alive "with juices like wine."

9: Hide

Writer: Neil Cross
Director: Jamie Payne
Originally broadcast: 20 April 2013

Cast

The Doctor: Matt Smith
Clara: Jenna-Louise Coleman
Alec Palmer: Dougray Scott
Emma Grayling: Jessica Raine
Hila: Kemi-Bo Jacobs
The Crooked Man: Aidan Cook

***Steven's Review*:** The second story of the season from Neil Cross, *Hide* is a very smart piece of work that keeps the audience on its toes – a nicely spooky haunted house story with character depth as well as creepiness, which turns into a time-travel-gone-wrong story, which twists again when you least expect it to become, of all things, an alien love story. A high-quality script is combined with excellent production, resulting in one of the best episodes of the season so far.

If the expansive panorama of *The Rings of Akhaten* two weeks ago was a grandiloquent, operatic production with full chorus, this episode is a chamber piece as intricately detailed as a string quartet, with Cross restricting himself throughout to just a handful of individual characters. The story is centred around the wonderfully named Caliburn House (a nod to Shakespeare's monstrous Caliban in *The Tempest,* and a hint of what's to come) on a dark and stormy night in 1974. Psychic researcher Alec Palmer is working with empath Emma Grayling to investigate a presence which has been documented as haunting this area for hundreds of years, even before this gloomy, forbidding mansion was built. Emma manages to make contact with an indistinct, screaming white figure, but their experiment is suddenly interrupted by the Doctor and Clara knocking on the front door.

The Doctor talks his way inside with a bluff about being some kind of government inspector amid a flood of exposition that shows he already knows all about Alec and Emma, including the secret espionage work that Alec was involved in during World War II. I could have done without the over-the-top clowning in this scene ("Oh, bliss… nice action on the toggle switches. You know, I do love a toggle switch. Actually, I like the *word* toggle. Nice noun, excellent verb…"), which is one of the few facets of Matt Smith's Doctor that often doesn't work for me. But it does at least contrast well with the Doctor's experiences later in the episode, when Smith will get to show some deeper emotions – including, unusually for the Doctor, fear. Of more importance is that, unlike *Cold War* last week, where the Doctor was given pre-existing knowledge of Skaldak's past simply in order to speed the narrative along, here the Doctor's info-dump about Alec and Emma will be justified in retrospect by the revelation at the end that (unknown to Clara) he came here deliberately.

Despite only half-accepting the Doctor's tale of being from the Ministry, Alec shows him the collection of notes and photographs he has assembled concerning the manifestations of the Caliburn ghost – otherwise known as the Witch of the Well. The whole setup is (as Cross has happily acknowledged) a direct homage to Nigel Kneale's 1972 drama *The Stone Tape* – even down to a detail like Alec's mention of the tins of spam left by servicemen stationed at the house during the war, found years later along with handwritten notes appealing to the ghost ("For the love of God, stop screaming"). *Doctor Who* has never been averse to taking already told stories and putting its own spin on them: in the 1970's the early Tom Baker years saw a number of stories inspired by famous horror movies, while Kneale's *Quatermass* stories – seminal works of British television science fiction in the 1950's – were plundered for the bases of several Jon Pertwee adventures. Alec's calm, deliberate tone as he tells the history of the Witch builds up an effectively creepy atmosphere, but then the first reversal of the story takes place, with a hint that the apparition might not be malevolent after all:

Emma: "She knows I'm here. I can feel her calling out to me."
Clara: "What's she saying?"
Emma: "'Help me…'"

The production design is excellent, and the direction from newcomer Jamie Payne is thoroughly effective at building the tension. Immediately after the dialogue quoted above, there's a wide shot of the four characters with an indistinct *something* passing quietly across the foreground. The Doctor and Clara go off to explore, and the house's dark, echoing rooms are full of shifting shadows thanks to being lit mainly by candles carried by the characters. The occasional glimpse of another presence lurking in the background is hair-raising.

But *Hide* has a lot more to it than just some creepy moments. The two guest stars both give wonderful performances. Dougray Scott is the embodiment of decency as the reticent war hero Alec. Jessica Raine's piercing eyes and quietly tense manner make it easy to believe in Emma's empathic talents. The title of the episode has multilayered significance, as they start to realize they have both been concealing their true feelings for each other.

Alec: "Experience makes liars of us all. We lie about who we are, about what we've done…"
Emma: "And how we feel?"
Alec: "Yes, always. Always that."

Entering the music room ("the heart of the house," according to Emma), the Doctor and Clara find a strange patch of coldness. The Doctor casually draws a chalk circle around it, which seems to trigger the strongest manifestation yet. When the tension rises as a loud, angry pounding noise echoes through the house, Clara has to tell the Doctor that while she might be a little bit terrified, he doesn't actually have to hold her hand. His response – "Clara… I'm not holding your hand" – is a lovely piece of multi-purpose scripting; it provides a laugh, combined with a scare as we get another glimpse of the mysterious presence, and is also a clever piece of foreshadowing for later.

The episode is very carefully paced, and knows when to relax the haunted-house antics and take a breath. A pair of parallel character development scenes, intertwined thanks to sensitive cutting between them, deepen the story and characters very satisfyingly. Alec tells the Doctor about his war work – not the facts, which the Doctor already knows, but his feelings about what he did ("I killed… and I caused to have killed") and how his involvement in ghost hunting is in some way a response to having survived the horrendous conflict ("It does tend to haunt you – living – after so much of… the other thing"). Matt Smith's face clearly shows how Alec's story resonates with the Doctor's own dark past. The warmth in Scott's performance as the Doctor asks Alec what he would say to those he sent off to their deaths if he could, and Alec simply replies, "Well, I'd very much like to thank them," is extraordinary. At the same time, Clara is teasing out Emma's attraction to Alec. Emma is worried that she might be seeing only what she wants to see, but Clara amusingly tells her that "it's obvious – it sticks out like a… big chin." Emma immediately asks the same question about Clara and the Doctor, but when Clara disclaims any such attraction the scene, which was threatening to become too cosy, takes an oddly ominous turn: "Good. Don't trust him. There's a sliver of ice in his heart."

What follows is a somewhat unusual interlude, as the Doctor and Clara go back to the TARDIS and embark on a journey through time, stopping at various points so the Doctor can snap photographs of the area. In most stories the TARDIS plays no part other than depositing the Doctor and his friends into the situation and taking them away again at the end; if it is used in the middle of a story, the writer always has to take care to address the implied question of why they don't simply leave and go somewhere else. In this case, the use of the TARDIS can be justified as being directly related to the Doctor's investigations. The sequence also serves the purpose of providing some more time to spend on exploring the relationship between the Doctor and Clara.

This is the first story Jenna-Louise Coleman recorded as Clara (even before her work on *The Snowmen*), and she's clearly still finding the character, falling back a little too often into generic perkiness – some of which is nevertheless amusing, like the moment of childish playacting when Clara wants the Doctor to *dare* her to explore the house. But she makes the most of a couple of telling scenes where Clara's more thoughtful side comes through – the scene with Emma already mentioned, and the moment here when the banter dies away at Clara's realization that the Doctor's investigating technique involves casually making a survey through the Earth's entire history. As she says, the Doctor's mastery of time means that everyone is like a ghost to him. When she presses him further ("What are we to you? What can we possibly be?") he tells her, "You are the only mystery worth solving" – leaving it nicely ambiguous whether he means humanity in general, or Clara in particular.

Returning to the house, the Doctor reveals that the "ghost" is actually a woman named Hila Tacorian from Earth's future. A pioneer in an early time-travel experiment which failed, she became trapped in a "pocket universe" adjacent to ours, where time passes at a vastly different speed. This is the only clumsy moment in this otherwise deftly constructed script, as the Doctor tells us all about Hila in a massive info-dump that comes out of nowhere. Rather than slowly gathering clues to work out what's going on, the Doctor suddenly seems to know everything about Hila already, and the photographs he took from the TARDIS end up being a mostly irrelevant slideshow. Nevertheless, it's still an effective twist as the story pivots from investigating a ghost to rescuing a trapped woman.

The Doctor's method of creating a portal into the pocket universe where Hila is trapped involves amplifying Emma's mental abilities, using a nice reference to the past for long-term viewers. (In another such reference, his trips to the far-past and far-future Earth made use of the orange spacesuit worn by David Tennant in 2006's *The Satan Pit* and 2009's *The Waters of Mars*.) From the end of the Jon Pertwee era in (appropriately) 1974 comes the blue crystal from Metebelis 3 – a name which, unfortunately, is jarringly mispronounced by Matt Smith, incorrectly emphasising the second syllable rather than the third. It was very surprising to see such an error being allowed through by a production team which has several people (showrunner Steven Moffat among them) with an encyclopedic knowledge of the Classic Series. (In a later interview, Moffat revealed that the mistake *was* noted and a redubbed version of the dialogue recorded, but owing to some miscommunication it failed to make it into the final episode.)

Even now that the story has opened out from the haunted house, the spooky atmosphere is successfully maintained. Entered through a portal filled with blinding light that recalls Steven Spielberg's *Poltergeist* (1982), the pocket universe appears as a cold, otherworldly, mist-filled forest floating in the void. The Doctor quickly locates Hila, who is being pursued by the same kind of misshapen creature we have seen glimpses of in the house. Its odd, scuttling movements make the "Crooked Man" (as the credits call him) genuinely unsettling. By the time the creature is finally revealed in full right at the end of the episode, later plot revelations have removed its menace, but it's still a wonderfully creepy piece of design – a twisted, warped version of a man that is probably near the limit of how scary a *Doctor Who* monster can be, given the large number of young children in the audience.

The Doctor manages to get Hila back to the real universe, thanks to an "echo" version of the house manifested by Emma. Characteristically, the Doctor gets distracted at a crucial moment by the realisation of what caused the loud pounding he heard earlier (the creature trying to get into the house) – and as Emma collapses, exhausted, the echo house disappears, leaving the Doctor marooned in the alien forest. Once past the goofiness of his opening scene, Matt Smith has been superbly watchable as usual, particularly now as he gets to show some real fear as the Doctor runs through the forest trying to evade the creature. It's interesting how much more vulnerable he looks without his bow tie (having used it to attempt to hold the doors of the echo house closed and keep the creature out).

Clara yells at Emma to re-establish the link, but it's Alec who finally gives her the strength to do so, openly committing to his feelings for her and thereby neatly bringing together the strands of the story. Clara returns to the TARDIS, hoping to use it to enter the pocket universe – which the Doctor had earlier rejected as too dangerous – and thereby rescue him. The curious antagonism between Clara and the TARDIS, first seen in *The Rings of Akhaten*, reappears. Earlier, she had told the Doctor of her feeling that the TARDIS didn't like her, which he humorously brushed off ("The TARDIS is like a cat. A bit slow to trust, but you'll get there in the end"). Now the ship refuses to allow her inside until the link is actually reopened by Emma. Even then, Clara's contribution to the Doctor's rescue is limited to screaming while being tossed around the console room as the TARDIS careens wildly through the pocket universe, the Doctor eventually escaping by clinging to its outside in a manner reminiscent of Jack Harkness in 2007's *Utopia*.

I greatly enjoyed the ingenious way the episode fakes us out with what appears to be the wrap-up scene, as daybreak finally arrives and the Doctor drops the revelation that Hila is actually Alec and Emma's remote descendant from the future. His advice to them to "hold hands and never let go" leads to the final realization – the monster was actually no threat at all; it had also become trapped in the pocket universe, and just wanted to be reunited with its mate in the house. ("Every lonely monster needs a companion" was also a nice reminder of the Doctor's ambivalent opinion of himself.) Particularly stylish is the abruptness of the ending – since we've already had a "farewell" scene, the episode simply cuts to black once the audience has been given enough pieces to put together the mechanics of the plot resolution for themselves.

But the most interesting aspect of the ending is the revelation that the Doctor deliberately came here in order to get Emma's opinion of Clara – helping out with the ghost was only a means to an end. He remains focused on unravelling the mystery of his new companion, but once again finds himself with no new information. For the moment, the show is deliberately keeping us at a distance from both the Doctor (which is normal) and his companion (which is not). We leave the episode with Emma's assurance that Clara is "a perfectly ordinary girl," but clearly there is something crucial about her that still remains hidden.

Steven's Classic Who DVD Recommendation: The 1977 tale *Image of the Fendahl*, starring Tom Baker and Louise Jameson, exhibits a number of uncanny parallels to this episode, with its story of psychic phenomena in an old country house, an empath among the locals, and even the same unusual use of the TARDIS to help with the Doctor's investigations. It is one of the Classic Series' most striking combinations of horror and science fiction, and is well worth checking out.

***Kevin's Review*:** *Hide* is probably my favourite episode of Series 7. Like Tom MacRae's *The Girl Who Waited* from 2011, this is an ideal of how brilliant *Doctor Who* can be, in its ability to create its own fantastically unique narratives. There's no other series on TV that could ever possibly carry off or even conceive of such a fabulous story as this. Yes, as Steven writes, Neil Cross was very inspired by Nigel Kneale in the writing of this episode, but the magic and madness of *Doctor Who* imbues his writing too. (Indeed, Cross originally intended to feature Kneale's infamous creation Professor Bernard Quatermass in this episode, but copyright restrictions prevented this, so he created the character of Alec Palmer instead.) So great is this script, that it's no surprise to hear that Moffat immediately commissioned Cross to write another. Neil Cross must be a *Doctor Who* fan (or an admirer at the very least), as the essence of our favourite Time Lord oozes through every scene of this script. Only a long-time fan could have thought of such an ingenious way to incorporate that infamous crystal from Metebelis Three that featured in the Classic Series Pertwee adventures *The Green Death* (1973) and *Planet of the Spiders* (1974).

As Steven notes, it's a bit of a shame that Matt Smith mispronounces 'Metebelis', but this is a rather minor blip in an otherwise perfect adventure. In addition to this, the lamp on top of the TARDIS uncharacteristically stays lit after materialisation. Another misstep that is not Neil Cross's fault was the decision to cast Dougray Scott as Palmer. Don't get me wrong, Scott gives an excellent performance, but surely it must have occurred to the production team that, as he's in his late forties, he's far too young to play Palmer? *Hide* is set in 1974, approximately thirty years after the Second World War, and unless Palmer was an exceptionally gifted and able teen prodigy, I don't see how he could possibly have had the responsibility of sending agents on dangerous missions. Indeed, although the agencies that the Doctor claims that Palmer worked for appear fictional – 'the Baker Street Irregulars', 'the Ministry of Ungentlemanly Warfare' – these are in fact nicknames for the SOE (Special Operations Executive) that ran clandestine missions in occupied Europe from 1940 to 1946. Palmer's upset at the prospect of having a project taken away from him by the ministry sounds similar to Churchill's order to destroy Colossus, the world's first electronic programmable digital computer, which played a huge role in the decryption of Nazi ciphers during World War II. (Dougray Scott, of course, starred as a Bletchley Park cryptanalyst in the 2001 film *Enigma*, which involved disrupting U-boat operations, just like Palmer here.) Although it is more plausible that Palmer would have run missions during the Korean War, the type of missions that he talks about, and his belief in the cause, confirms that he won his Victoria Cross in the Second World War. It's possible that the production team originally intended to add prosthetics to Scott so that he looked ten years older onscreen. Indeed, this seemingly impossible age gap between himself and Emma would provide an additional explanation as to why he cannot see the real woman in front of him while hunting for his ghost, and why he's still asking the Doctor at the end, "Well, what's supposed to happen? I mean, what do we do now?" In this light, it's interesting that Emma asks if Clara has any romantic feelings for the Doctor, as I've argued previously in the book that Moffat must have culled any notion of romance between the real Clara and the Doctor due to his decision to cast an older actor in the role following the departure of Matt Smith. The age gap between Jenna-Louise Coleman and Peter Capaldi is similar to that between Jessica Raine and Dougray Scott, but that doesn't seem to stop Emma from harbouring romantic feelings for Palmer, or the Doctor and Clara from pushing them in that direction.

At first, I thought the romantic ending for the Crooked Man was a bit of a bolt out of the blue, an unwelcome interruption from one of those sentimental moments that *Doctor Who* has borrowed wholesale from *Star Trek: The Next Generation* (the resolution of *Encounter at Farpoint* springs to mind). However, this idea of love surviving our inevitable deaths, through the genes that we carry on to the next generation, is a lovely poetic image. At the end, the Doctor reasserts Emma's pronouncement that love will always survive: "That's why the psychic link was so powerful. Blood calling to blood, out of time. Not everything ends. Not love. Not always." Or as Virgil wrote, "Love conquers all." Neil Cross presented us with a similar poetic metaphor in *The Rings of Akhaten*: "The soul's made of stories, not atoms. Everything that ever happened to us. People we love, people we lost. People we found again against all the odds." In this speech, the Doctor seems to be making a subtle allusion to his rediscovery of Clara, as someone he found "again against all the odds". Of course, we know from the resolution of this episode that the Doctor's main reason for visiting is to find out more about Clara's story. Emma's assertion that Clara is just an ordinary girl is perplexing to the Doctor. However, rather than the setback that this seems to be for the Doctor, this is actually a confirmation that this Clara is the original, for she is not one of the ghostly splinters that have scattered throughout the Doctor's timestream. At this point though, the Doctor still can't see beyond the mystery of how the same woman can live and die in several time streams. (I must mention at this point that Jessica Raine, who is splendid in the role of Emma, went on to play an even more pivotal role in 2013 when cast as Verity Lambert, the first producer of *Doctor Who*, in Mark Gatiss's dramatization of William Hartnell's years on the show, *An Adventure in Space and Time*.)

I thought that the characterisation of Clara was brilliant in this episode. For me, this is her best adventure of the series, along with *Asylum of the Daleks* and *The Snowmen*. Clara's interplay with the Doctor is very good, and I loved the high-fives that they give each other from time to time. Clara has some excellent interplay with the TARDIS when she gets to speak to its Voice Visual Interface, which confirms that the TARDIS does not like Clara, as first seen in *The Rings of Akhaten*, albeit via some vindictive dialogue. As I have previously written, Clara loses some of her sparkle once she no longer has flirtatious banter to fall back on, and the production team mostly compensates for this by getting her to prove her worth by doing earnest deeds. However, Cross gives her some excellent character development here, as he shows how scared she can be during her adventures with the Doctor, much like the disquiet Clara displayed after seeing the dismembered submariners in *Cold War*. Yet the production team do not present Clara as the stereotypical screaming 'frozen in the headlights' female companion of old. Although she may well cry in fear, the Doctor cries in fear beside her in this episode.

Indeed, I believe that *Hide* is very much Cross's love letter to the mid-70's Golden Era of *Doctor Who*, which was redolent of gothic horror. 'Hide' doesn't just refer to people hiding their feelings, it's also an allusion to *Doctor Who*'s classic mantra of '*hiding* behind the sofa'. This adventure is the first one in a long time that has made me feel genuinely unsettled and disturbed, as the production team ratchet up the fear quotient in this anniversary year. The way that director Jamie Payne shoots the 'Crooked Man' is really quite startling. Indeed, all of the creepy forest sequences in the pocket universe seem redolent of Tim Burton's 1999 version of *Sleepy Hollow*. In some ways, this reminded me of part of the *Blake's 7* episode *Trial*, where Blake, grieving from the death of one of his fellow freedom fighters, teleports down to a deserted planet. Unfortunately, this planet is a living entity that absorbs all 'parasites' on its surface like Blake… Watching this drama now as an adult is somewhat spoiled by the ridiculous costume that an alien in this episode wears, but this scenario very much appealed to my youthful imagination, just as I'm sure that countless young *Doctor Who* fans will remember *Hide*'s pocket universe for many a year. When I watched this episode again, I did so while wearing headphones. Consequently, I must praise the sound effects, which were just as brilliant as the visual effects. It was also great to hear the TARDIS's cloister alarm bell ringing again, since this is always a good sign that the Doctor is in considerable danger.

There's also a good bit of humour in this episode. I very much liked Clara's claim that she and the Doctor are *Ghostbusters*! (The Doctor evidently pre-warned her that they would be visiting a haunted house.) One theme that runs through this series is that of the "oldest question in the universe", so it's quite funny to see Palmer unconsciously subverting this by asking "Doctor what?" When Emma objects to the Doctor labelling her as Palmer's 'companion', the Doctor obliquely refers to second-wave feminism by replying: "It's 1974. You're the assistant and non-objective equipment. Meaning psychic." Of course, there is irony here, as Emma wants nothing more than to be Palmer's romantic partner. It's also amusing when the Doctor waxes lyrical about the loneliness of empathic psychics, while Emma (like Jex in *A Town Called Mercy*) is "still in the room". I'm not quite sure what the inhabitants of Carlisle will make of their town being called the "opposite of bliss", but as a proud native of a town (Slough) combusted in literature by a poet laureate, I'm sure that this slight will live long in their minds! There's an amusing reference to the TARDIS hatstand, which has now disappeared from the console room. Perplexingly, the Doctor again roots about in the cupboards at the bottom of the time rotor, as if this is his only storage area, which is a bit strange in the episode that precedes *Journey to the Centre of the TARDIS*.

More pointed though is Clara's statement: "So I am a ghost. To you, I'm a ghost. We're all ghosts to you." It follows that this is an unconscious reference on Clara's part to her being the "woman twice dead", the ongoing mystery in this second part of the series. Not only is Clara's body 'in the ground' in a whole multitude of places, but (as we know from the series finale) the Doctor's own corpse is also 'out there' (if not in the ground). The Doctor's demonstration of the pocket universe's relationship with ours using two balloons is quite reminiscent of the Fourth Doctor's explanation to Leela of the TARDIS's dimensional transcendentalism in *The Robots of Death* (1977). The Doctor's "make do and mend" psychochronograph could be a reference to Philip Sandifer's *TARDIS Eruditorum*, aka "A Psychochronography in Blue", which I've seen in the Kindle store, and now that I've had a chance to read a bit of it – thanks to Cross's mention of a psychochronograph – I must say that it looks thoroughly intriguing. At the end of the episode, there's an amusing inversion of the Grandfather paradox (said to negate the possibility of time travel, as time travellers would be forever popping off to the past and accidentally killing their grandfathers before they'd had any children). Contrary to the paradox, the Doctor announces that Hila is Emma and Alec's descendant, thereby 'accidentally' ensuring that these two shy lovebirds will finally get it together in order to ensure the eventual existence of their time travelling progeny.

However, as Steven writes, the Doctor's contention that "Every lonely monster needs a companion" is an obvious reference to himself. Throughout this episode, the Doctor is implicitly compared with Alec, the war hero haunted by what he's seen, for the Doctor is himself a similar beast. As we will know from the War Doctor later on this year, the Doctor has similar misgivings about the many people that he has sent to their deaths (although the Doctor actually killed them, rather than just sending them on suicidal missions). Like Alec, the wounded Doctor has ended up in "a lonely old house, looking for ghosts." This is one of the many reasons why this episode is so brilliant, as not only does *Hide* conjure with a whole miscellany of new themes, but it also fits seamlessly into the narrative of this series.

Like Steven, many fans have taken *Hide* to be an allusion to Shakespeare's *The Tempest*. However, unlike Steven, this is seems to be due to many fans mishearing 'Caliburn' as 'Caliban'. Since I can't find any documentary evidence about Cross being influenced by *The Tempest*, I'm not sure if he intended any such allusion. Yet I can see how tempting it is to make this inference, as I've often thought of the Doctor as being similar in some ways to Prospero, the main character of *The Tempest*. Like the Doctor here, the sorcerer Prospero is nearing the end of his life, and has magical powers. Unlike the Doctor, Prospero is keen to ensure his inheritance and legacy live on, while the Doctor is actively removing all trace of his activities from every database in the universe, and the Doctor's wand (his sonic screwdriver) doesn't work in the pocket universe. As the title of Shakespeare's play suggests, there is a huge storm in *The Tempest*, as here; however, the storm in *Hide* is merely a traditional staple of the haunted house story. While the TARDIS faces a stormy time vortex during its trips into the pocket universe against the Doctor's wishes, Prospero purposely conjures up a storm to strand the ship of his usurpers. I suppose Hila could be the pocket universe's Ariel, and the 'Crooked Man' its Caliban, but this is stretching the pocket universe's balloon fabric a bit too far in this analogy. Besides, 'Caliburn' is also a variant on 'Excalibur', but there doesn't appear to be any Arthurian myth at play here. The image of the ghost from Palmer's photos is much akin to Edvard Munch's *The Scream*, the painting, which, of course, inspired Moffat in his creation of the Silents.

Then again, Palmer does reveal that an alternative name for the apparition that haunts the house is the 'Caliburn ghast'. Now, 'ghast' is a term that H. P. Lovecraft used to label a breed of monster in *The Dream-Quest of Unknown Kadath* (1927):

> After a moment something about the size of a small horse hopped out into the grey twilight, and Carter turned sick at the aspect of that scabrous and unwholesome beast, whose face is so curiously human despite the absence of a nose, a forehead, and other important particulars.

This sounds quite a bit like the 'Crooked Man'of *Hide*, although he does have a nose (albeit in a slightly different place than you'd expect from a human face). The ghasts are carnivorous, which probably explains why the Doctor fears that this beast will consume him. Lovecraft's beasts are also cannibalistic, and it's interesting to note here that Shakespeare derived the name of Caliban from 'cannibal', inspired by tales of sailors encountering such fearsome people amongst the inhabitants of the New World. It's possible that the references to the ghast are actually horrified reactions to the sight of the Crooked Man's lover, instead of the ghost (who also unwittingly horrifies all who see her). However, as we know from the resolution of this splendid tale, this Crooked Man is a real softy at heart, and is now probably living out his nursery rhyme life in a little crooked house with his crooked wife and crooked mouse.

10: Journey to the Centre of the TARDIS

Writer: Steve Thompson
Director: Mat King
Originally broadcast: 27 April 2013

Cast

The Doctor: Matt Smith
Clara: Jenna-Louise Coleman
Gregor van Baalen: Ashley Walters
Bram van Baalen: Mark Oliver
Tricky: Jahvel Hall
Time Zombies: Sarah Louise Madison, Ruari Mears, Paul Kasey

***Steven's Review*:** Thanks to its immediately intriguing title, *Journey to the Centre of the TARDIS* was one of the most highly anticipated episodes of this season. But in fact, although it delivers a nicely twisty plot and some memorable moments, it turns out to be a surprisingly inconsequential story. While not quite at the level of "she woke up, and it was all a dream," the resolution does cheerfully banish most of what we're shown in the course of the episode to the land of non-existence. Apart from a couple of moments between the Doctor and Clara that might possibly have repercussions later, this is as much a 'filler' episode as writer Steve Thompson's previous story *The Curse of the Black Spot* in the 2011 season.

The set-up is very straightforward. The TARDIS is spinning through space with its shields temporarily down; the Doctor has stripped the ship's operation down to basics as part of an effort to allow Clara to become more familiar with it (picking up on the "Clara versus the TARDIS" thread from earlier episodes). The time machine is noticed by a trio of scavengers operating a huge salvage ship. They ensnare it with a "magno-grab" and haul it aboard, badly disrupting all its systems as explosions go off all around the console room. The Doctor is somehow thrown outside of the TARDIS entirely, while Clara is lost in its vast, labyrinthine interior. He rapidly recovers, sizes up the situation, and enlists the help of the scavengers to find her by promising them the richest salvage haul of their lives. Once they're all inside the TARDIS, he ensures their co-operation by locking them in, with a self-destruct timer ticking down, giving them thirty minutes to help him find Clara. ("Don't get into a spaceship with a madman. Didn't they ever teach you that?")

The Doctor: "Salvage of a lifetime. You meant the ship… I meant Clara."

Like last week's *Hide*, this is another story with a very small cast list; apart from the Doctor and Clara, the only other speaking characters are the three scavengers, the Van Baalen brothers. Unfortunately, unlike *Hide*, which boasted two superbly watchable performances, this episode exhibits an uncharacteristic lapse in the quality of *Doctor Who*'s guest casting. Ashley Walters as Gregor, the leader, does a reasonable enough job (though no more than that), but Jahvel Hall as Tricky, the youngest one, is wooden and clearly inexperienced. The script gives him a justification for adopting a robotic manner, but that doesn't make up for some of his more mumbled and hard to understand line readings. Mark Oliver as Bram, the big, slow one, is perhaps even worse – the character is obviously supposed to be of limited intelligence, but it often comes across as if the actor is reading his lines off cue cards.

At the start, the story hides the fact that Tricky is actually related to the other two. The big reveal comes quite late in the episode, when the Doctor shames Gregor into confessing that Tricky is actually his younger (and smarter) brother, to whom their father was intending to pass on the leadership of the outfit. When his eyes and voice box were destroyed in a salvage accident and his memory damaged, Gregor and Bram seized the opportunity to make him think he was their android servant ("It was a joke. It was just a stupid joke… We did it to relieve the boredom"). This rather sadistic practical joke is about the only bit of character development the Van Baalens receive. It's also possibly the most ridiculous plot twist since 1975's *The Android Invasion* expected its audience to believe that a human astronaut had spent two years wearing an eye patch given to him by his alien captors without noticing that the eye underneath it was in fact perfectly functional. A moment's thought will make any viewer realise that the deception couldn't possibly be sustained over any length of time. It's no wonder that the Doctor says to the Van Baalens, "You know, I've got to tell you… I won't be needing you in my quiz team," when he eventually reveals that his TARDIS self-destruct timer was nothing but a clever bluff.

The real star of the episode is the TARDIS itself. It's surprisingly rare for the show to devote screen time to the Doctor's vessel – normally, it's literally just a vehicle to get the Doctor and his friends into and out of each story. In all the nearly seven hundred episodes of the Classic Series, there are perhaps a dozen where the interior rooms and passageways of the TARDIS (beyond the main control room) are important to the plot. Aside from a few corridors (and the reuse of the old Eccleston/Tennant control room) in 2011's *The Doctor's Wife*, this is the first time that the new series has given us an extended exploration of the TARDIS. That episode did not attempt to present the TARDIS interior as perilous in itself; the threat came from an external entity that had possessed the ship. Here, there's a sense of real danger – even the Doctor seems uncertain what lengths the TARDIS might go to in order to protect itself from those who would tear it apart. The Doctor, Gregor and Tricky find themselves trapped in an illogical maze of corridors that keep leading them back to the same spot, and menaced by strange zombie-like creatures. These crude, featureless humanoids lurching through the TARDIS interior recall the "antibodies" created as a defence mechanism by another piece of sentient architecture, the living city in 1974's *Death to the Daleks*.

Clara, nursing a hand burned in the original explosions, finds a storeroom full of old props like Melody's cot and Amy's model TARDIS which were featured in the 2011 series. Also lurking in there is one of the zombies, which pursues her through the corridors. The production design manages to create the appropriate sense of scale, suggesting an endless maze linking any number of imposing spaces. Clara goes past an observatory and a swimming pool (giving us a glimpse of something which has been mentioned in passing several times in previous episodes), before finding an enormous library – with a lovely unexplained touch of a row of bottles labelled *Encyclopedia Gallifreya* which apparently store knowledge in liquid form. Also impressive is the architectural configuration chamber, which Gregor finds with the aid of a hand-held sensor that apparently possesses the handy property of being able to analyse any piece of technology and put a value on it – a very naive idea, which is no more believable here than it was in last year's *Dinosaurs on a Spaceship*. He takes one of the "circuits" – which appear as glowing glass balls attached to a huge tree-like structure – over the Doctor's protests and warnings. Meanwhile, Bram is back in the console room, with orders from his brother to start dismantling it. Another fan-pleasing moment comes when the console is breached and memories start floating out – in the form of lines of dialogue from previous stories that were spoken in the TARDIS console room. They are deliberately kept soft and indistinct, but a couple of them date back to the very first TARDIS scene in 1963.

Bram is caught by one of the zombies as he continues to attack the console, while Clara discovers multiple "echo" versions of the console room (created as defensive misdirection by the TARDIS). When the Doctor, Gregor and Tricky find themselves in another such "echo" room, he is able to utilise some convenient technobabble to rescue Clara from an advancing zombie and pull her through to rejoin them. Their reunion is not as joyous as he was expecting – she throws a punch at him, furious ("Why have you got zombie creatures? Good guys do not have zombie creatures – rule one, basic storytelling!"). At this point, all Gregor wants to do is get out, particularly after the Doctor admits he was lying about the self-destruct. There's an unfortunate glibness here, in that neither Gregor nor the Doctor seem to be at all bothered by Bram's demise stemming from the Doctor's little practical joke – no doubt due to the writer being aware that the story will end with Bram alive again, even though the characters don't know that. But then it turns out that the TARDIS engine really is damaged and about to explode – and so they need to go back into the maze, embarking on the journey of the episode's title.

There's a frustrating arbitrariness about some of the plotting in this episode, especially in this stretch, as Steve Thompson contrives to separate Clara (again) from the others for no reason, and she starts to see flashes of previous events. The Doctor quickly finds her once more, explaining that the TARDIS is "leaking" some of the recent past through "time rifts" – damage caused by the magno-grab. Then they're threatened by giant rods thrusting randomly through the walls, like something out of a video game level. Tricky gets pinned to the wall by a rod and yells for Gregor to cut his arm off – which is when the aforementioned ridiculous revelation about his true nature comes to light. Finally, the Doctor leads them to the Eye of Harmony chamber, the power source of the TARDIS – an impressive combination of practical effects, lighting and CGI – where they are trapped by zombies banging on both doors. Annoyingly, the Doctor's emphatic statement that they can only survive for a minute or two in here (made literally just a couple of minutes before they entered) gets immediately forgotten about, in favour of having a long climactic action scene. It emerges that the zombies are actually future versions of themselves, burned by the forces in this chamber – the future, as well as the past, is leaking through the time rifts. To avoid their fate they need to somehow interrupt the timeline, but Gregor and Tricky fail, and only the Doctor and Clara are left to escape from the two newly-created zombies.

With all the extraneous parts of the plot now cleared away, the best scene of the episode for both Matt Smith and Jenna-Louise Coleman comes when the Doctor finally confronts Clara about his experiences with the different versions of her. The episode plot and the season arc plot neatly reinforce each other; in the Eye of Harmony chamber Clara, thinking they were about to die anyway, had demanded answers about the zombies from the Doctor. His refusal was shot through with guilt ("I brought you here to keep you safe but it happened again. You died again." "What do you mean, *again*?"). Now, on the illusion of a cliff edge, the Doctor turns the demand back on her. Smith convincingly conveys the Doctor's frustration at having worried over this conundrum for ages now ("What are you, eh? A trick? A trap?"). He still doesn't get any answers, but his relief at realising that she knows no more about it than he does is palpable.

Director Mat King, a newcomer to *Doctor Who*, seizes the opportunities afforded by this story for some self-consciously showy camera work. The many different TARDIS corridors the characters travel through (the same set reused, of course) are kept distinct thanks to simple but effective lighting tricks, while a constantly moving camera, skewing from side to side, ensures they remain an unsettling environment. The zombies are shot with a blurring filter to maintain their shadowy threat. We even get a new perspective on a familiar set with the striking initial shot of the camera continuously backing away from the Doctor and Clara as they briskly circle the console, bantering. When the Doctor convinces Clara that they have to jump off the cliff, and they land in the TARDIS engine room, the image of them walking through a cloud of shattered components, frozen in a white void, is one of the highlights of the story.

The Doctor realises it's up to him to save the TARDIS, but he has no idea how ("She's always been there for me, now it's my turn") until Clara moves to hold his hand – a probably unintentional duplication of *Hide*, which has a similar turning point. The burns on her hand provide the solution – they're the impression of a message burnt into the remote control for the magno-grab by the Doctor, tossed through a time rift to his past self, which Clara picked up in the opening scene. The Doctor locates a suitable rift, and this time manages to talk to his previous self rather than just tossing the remote. The earlier Doctor now uses the remote to deactivate the magno-grab field, thereby negating the whole sequence of events. Thompson's circular story structure is actually quite a clever piece of plotting (as could be expected from one of the creators of the intricate narratives of *Sherlock*), but it does require close attention from the viewer to catch all the details. Crucial links in the chain of events like the Doctor initially obtaining the magno-grab remote by picking Gregor's pocket when they first meet, or him burning the message into it with his sonic screwdriver, are not dwelled on at all, but pass by in a flash. Compared to something like Steven Moffat's *Blink* – one of the best ever examples of this kind of puzzle-box plot – keeping up with this episode was hard work.

As the TARDIS flies on, now ignored by the salvage ship, there's an unexplained *Twilight Zone*-style twist in the tale – we see that Gregor now treats Tricky as a proper brother, not a robot. It seems that not everything was completely reset, and the tinge of conscience the Doctor detected in Gregor has been strengthened as a result of their encounter – even though that encounter now never happened. By contrast, Clara is back to her usual relaxed bantering with the Doctor in the final scene, while he feels the need to seek some reassurance:

The Doctor: "I need to know if you feel safe. I need to know you're not afraid."
Clara: "Of?"
The Doctor: "The future. Running away with a spaceman in a box. Anything could happen to you."
Clara: "That's what I'm counting on."

Earlier, we saw what could be a portent of things to come when Clara apparently came across something significant (the Doctor's real name, perhaps?) written in a book – *The History of the Time War* – in the library ("So that's who…" she says to herself, cryptically). Given the "reset button" ending to the episode, it remains to be seen how much Clara actually remembers of the experience, but one way or another, it seems answers are on the way.

Steven's Classic Who DVD Recommendation: 1978's *The Invasion of*

Time, starring Tom Baker and Louise Jameson, also devotes a significant part of its six-episode running time to a chase through the corridors and rooms of the TARDIS. Unfortunately, it was a story whose production was seriously marred by both budget troubles and strike action, which meant that its portrayal of the TARDIS interior is a far cry from the labyrinth of wonders shown in this episode.

***Kevin's Review*:** Oh dear. From the sublime to the ridiculous, as the old cliché goes. Steven Moffat intended the episodes in the first part of Series 7 to be mini-movie blockbusters. *Journey to the Centre of the TARDIS* seems to hark back to this theme, albeit in a very B-movie kind of way.

The discordant note starts at the very beginning, when Murray Gold's music that accompanied the reveal of the vast spaceship at the beginning of *The Doctor, the Widow and the Wardrobe* is recycled here. The Van Baalen brothers' salvage ship, while impressive, is significantly shorter than the vessel that featured at the beginning of the 2011 Christmas Special, which means that Gold's music rather loses its epic feel. I'm all for the recycling of TV music when it can add poignancy and emotional depth to a scene, but in this instance, the production team would have been better off commissioning a new piece of music.

It is indeed quite unfortunate that this story follows on after *Hide*, especially since the preceding episode was uniformly brilliant. In addition to this, while the story opens with Clara expressing her feeling that the TARDIS doesn't like her (a theme that began in *The Rings of Akhaten*), the Doctor's suggestion that Clara should talk to the TARDIS is one that was already realised in *Hide*. The Doctor suggests that Clara should 'talk' with the TARDIS by piloting her, while ignoring the rather simpler option of firing up the TARDIS's Voice Interface again. Obviously, the interface isn't the essence or 'soul' of the TARDIS (which was personified by Idris in *The Doctor's Wife* last series), but it is still possible to derive some characterisation or anthropomorphism from it. Following her rather rollercoaster ride in the TARDIS during the previous episode, it's not surprising that Clara is reluctant to take the 'wheel'. (Although the TARDIS invited Clara on board during its trip to the pocket universe in *Hide*, the TARDIS flew itself, instead of Clara being at the wheel.) Indeed, the TARDIS must still be feeling the ill effects of its trip to the pocket universe, judging by how easily the Magno-grab damages it. Actually, I'm being far too fair on writer Steve Thompson here. In an episode that should be all about displaying the sheer awesomeness and wonder of the TARDIS, Thompson instead greatly weakens our impression of our favourite ship by making it so impotent and fragile in this episode. No matter whether the TARDIS's 'shields' are down, it shouldn't be disrupted by something so innocuous as a magnetic grabbing tool. Indeed, if the Magno-grab is so dangerous as to wreck the contents of a vessel as advanced as the TARDIS, then why are the Van Baalen brothers using it? It must surely destroy a sizeable chunk of all the salvage that they come across! Having written that, in the Classic Series, the Doctor was able to make the TARDIS inoperable by merely removing a fluid link (in 1963's *The Daleks*). A broken spring in the "Fast Return Switch" was all that was needed to send the TARDIS hurtling to its doom in *The Edge of Destruction* (1964). Despite the cause of the danger in this latter serial being so ludicrously small, this story did at least introduce the notion that the TARDIS is alive, and that it could affect the psychology of its crew when threatened with imminent destruction. Although the revamp of the TARDIS first shown in *The Snowmen* removed most of the 'make-do and mend' elements that the Doctor had utilise to clutter up the console, the Doctor still uses a key with the rather human label 'Smiths' to shut the TARDIS down to its 'basic mode'.

Although Clara suggests that the Doctor is "one of those guys who can't go out with a girl unless his mother approves", there is no suggestion that she is entertaining a romantic relationship between her and the Doctor. (Yet it's an amusing thought that she metaphorically alludes to the TARDIS as the Doctor's 'mother', instead of his would-be wife, as suggested in *The Doctor's Wife*.) I found Thompson's characterisation of Clara in this episode to be rather humourless and earnest. This is understandable, I suppose, in an episode where she faces real peril. Then again, she's faced danger in other episodes this series with far greater humour and energy.

In one of many bizarre incidents in this episode, Tricky's augmented eyes spot the Doctor's boots (and legs) sticking out from under the TARDIS like a veritable Wicked Witch of the East. Obviously, it's inconceivable that the Doctor would walk out of the TARDIS without Clara; however, it's even more unbelievable that he would have been thrown out of the TARDIS. It's also ludicrous that the TARDIS is leaking fuel, especially as it seems to be invisible. Given the Doctor's attachment to the TARDIS, it's surprising to see that he so easily offers his vessel to the Van Baalen brothers as scrap. Although the Doctor later emphasizes that he meant Clara when he was talking about "the salvage of a lifetime", the Doctor does definitely offer up the whole TARDIS up as scrap first in order to get their help in retrieving Clara. This is a good sign of how much Clara means to the Doctor; however, as we will see later in the episode, her value to him is still as "the only mystery worth solving" instead of a reflection of his having an enhanced personal regard for her, which the Doctor has seemingly yet to develop. Although the Doctor makes a big thing later of "Salvage of a lifetime. You meant the ship. I meant Clara", Gregor only dubiously mentions the "salvage of a lifetime" when faced with the TARDIS's unimpressive exterior, and the Doctor's previous suggestion of: "If you help me get her out, you get the machine, all the scrap, eh?" Perhaps Thompson meant for Matt Smith to deliver this line in a sarcastic tone. Meanwhile, back in the TARDIS, Clara pointlessly ignores a warning light and opens a door, causing an explosive backdraft, an act so dumb that it possibly relegates her from the Doctor's quiz team also. Prior to this, Clara has somehow been thrown clear of the TARDIS console room due to the activation of the Magno-grab, but doesn't sustain any additional injuries… Meanwhile Gregor, who must have seen thousands of ships with artificial gravity in his time, reveals how dumb he is when expressing his surprise that the TARDIS has gravity.

As we have seen from the past 50 years, the Doctor is very capable, so it is surprising when he decides that he needs the help of three strangers to find Clara, especially as this will inevitably involve a great deal of his precious time explaining aspects of his alien ship to them. So, in order to bring the Van Baalens' focus to the job in hand, the Doctor conjures up his fake 'self-destruct' act. Although the Doctor will later say that this show was all down to "the old wiggly button trick", the countdown that he shows onscreen is also an integral part of this façade. I guess that in ordinary circumstances, if you wanted to rescue people from a wrecked ship, then seeking the help of a salvage team would be an obvious step. However, the Van Baalens have already shown how greedy and unscrupulous they are in their negotiations with the Doctor and their use of the Magno-grab. This 'locking in of people until the problem is solved' is an approach that the Doctor has seemingly borrowed from Professor Lidenbrock in Jules Verne's 1864 novel *Journey to the Centre of the Earth* (from which Thompson uninspiringly derived the title of this episode). At the beginning of Verne's story, Lidenbrock locks in everyone in his house (including the maid) without food until he successfully cryptanalyzes a cipher (which fortunately his nephew succeeds in doing). Although this episode doesn't feature the dinosaurs from Verne's novel, it does feature the proto-human zombies that terrorize our heroes, along with the exploding star of the Eye of Harmony, which is akin to the fiery magma you'd expect to find at the Earth's core. As the countdown that the Doctor has set to focus the Van Baalens' attention will last 30 minutes, the events in the rest of the episode are supposed to happen effectively in 'real time', as there is half an hour left to play in this story. In this way, the set-up of this story is akin to Chris Chibnall's 2007 story, *42*, which was also set in real time. Then again, following the TARDIS's extreme reaction to this dire situation, what is and isn't happening in 'real time' becomes questionable.

It's interesting to see that Clara comes across the Doctor's cot as she wanders through the damaged TARDIS. The cot first appeared in 2011's *A Good Man Goes to War*, along with hints about its importance that have yet to materialize. I have previously speculated that the most obvious reason for the Doctor's retention of the cot was that Susan, the Doctor's granddaughter, must have been a baby when the Doctor originally escaped from Gallifrey. At one point, I even thought that Clara was probably some reincarnation of Susan, but obviously, we know now that this is not the case. There's also one of the models of the TARDIS that Amy (presumably) made as a child. The zombie that originally chases Clara is the one that is holding its hand on its face; we later learn that this zombie is the Doctor. So, in this story, the Doctor is metaphorically hunting down Clara (by investigating her origins) and actively pursuing her, albeit in zombie form.

When Bram removes one of the panels from the console, we hear many echoes from the past talking about the abilities of the TARDIS. Bram seems to not hear any voices, so it's a moot point as to whether they are real or no; possibly they're just audio echoes of previous events, just like the visual echoes of the more recent past that Clara will see later on in this episode. In any case, it is a lovely bit of nostalgia in the 50th Anniversary year to hear Susan, Jo Grant, Amy, Ian Chesterton, the Third Doctor, the Fourth Doctor, and the Ninth Doctor talking about the TARDIS. I presume that Michael Pickwoad's design of the new TARDIS console took into account the requirement for Bram to remove at least one of the panels in this episode. Gregor's avarice awakes when he learns about the TARDIS architectural reconfiguration system. “A machine that makes machines?” he asks, apparently oblivious of 21st Century 3D printing technology. Despite Gregor’s theft of a circuit, it is apparently this device that reconfigures the TARDIS’s architecture to prevent Gregor escaping from the ship with the circuit. Another duff script point occurs when Gregor threatens to burn the TARDIS, which seems to work, as the TARDIS allows Gregor to exit from the architectural reconfiguration system. The Doctor’s labelling of the architectural reconfiguration system as “living metal” could hark back to the similar Gallifreyan metal Validium, which played a central role in the 25th Anniversary adventure, *Silver Nemesis* (1988). Professor Kettlewell used a more prosaic type of living metal to build the titular Robot in Tom Baker’s debut in 1974.

The Doctor’s library is truly spectacular. The book, *The History of the Time War*, is, of course, a bit of a teaser. In the previous two series of *Doctor Who* under showrunner Steven Moffat, the Doctor’s companions were unable to read Gallifreyan, presumably because the TARDIS translation matrix doesn’t need to translate the Doctor’s own language. However, not only is Clara able to read *The History of the Time War*, she also conveniently comes to a page that apparently reveals the true name of the Doctor. I guess this is quite like the clever bit in *The Snowmen* when the Doctor discovers an important part of Simeon’s plans by tossing his scrapbook in the air to find the “most opened file, most viewed page”. Similarly, Clara would seem to have opened one of the most viewed pages in *The History of The Time War*. As the old cliché goes, ‘history is written by the winners’. In this instance, the only apparent ‘winner’ in the Time War would seem to be the Doctor. Indeed, no one else apart from the Doctor would have witnessed all the events of the Time War. From the seals of Rassilon on the cover, it is evident that that this book was written from a Time Lord’s perspective. Since the Doctor is the last remaining Time Lord at the end of the Time War, one can only deduce that he wrote this book. As we know from the resolution of this series and this incarnation of the Time Lord, the Doctor’s real name is a dangerous secret. This would tend to suggest that the Doctor wrote this history for himself in Gallifreyan. Then again, since this Doctor knows that he does not have much longer to live (as he is at the end of his regeneration cycle) it’s possible that he wrote this book in another language (such as Clara’s English), for what is the point of writing a history if there's no one who can read it? The Doctor will later say that he rushed his bluff of the Van Baalen brothers; however, this scene – where Clara says, "So that's who…" – while seemingly more important in the grand scheme of things, is far more rushed. Then again, River Song is an archaeologist/historian who is intimately associated with the Doctor, who knows Gallifreyan, who has written about him before, and who knows his name, so she must have written this book and presented the only copy to the Doctor. Indeed, it would have been very egotistical for the Doctor to write about himself in the third person otherwise. The *Encyclopedia Gallifreya* on the other hand, seems to be an audio database of knowledge via a magical liquid medium. In other words, it is this series' 'Harry Potter moment'.

Since the redesign of the TARDIS first shown in *The Snowmen*, the Doctor, despite owning a ship of infinite size (as revealed in this episode) has been bizarrely keeping clothes in the cupboards at the base of the time rotor. Having written that, if you do have an infinitely sized ship, then I suppose it would make sense to have everyday items like clothes close to you. However, Bram now reveals that these same 'cupboard' doors are just another entry point into the TARDIS's inner workings. (Readers of our guide to the 2010 season may recall that I similarly moaned about the inconsistent look of the TARDIS communicators that year.)

It's interesting that when the Doctor first encounters the conjoined zombie of Gregor and Tricky, the Doctor says "I'm sorry" to it, revealing for the first that he knows more about these creatures than he's letting on, much to the frustration of Clara later. As Steven writes, Mat King's direction of this episode is very effective, despite the duff elements of the script. I particularly enjoyed the 'echo rooms' scene in the TARDIS console room, which I thought that King very effectively realised. It does seem to be more than a little derogatory for the Doctor to define Clara as 'Lancashire Sass' (i.e. a cheekily rude Lancastrian person), especially in this episode, where Clara seems more earnest rather than charmingly cheeky. (It's interesting to note here that the real Clara Oswald derives from the same part of the UK as Jenna-Louise Coleman. As we saw in *The Snowmen*, Coleman is capable of speaking in cockney and Received Pronunciation, but I guess it's just easier to deliver Steven Moffat's machine-gun pace scripts in Coleman's own accent. In this light, we'll probably find out that Peter Capaldi's Doctor was born in a Scottish part of the TARDIS!) Indeed, there's anger more than cheeky sassiness behind Clara's punch to the

Doctor's chops here. I may be wrong, but this scene, where Clara's zombie alter ego corners her, is possibly the one scene in 21st Century *Who* where a female companion screams in abject terror when confronted by a monster. Cornered as Clara is up against a wall, this image is very reminiscent of that first iconic scene of a female companion's scream of terror in *Doctor Who* – that of Barbara Wright when confronted by a Dalek for the first time in *The Daleks* (1963). Special praise must go to zombie Sarah Louise Madison and director Mat King for making it very clear in this scene that it is the zombie version of herself that is chasing Clara in this scene, rather than the Doctor-zombie who was previously pursuing her.

Then we get to the dumb scene where Tricky is speared through the shoulder by one of the warping fuel rods, and he learns that he is not an android after all. As Steven writes, this is reminiscent of a similarly wretched scene from *The Android Invasion* in 1975. Perhaps if Tricky had more of a robotic, artificial voice to go along with his augmented eyes, then one might have understood his mistaken belief that he is an android. Although one would have thought that this realisation of his humanity would have struck the first time he felt hungry or needed to go to the loo. For instance, soon after Bram has called him an 'android' for the first time, at the very beginning of this episode, we see Tricky drinking from a can. Either Tricky's near fatal accident happened very recently (i.e. within the last 24 hours), or he has qualified his status as being akin to that of the more organic replicant androids represented by Ridley Scott in his version of *Blade Runner* (1982). Indeed, in that movie, the idea that Deckard could have been an android all along is not ridiculous, since the Replicants are, in many ways, more human than the humans. Nevertheless, unless shock has kicked in, the fuel cell spearing Tricky in the shoulder should be a massive indicator to Tricky that he has the capacity to feel pain. It's also incongruous in this scene that Tricky's wound does not bleed, and that he's still able to move fairly freely later on, to the extent of overpowering the conjoined zombie. Despite his dumb plotline, I think that Jahvel Hall does give a good performance as Tricky, and very successfully makes him the most likeable of the Van Baalen brothers. Mark Oliver's performance isn't great, but then Thompson doesn't provide him with great material to work with. The fact that the Doctor has been hinting all along that he doesn't think that Tricky is an android also makes the revelation that he is human a bit redundant.

It's interesting to see that an aspect of the Eye of Harmony is still an integral part of the TARDIS's architecture. Now that the 'make do and mend' TARDIS console, and the Doctor's 'romantic' relationships with companions appear to be at an end, it would seem that the Eye of Harmony's presence within the TARDIS is the one innovation that still remains from the 1996 *Doctor Who* TV movie. While the temperature in this room is highly dangerous, it's laughably easy for the zombies to break through the glass panels in the doors, so they can't have been made of a very strong material.

Although the Doctor shows his frustration at his inability to discover Clara's true nature, following his confrontation with her in this episode, he's more willing to accept that she is "just Clara". However, as we will know for sure by this series' finale, she isn't "just Clara", for this Clara is the original. Yet the Doctor doesn't realise this yet. Although the Doctor rewrites time in this episode, due to his telepathic link to the TARDIS, he will not forget that this rather startling confrontation has taken place, as we learn later in *The Name of the Doctor*, when Clara recalls this stand-off.

As Steven points out, Thompson has plotted his finale quite intricately, perhaps too much so, because it's very difficult to spot all the details on first viewing. For instance, the Doctor's inscription of "Big Friendly Button" on the Magno-grab remote via his sonic screwdriver isn't really shown. The Doctor also perfects his previous plan by physically entering the Time Rift to shout to his previous self. Where this all falls down though is in the Doctor's exclamation that "I need to find the music"; this doesn't make sense, because he shouldn't have heard the Van Baalens playing rock music on their ship when they operated the Magno-grab. I know that we hear their rock music in the background in the TARDIS console room in the beginning, but it's very unlikely that the music could have travelled through the vacuum of space, and then somehow penetrated the TARDIS console room. It's also implausible that the Magno-grab remote could work within the confines of the TARDIS, or even that such a powerful device would have a remote control at all. In addition to this, the Magno-grab remote becomes red-hot when the Doctor thrusts it into the time rift; so much so, that the Doctor's "Big Friendly Button" inscription burns Clara's hand. Yet, although he screams in agony, the past Doctor's skin does not appear to burn when he appears in the time rift. Then again, the Doctor did describe Clara's skin as being "beautiful fragile human skin", implying that it is more susceptible than his own. On the other hand, since one of the zombies is the Doctor, we learn that his skin will eventually burn in exactly the same way as the humans' do. Then there is the notion that Gregor has remembered the Doctor's appeal to his decency, despite the fact that he will never get to know the Doctor now that our favourite Time Lord has rewritten time. Could this be a hint that Clara will still remember the Doctor's real name despite his rewriting of time? If so, then it is not played out in the rest of the series. Then again, it seems that the Doctor's influence goes way beyond this, as the picture of the Van Baalen brothers is now shown to be complete, with Tricky now back in his rightful place in the photo. Gregor's spark of decency does appear to be somewhat limited though, as Bram still calls Tricky "robot", so suggesting that they still carry out their cruel 'impractical' joke on their little brother. However, the suggestion is that Gregor won't let Tricky go on believing this stupid lie in the long term.

I'm sure *Journey to the Centre of the TARDIS* will have been a big hit with younger viewers, especially as the zombies are very effectively realized, and are quite scary in places. (As mentioned before, the production team seem to have raised the horror quotient in this Anniversary year.) I remember being impressed by *The Invasion of Time* when I was a child, especially with the surprise reappearance of the Sontarans, and the chase through the TARDIS really fired my imagination. Given that modern *Doctor Who* visuals, costumes, and sets are far more impressive than in the days of the Classic Series, I'm sure that this adventure will stay in the mind of younger viewers for a long time. At least Steve Thompson foregrounded the "Big Friendly Button" at the beginning of the episode, unlike the dodgy-looking Sontarans that appeared out of nowhere at the dénouement of *The Invasion of Time*. Having written that, any half-decent script editor would have spotted that the Tricky android subplot was a bit of a non-goer from the start, and would hopefully have come up with a more convincing reason as to why the Van Baalens couldn't get on. In this pivotal Anniversary year, it would also have been interesting if Thompson had called the salvage team the 'Foreman Brothers', instead of making them sound like a Californian rock band from the 70's.

Kevin's Classic Who Comic Book Recommendation: Fans of the Doctor's comic book adventures may be interested to know that there's quite an interesting and amusing Fourth Doctor story (his penultimate) in a similar setting called *Junkyard Demon* (1981). I remember this as being rather startling at the time, especially since

Mike McMahon and Adolfo Buylla's art was radically different from that of the great Dave Gibbons. Despite my initial disgust at this radical departure from the normal *Doctor Who magazine* comic strip, I recalled this funny little adventure with great fondness while watching *Journey to the Centre of the TARDIS*.

11: The Crimson Horror

Writer: Mark Gatiss
Director: Saul Metzstein
Originally broadcast: 4 May 2013

Cast

The Doctor: Matt Smith
Clara: Jenna-Louise Coleman
Mrs Gillyflower: Dame Diana Rigg
Ada: Rachael Stirling
Madame Vastra: Neve McIntosh
Jenny: Catrin Stewart
Strax: Dan Starkey
Angie: Eve De Leon Allen
Artie: Kassius Carey Johnson
Edmund & Mr Thursday: Brendan Patricks
Amos: Graham Turner
Effie: Olivia Vinall
Abigail: Michelle Tate
Urchin Boy: Jack Oliver Hudson

Steven's Review: With *The Crimson Horror*, the new series of *Doctor Who* notches up its 100th episode. It's an achievement that would have seemed outlandishly improbable at the beginning of 2005, the year of the revival that would turn the show from a fading memory into a pop culture juggernaut that displays no sign of slowing down as it approaches its 50th anniversary. Writer Mark Gatiss, who helped to launch the new series with a story set in the Victorian era (*The Unquiet Dead*), revisits one of *Who*'s favourite time periods with a wonderfully vibrant tale which provides splendid entertainment in itself, but also ties into the ongoing arc of the season.

Gatiss's second script this year is entirely different in feel from *Cold War*, which achieved its effect by keeping characters, events and environment as realistic as possible. Here, right from the start we are plunged into the lurid world of the Victorian "penny dreadful". In the Yorkshire of 1893, a pair of young investigators, Edmund and Effie, are posing as husband and wife while they attempt to uncover the secrets of Sweetville – a community created by wealthy factory owner

Mrs. Winifred Gillyflower. A stern fundamentalist who delivers harsh sermons railing against the "moral decay" of the grim new industrial cities growing across the north of England, she is gathering recruits for her new "perfect" town – but once inside, they are never heard from again. Edmund soon comes to a sticky end, and as Mrs. Gillyflower archly confronts Effie ("We're so very sorry for your loss"), there's no doubt who the villain of this melodrama is going to be.

Edmund's brother (amusingly, played by the same actor) later finds and examines his dead body – its flesh now stained a bright crimson. Gatiss doesn't give him a first name; instead, with a nod and a wink in the direction of G.K. Chesterton, he is referred to only as "Mr. Thursday". Unlike several other recent episodes, even the minor characters of this story are vividly drawn; the crude, leering mortuary examiner is a delight, as is the running gag of Mr. Thursday fainting whenever he sees anything he can't cope with – which is destined to happen a lot, after he goes to London to engage Madame Vastra to investigate his brother's death. He tells her of an old legend that the last image recorded by the eyes of a dying man can be recovered. Vastra scoffs, but he presents her with photographic evidence – the last thing Edmund saw… was the Doctor.

For the first third of the episode, that enigmatic image is the only sign of the show's title character; the story benefits immensely from keeping him mysteriously offstage, and being told almost as a tale from a spin-off series starring Vastra, Jenny, and Strax – picking up from where we last saw them in *The Snowmen.* In the exaggerated reality of this episode, a lizard-woman detective, her wife/maid who is also a martial arts expert, and a Sontaran warrior who serves as their butler don't feel at all out of place. As they head north to find the Doctor and investigate Sweetville, Strax is wonderfully comic, as always, with his trouble grasping the concept of gender and his eagerness to deploy high-tech weaponry as the answer to every problem. After convincing him that they need to be a little more subtle, Vastra sends Jenny in to infiltrate the place. After sitting through Mrs. Gillyflower's presentation – at which she reveals her daughter Ada, apparently "blinded in a drunken rage, by my late husband" – Jenny volunteers to join the recruits.

Strax: "But how will she locate the Doctor?"
Vastra: "To find him, she need only ignore all KEEP OUT signs, go through every locked door, and run towards any form of danger that

presents itself."
Strax: "Business as usual, then."

What Jenny finds as she investigates the factory is that the place is empty – there's just a battery of large gramophones emitting factory noises. She finds her way to a mysterious room containing a "monster" which we earlier saw Ada feeding through a floor-level hatch in the door (an image which is no doubt a deliberate homage to a similar moment in 1989's *Ghost Light*). She picks the lock, and the Doctor is revealed – an all but paralysed victim of Mrs. Gillyflower's "crimson horror", his skin like hard plastic. As Jenny guides him away, they pass by a room where Mrs. Gillyflower's minions are immersing some of the new recruits in a vat of red liquid which apparently preserves them in some way, almost like turning them into mannequins.

With the aid of his sonic screwdriver, Jenny helps the Doctor return to normal. Matt Smith, having had fun doing some zombie acting, switches to exuberant mode as the Doctor bounds around Jenny, even seizing her for a kiss (and naturally, earning himself a slap). In a long flashback, which is playfully presented by director Saul Metzstein in the style of jerky, sepia-toned old movie footage, the Doctor tells the story of what happened after he and Clara arrived here. He was trying for London rather than Yorkshire 1893, obviously intending to bring Clara to Vastra – who saw another version of Clara die in *The Snowmen* – to get her opinion of her. For Classic Series fans, Gatiss throws in a couple of callbacks to Tegan Jovanka, companion to Peter Davison's Doctor in the early 1980's – there's a reference to him spending a long time "trying to return a gobby Australian to Heathrow Airport," and "Brave heart, Clara" is an adaptation of a catchphrase of that time. They run across Edmund, who shows them an earlier victim of the crimson horror (in a mortuary scene that brings to mind the 1977 classic *The Talons of Weng-Chiang*). The Doctor mentions the old Romany superstition about a dying man's last sight (yet another homage, this time to his use of the same idea in 1975's *The Ark in Space*); in a clever, Steven Moffat-like twist, this is no doubt the source of Mr. Thursday's own belief, passed on to him by Edmund before he started his own ill-fated investigation into Sweetville after the Doctor disappeared.

The flashback continues as we see the Doctor and Clara – posing as "Mr. and Mrs. Smith", complete with Yorkshire accents – enter Sweetville and meet Mrs. Gillyflower. Their pleasant tour of the premises is suddenly ended as they find a bizarre tableau of preserved victims. They are captured and taken to be processed; Clara successfully makes it through the ordeal, while the Doctor is among the crimson-stained rejects that Mrs. Gillyflower instructs Ada to dispose of in a nearby canal. But thanks to his non-human nature, the Doctor is still (just) capable of movement, and Ada hides him away. Finally (in a rather spurious piece of plotting – Gatiss is not as practiced at connecting up these out-of-sequence narratives as Moffat is) the dying Edmund bursts into the Doctor's room, providing him with his final sight of the Doctor that kicked off the whole story.

With the flashback concluded, the Doctor finishes up his explanation to Jenny, telling her they have to find Clara. ("But Doctor, Clara's dead… isn't she?" "It's… complicated.") Meanwhile, in a street outside, we have a comedy scene with Strax threatening his horse for getting him lost and pulling out his blaster to deal with it ("The fourth one this week… and I'm not even hungry"). He is approached by a street urchin who gives him directions in a strangely stilted manner – "Turn around where possible. Then, at the end of the road, turn right. Bear left for a quarter of a mile, and you will have reached your destination." Strax asks the boy's name, and he replies, "Thomas Thomas" – the rather laboured joke being that TomTom is the brand name of a leading European satellite navigation system. It's a mildly amusing punchline, but I don't think it was worth pushing the actual story aside for almost a whole minute to tell it.

Jenny and the Doctor find Clara, in another preserved tableau under a giant bell jar, which the Doctor smashes with a handy chair. While Clara is being revived, Jenny fights off an attack from Mrs. Gillyflower's minions, the sight of her leather catsuit as she strips off her prim Victorian attire provoking a sneaky ribald joke involving the Doctor's sonic screwdriver. Strax arrives to complete the rout of the enemy, and Vastra has to calm him down. When she accuses him of being overexcited thanks to "eating Miss Jenny's sherbet fancies again," his "Noooo…" is hilarious, like a caught-out naughty child. With the Doctor's team now all together again, including Clara ("I know who you think she is, but she isn't. She *can't* be"), they can start fighting back. Pleasingly, Vastra's involvement in the story turns out to be more than just a whimsical reuse of a popular character; when she obtains a sample of the crimson fluid from the mortuary, the Silurian realises she has seen it before – about 65 million years ago. She provides the Doctor with the crucial information about a leech-like parasitic creature from her own era that secretes the red venom, which Mrs. Gillyflower is using for her own purposes.

Gatiss expertly controls the shifting tone of the episode throughout – after starting with a brief nod to realism with the Victorian social and industrial background, the story has kept getting wilder and wilder. By the time it emerges that Mrs. Gillyflower's plan is to launch a rocket full of the toxic red substance up the chimney of her faux-factory into the atmosphere, then explode it, which will kill everyone except her chosen "pilgrims", and that the source of the poison is an ancient parasite symbiotically bonded to her chest (her "silent partner", that she calls "Mister Sweet"), *The Crimson Horror* has become a full-blown steampunk action adventure.

The roles of Mrs Gillyflower and Ada were specially written by Gatiss for Dame Diana Rigg (who gained fame in the 1960s series *The Avengers* for exactly the sort of leather-clad kung-fu heroics that Jenny indulges in here) and her real-life daughter Rachael Stirling – the first time they've worked together. Both acclaimed actresses clearly relished the opportunity to portray this rather perverted mother/daughter relationship. Rigg's character is the more straightforward of the two, but she still has quite a range to cover, from the imperious self-righteousness at the beginning of the episode (under a thin veneer of Victorian philanthropy) to the out-and-out insanity of her final moments. Rigg hits the right levels all the way through, making the most of Gatiss's rich dialogue – such as when she rebuffs a stricken Ada with, "Kindly do not claw and slobber at my crinoline. You know I cannot bear to look at sick people" – without pushing so far that the character topples over into pantomime. Particularly delightful is her response when the Doctor confronts her with the fact that in the wrong hands, the red poison could destroy the world. She simply holds out her hands to him and gleefully says, "Do you know what these are? *The wrong hands*!"

For me, though, the star performance of the episode is Stirling's. Ada starts out seeming purely grotesque, with her filmed-over, sightless eyes and horribly scarred face, but becomes a steadily more rounded and human character as the story progresses. The lonely Ada conceives an affection for the paralysed Doctor, only to be devastated when she loses her "monster". She is confronted by her mother, who is disgusted at her having formed an attachment to a "reject" and alarmed that her plans may be threatened; she casts off her daughter, leaving her sobbing on the floor ("The bright day is done, child. You are for the dark"). Stirling is particularly captivating in her scenes with Matt Smith as the freed Doctor returns to Ada and shows compassion for her.

In her own way, Ada is as strong-willed as her mother, and she turns on her fiercely after the Doctor goads the old woman into admitting she experimented with the venom on Ada. In this confrontation scene, Matt Smith gets to deliver one of his more memorable lines as the Doctor declares succinctly to Mrs. Gillyflower: "I'm the Doctor, you're nuts, and I'm going to stop you." Clara smashes the rocket controls, but the old woman takes Ada hostage at gunpoint and heads to the "secondary launch control" which all the best villains have in stories of this type. The climax takes place in the chimney containing the rocket, as Ada eventually gets away from her mother when she launches the device (the story skating blithely over the implausibility of anyone in the chimney surviving such a blast-off). Fortunately, Vastra and Jenny have had time to remove the cargo of venom, and the crazed old woman, facing the ruin of her plans, tries to shoot the Doctor. But Strax has reached the top of the chimney, and shoots the gun from her hand, sending her toppling over a railing to the floor far below. In an appropriately grotesque but satisfying conclusion, the parasite detaches itself from the dying old woman and is beaten to death by Ada. ("Forgive me, my child." "Never!" "That's my girl…")

Jenna-Louise Coleman hasn't had much to do as Clara this week; apart from looking pretty (again) in her Victorian attire, her main purpose is to bring the plot threads from *The Snowmen* back to the surface. In the wrap-up, after the Doctor has a final uplifting exchange with Ada, who is determined now to make something better of her life, Jenny presses him again about Clara – and he is surprisingly cheerful as he all but admits that this avenue of investigation into the mystery of his companion has turned out to be another dead end. (Unfortunately, there's a rare directorial blemish in the staging here: perhaps because it was clearly pouring with rain while this scene was being filmed, Ada is stuck standing right next to Jenny and the Doctor as they discuss a private matter that has nothing to do with her.) As Vastra and Strax prepare to store the captured venom away in a vault, there's a final gag as Mr. Thursday comes up to them while they watch the TARDIS dematerialise – only to faint again.

The show is still managing to put off telling us what's really going on with Clara, but right at the end of the episode, the arc-plot starts moving at last. Clara returns to the present-day home of the children she is taking care of, only to discover that they've found photographic evidence on the internet of her jaunts with the Doctor to the past – including one in Victorian London that she knows nothing about…

Classic Who DVD Recommendation: For another overstuffed extravaganza of Victoriana, check out the final story ever made (albeit not the last one broadcast) for the Classic Series: the wonderfully intricate and macabre *Ghost Light* from 1989, starring Sylvester McCoy and Sophie Aldred.

Kevin's Review: *The Crimson Horror* is interesting in its rendition of 'Victorian values'. From the *Victory of the Daleks* edition of *Doctor Who Confidential*, we know that Mark Gatiss is a writer that puts a lot of research into his work, but I think that in this instance, it has resulted in a mishmash of an adventure. There are some excellent aspects of *The Crimson Horror*, but ultimately, I don't think these blend well enough for Gatiss to present us with a coherent narrative. In Classic Series terms, this story is more *The Stones of Blood* (1978 – the 100th *Doctor Who* adventure with a splendid opening, but a disappointing conclusion) than *Horror of Fang Rock* (1977 – a classic "base under siege" story redolent with "Victorian values", albeit with a monster that looks less than convincing to modern eyes).

Some of the incidental details that Gatiss mentions are quite interesting. For instance, the Doctor mentions that Sweetville is supposed to be a match factory. The manufacture of matches in the late Victorian era was very controversial, as one of its main and most economical ingredients – white phosphorus – emitted a vapour that caused "phossy jaw", which could lead to toothaches, swelling gums, abscesses in the jawbone, and, in extreme circumstances, brain damage. In the most severe cases, the only remedy was for surgeons to remove the afflicted jawbone. In 1906, the Berne Convention banned the industrial use of white phosphorus, so ending the scourge of phossy jaw. A forensic detail that is quite similar to the bodies that display the "crimson horror" here is that bones afflicted with phossy jaw would glow a greenish colour in the dark. So, it's not a big surprise when Edmund's investigations lead to the gates of Sweetville, as the "crimson horror" has all the hallmarks of an industrial accident. Indeed, a more expensive (but safer) alternative to white phosphorus was red phosphorus, so it would be natural enough for an investigator like Edmund to assume that the "crimson horror" was some kind of previously undiscovered side effect of Mrs. Gillyflower's use of red phosphorus in her match manufacturing process. As Amos says, "Them new manufacturers can do horrible things to a person".

Gatiss contrasts Amos's similar apparent use of the new chemical formaldehyde (itself very toxic) to preserve dead things to Mrs. Gillyflower's use of the red venom to preserve living beings. The Victorians used bell jars to help preserve and present taxidermy exhibits, and Mrs. Gillyflower seemingly uses bell jars in a related way. However, you usually pump air out of bell jars to create a vacuum, rather than pumping air into them, as seemingly occurs onscreen in *The Crimson Horror*. Presumably, this is an indication on Gatiss's part that Mrs. Gillyflower's vision of a future race of 'perfect' pilgrims, while impressively prim and proper in tableau form, would turn out to be far less ideal in practice. As an aside, I must note that it is fortunate for this episode that the Victorians were so keen on having comprehensive undergarments such as long johns, as even today, it probably wouldn't have been quite proper for Matt Smith or the extras to go wandering around in boxer shorts! It's also just as well that the Doctor has unusually gone to the trouble of adopting the full costume of the local society here, so that he would not look out of place among Sweetville's pilgrims, to the extent of wearing long johns. Not that the Doctor's usual style of dress would look out of place in the Victorian era, given that he has always tended to get his fashion sense from this time. It seems too that the Doctor's long johns contains the fabric that never wears or stains invented by Alec Guinness's character in the Ealing Comedy, *The Man in the White Suit* (1951).

Given that match manufacture was such a hazardous industrial process, one could be surprised as to why so many 'pilgrims' sign up to live in Mrs. Gillyflower's community. However, one of the main opponents of Bryant and May's use of white phosphorus in match manufacture in the late Victorian era was the Salvation Army, who even went to the trouble of setting up their own rival red phosphorus match factory. Another clue that Mrs. Gillyflower is supposed to be some kind of Salvation Army adherent is her accusation that her late husband blinded Ada in a *drunken* rage, as the Salvation Army was one of the main proponents of temperance and abstinence from alcohol at this time. Music is an integral part of Salvation Army services; in this way, Mrs. Gillyflower and her pilgrims anachronistically sing *Jerusalem* (Sir Hubert Parry didn't set William Blake's 1808 poem *And Did Those Feet in Ancient Time* to music until 1916). The

Salvation Army's main aim was to provide relief to the destitute, of which there were many in Victorian England. However, Mrs. Gillyflower seems to have a slightly different agenda, as Vastra states that she is "only interested in the fittest and the most beautiful". Indeed, Mrs. Gillyflower seems to have a Social Darwinist or Eugenics approach in her 'unnatural' selection of her pilgrims. As Mrs. Gillyflower later says to Ada in a pivotal moment, "You know I cannot bear to look at sick people." It becomes clearer later on that Mrs. Gillyflower has only 'borrowed' the contemporary religious and temperance discourse to promote her own dystopian vision of the future (for she will later hypocritically offer the Doctor "a glass of Amontillado"). Mrs. Gillyflower also implicitly compares her silent partner Mister Sweet with the Biblical God when she says, "Mister Sweet is always with us". Indeed, this is literally true, as she reveals that her 'deity' – Mister Sweet – has adhered himself, leech-like, to her chest.

Although Mrs. Gillyflower's vision of the future and the "coming apocalypse" hardly seems to be a barrelful of laughs, it is not surprising that so many pilgrims sign up, for at least they would have better living conditions in Sweetville than they would in a Victorian slum. Indeed, Gatiss's model village for Sweetville seems to be Bourneville, the community that the Cadbury brothers built to provide improved living conditions for their workers, with the first land bought in 1893, the year in which Gatiss sets *The Crimson Horror*. As chocolates are 'sweets', you can see Gatiss's likely derivation of the name *Sweet*ville. Incidentally, the Cadburys were Quakers, and proponents of the temperance movement, which is why they built no public houses in Bourneville. It's interesting that Mrs. Gillyflower chooses to sing *Jerusalem* at the recruitment drive, as Blake's poem is often taken to mean that a Second Coming of Christ to England would create a heavenly paradise that would be in great contrast to the "dark Satanic mills" (as Blake put it) of the Industrial Revolution. Of course, Mrs. Gillyflower isn't being hypocritical for promising paradise in the form of a "dark Satanic mill", for we later learn in this episode that the mill is an empty façade of industrialisation. (Although the chimney houses a rocket – the delivery system for the "coming apocalypse" – that Mrs. Gillyflower has presumably built there.) When Mrs. Gillyflower launches the rocket via the secondary controls, she again anachronistically sings a Christian hymn. Although John Bunyan wrote the original words to the hymn, *To Be a Pilgrim*, in *Pilgrim's*

Progress (1684), the variant that Mrs. Gillyflower sings here is from the 1906 *English Hymnal*. In addition to this, Ralph Vaughan Williams composed the new tune to go along with the new arrangement of the words that Mrs. Gillyflower sings here. So, Mark Gatiss has employed some good old-fashioned dramatic licence in his use of two British hymns with jingoistic overtones in this episode. It's interesting to note that this is the second of three parodies of Christianity in *Doctor Who* during 2013, with the third being Moffat's ongoing representation of the Church in Matt Smith's final adventure, *The Time of the Doctor*. As I have previously mentioned, Mrs. Gillyflower only 'borrows' Christian millenarian discourse about the "End of Days". Similar Christian societies, such as the Jehovah's Witnesses, have predicted when the "End of Days" will come, and when these days have come and gone with no incident, they have tended to predict a new date. However, unlike Jehovah's Witnesses, the "wrong hands" of Mrs. Gillyflower have the power to bring the "coming apocalypse" about...

Like Steven, I think that Dame Diana Rigg does a brilliant job of bringing Mrs. Gillyflower to life. Again, I must say how fabulous it is that *Doctor Who* is now able to attract such acting 'royalty'. Dame Diana shows she is game for anything here by agreeing to take on a such an unusual role. When I first watched this episode, I thought that the prosthetic model of Mister Sweet was quite poor, to the extent that it looked like a 'joke' monster from sci-fi comedy *Red Dwarf*. Steven criticised the memory worm from *The Snowmen* for being none too convincing. However, I didn't mind the appearance of the memory worm, because Moffat mostly used it as a device for comic effect. Now that I've watched the episode again, Mister Sweet's appearance is not as bad as I originally thought. However, I still think that he's one of the most poorly executed monster designs in 21st Century *Who*. I was also a bit irritated that the production team again showed the lamp at the top of the TARDIS as still illuminated long after materialization in Yorkshire. Another aspect that I found less than convincing was the set-up for the optogram of the Doctor in Edmund's eye, as Edmund would have had to negotiate the narrow stairwell to the Doctor's cell in his death throes. In addition to this, in order to keep her 'monster' a secret from her mother and the pilgrims, Ada would have had to carry Edmund's body down that same stairwell. There also seems to be a big flaw in Mrs. Gillyflower's plans: if you desire to keep the 'rejects' from your industrial preservation process secret, then it's probably better to get your mute and very obedient pilgrims to dispose of the bodies in the canal instead of delegating this responsibility to your blind daughter… It's also interesting to see that when Ada learns that it was her mother who blinded her as part of her insane plot, she adopts some rather misogynistic language to attack her mother (along with her cane), using 'virago' here to accuse Mrs. Gillyflower of being something akin to a "mannish upstart". Rachael Stirling does a brilliant job of realising Ada, and the stilted way in which she moves her head during her first reveal at one of Mrs. Gillyflower's recruitment drives is quite startling. I'm sure Stirling and her mother must have had some great fun on set!

Gatiss mostly does a good job of bringing the Paternoster gang to life again, although his characterisation of Strax isn't quite as good as Moffat's. It's excellent to see Jenny getting quite a bit of screen time in this episode in the absence of Clara. As Jenny is Vastra's wife, it's fitting that she slaps the Doctor when he kisses her. (This is the second episode in a row where the Doctor's been struck by one of his companions!) If the Doctor's original motivation in taking Clara to Victorian London was to get an insight on her from Vastra, then our favourite Homo Reptilia doesn't provide any illumination on the mystery of Clara. Instead, it is Jenny that is constantly reminding the Doctor throughout this episode that the Clara the Paternoster gang knew is dead (so reinforcing Clara's mysterious origins). Indeed, it is possible that the Doctor's only reason for taking Clara to London in 1893 is to see if she has any 'memory' of the events of 1892… If this is so, then this would have been a very cruel thing to do to Captain Latimer and his children, if they happened to encounter Clara again… Alternatively, it's possible that the Doctor only wanted to gauge Clara's reaction to seeing Vastra, a Silurian at large in Victorian England. Clara's surprise at her first sight of Vastra is seemingly enough to convince the Doctor that this Clara hasn't met her before.

I was mystified as to why Strax picks up the street urchin Thomas Thomas. As I'm not a driver, it didn't occur to me that it was a play on the TomTom navigation system. Now that I know that it is, this doesn't make the joke any less lame, and a rather poor excuse to include a child actor in this episode, although Jack Oliver Hudson's performance is very good. Similarly, at the end of the episode, there is an even poorer excuse for children to have a free trip in the TARDIS when Angie and Artie blackmail Clara with historical photos that they have found that feature her. When I first saw this, I thought that this was an even less credible plotline than the Tricky/android one from the previous adventure. Why would Angie and Archie automatically assume that Clara is anything as esoteric as a time traveller just because they have found some photos of her in period costumes and settings? (The Silence obviously haven't been around the Maitlands' house long enough to make them forget all the extraterrestrial happenings that the Doctor gets involved with.) For someone who has been keen to remove his name from all intergalactic databases, the Doctor has been remarkably careless to allow people to photograph him so often. (It's the Doctor's presence in some of these photos that is the confirming evidence for the Maitland kids that it's Clara in the photos, instead of someone who just looks like her.) Indeed, it looks as though the Doctor's investigation into the mystery that is Clara Oswald has made him careless, for the TARDIS's repeated visits to the Maitland household were bound to attract attention at some point. The stilted and unnatural postures in these photos almost make them look like early Victorian daguerreotypes, albeit very colourful ones. Unlike Steven, I don't think there's any big revelation or plot development when Clara blurts out that she's only ever been to Victorian Yorkshire, not London, as Clara could easily explain this away to herself by believing that this photo is from a trip to Victorian London that she has yet to make. However, her exclamation does unwittingly confirm Angie and Artie's belief that she is a time traveller... So, a lot of the incidental details in this story are quite interesting, to the extent that my review of *The Crimson Horror* is a lot longer than I thought it would be. However, given that there was room in the episode for some unnecessary padding (the TomTom joke), Mark Gatiss could have explored some of these themes in more depth, and produced a much more substantial episode. For instance, I don't think that the reference to 'Mr. Thursday' is a very significant nod to G. K. Chesterton, unless Mark Gatiss views this story as being something of a metaphysical whimsy, similar in style to *The Man Who Was Thursday*. As it is, *The Crimson Horror* has some truly great moments, but the sum of these does not make for an overly compelling narrative.

12: Nightmare in Silver

Writer: Neil Gaiman
Director: Stephen Woolfenden
Originally broadcast: 11 May 2013

Cast

The Doctor: Matt Smith
Clara: Jenna-Louise Coleman
Angie: Eve De Leon Allen
Artie: Kassius Carey Johnson
Webley: Jason Watkins
Porridge: Warwick Davis
Captain: Tamzin Outhwaite
Beauty: Eloise Joseph
Brains: Will Merrick
Ha-Ha: Calvin Dean
Missy: Zahra Ahmadi
Cyberman: Aidan Cook
Voice of the Cybermen: Nicholas Briggs

***Steven's Review*:** After the almost universal acclaim (and a clutch of awards) for *The Doctor's Wife* in 2011, the next episode from Neil Gaiman had a high standard to live up to. Unfortunately, *Nightmare in Silver* falls short by some distance. Inconsistencies of tone, shallow guest characters, and a grab-bag of ideas that are presented but not developed render it as insubstantial as candyfloss – watchable enough, but making no impact at all, even when it tries to bring a new fearsomeness to the Doctor's second-most famous enemies, the Cybermen. Revolving around the fate of two children, at times it feels more like an episode from the late lamented *Doctor Who* spinoff series for kids, *The Sarah Jane Adventures*.

At the end of last week's episode, the children that Clara is looking after, Angie and Artie, found out about her travels with the Doctor, and he has now apparently been cajoled into giving them a trip in the TARDIS. The story starts with a tone of whimsical, *Willie Wonka*-ish fantasy as the Doctor brings Clara and the children to Hedgewick's World, showing off a "golden ticket" which he happens to have to the universe's biggest amusement park. Unfortunately, they arrive at a time when the place has been closed down for months due to mysterious disappearances. Angie, the older of the children, is unimpressed with the Doctor and his "stupid box". With Matt Smith turning up his Doctor's hyperactive wackiness in response, this initial section is very "kids' TV" in feel. Given that they're only here in the first place because of their threat to expose Clara, Angie in particular is difficult to like. She comes over as a petulant teenage brat, demanding attention while determined to be unimpressed with everyone and everything she encounters. Artie is easier to empathise with, but neither of the two young actors rises above the level of mere adequacy, and it's probably just as well that they end up being shunted to one side for most of the episode.

They encounter a stranded showman, Webley, who is in hiding, keeping out of the way of a platoon of soldiers guarding the place. A typically quirky Gaiman character, Webley takes them into his "world of wonders", a museum of curiosities that includes a faithful recreation of the famous fake "automaton" chess player with which Wolfgang von Kempelen mystified spectators throughout the courts of Europe in the late 18th century – except that in place of von Kempelen's Turkish figure, Webley unveils a Cyberman sitting at the chessboard. It's a cute way to introduce the creature and launch us into the opening titles, but this whole initial sequence is very slow-paced. The "kids' day out" feel continues as we watch Artie play a chess game against the Cyberman, after which the Doctor reveals that (just as in the 18th-century original) the thing is actually a puppet being worked by an operator concealed inside the chess table, and then the children get to have some fun on the "Spacey Zoomer" anti-gravity ride.

The story finally gets under way when the Doctor becomes intrigued by some "funny insects" he has noticed – centipede-like mechanical creatures crawling over some of Webley's exhibits. It soon becomes apparent (to the audience, at least – the characters take somewhat longer to catch on) that these "Cyber-mites" are infesting the dormant Cybermen in Webley's collection and bringing them back to life. The showman is captured by a force of Cybermen who have a hidden base on the planet, after which the fantasy element that loomed so large at the start of the episode quickly dies away to nothing as Webley is reduced to spouting exposition at the Doctor on behalf of his new masters. In this future time period, when the Cybermen are engaged in a huge war against a galaxy-spanning, Roman-style human empire (a nice callback to a throwaway line in 2005's *The End of the World*), the creatures have established themselves in secret on Hedgewick's World to repair their casualties and replenish their population by using the patrons (hence the disappearances which led to the closing of the amusement planet).

Unfortunately, the writer has to resort to some blatant idiot plotting to kick-start the story into motion. No justification is even attempted for why the Doctor makes the children bed down in Webley's museum while he investigates instead of letting them rest safely in the TARDIS (which they were just about to enter as he started his poking around). He insists that they stay in this unfamiliar environment for no reason other than the plot requiring him to. Soon after, with a similar lack of motivation, Angie simply declares herself bored and wanders off to talk to the soldiers, leaving her brother alone – whereupon he is, to no one's surprise, immediately taken by the Cybermen.

One of Gaiman's stated objectives for this episode was to make the Cybermen scary, and they certainly display some impressive new capabilities. The costumes have been streamlined and improved, giving them the ability to move fast for the first time ever. What's more, when the Doctor, Clara, Angie and the soldiers are attacked by a Cyberman, it is able to use a *Matrix*-style "bullet time" effect to evade their weapons fire, pluck Angie out of the midst of the group, and carry her off before they can react. Gaiman also revisits the idea seen in 2010's *The Pandorica Opens* that the Cybermen have the ability to detach their heads or hands, which can then act independently. Unfortunately, the big problem with their presentation here is that it makes them not so much derivative of the Borg from *Star Trek* as identical to them (rather ironically, given that when the Borg first appeared in the late 1980's they were criticised as obvious rip-offs of the Cybermen). Their Cyber-mites cause eruptions of metallic appliances on the faces of their victims, and they have gained the ability to instantly adapt to any tactic used against them – their new catchphrase is "Upgrade in progress". Compared to their previous appearances, it's quite an increase in threat level when the standard recommended method of dealing with them is now a planetary implosion.

The Doctor follows the Cyberman that kidnapped Angie, leaving Clara in charge of the soldiers (having earlier used his psychic paper to pass himself off as a Proconsul of the empire). He finds a transmat link to the Cyber base, and simply walks into the enemy stronghold – a rather rash course of action, occasioning a humorous exchange between Clara and the captain of the troops ("I trust the Doctor." "You think he knows what he's doing?" "I'm not sure I'd go that far"). Once inside, he finds the two children, taken over and placed into "walking comas" by the Cybermen, as well as the assimilated Webley, who tells of the Cybermen's particular interest in using children as a source of inspiration for their controlling intelligence, the Cyber-Planner ("A child's brain, with its infinite potential, is perfect for our needs") – the same idea previously used by another long-term enemy of the Doctor, in 1988's *Remembrance of the Daleks*.

Webley: "We needed children. But the children had stopped coming. You brought us children. Hail to you, the Doctor – saviour of the Cybermen."

The Doctor gets infected by the Cyber-mites, and his mind becomes a battleground for a contest of wills between him and the Cyber-Planner. This turns out to involve a lot of scenes of the Doctor talking to himself (and ultimately playing chess against himself), which would have been very dull had Matt Smith not absolutely gone for broke with his performance. He gets to spend a great deal of time acting against the Cyber-version of himself, both in split-screen, and by simply switching characters as the camera angle changes. His shouting and sneering as the Cyber-Planner is an odd way to depict what is supposedly an emotionless machine intelligence; it's almost as if the Cyber-Planner has been infected in turn with the Doctor's hyperactive personality, dubbing itself "Mr. Clever" and burbling with pleasure about the capabilities it's finding in the Doctor's memories. Smith's energetic performance, like so much of this episode, seems geared more toward the children in the audience than the adults, but it certainly gets across the idea of the Doctor only just holding back the swamping of his mind by an entity of the same level of power.

While the Doctor is thus occupied, Clara leads the soldiers in trying to hold off the steadily growing army of Cybermen. Jenna-Louise Coleman does well at showing Clara's quick thinking as she smoothly takes command of the troops and comes up with ideas for dealing with the creatures. In order for her air of authority over them to be plausible, they are portrayed not as hardened soldiers, but as a collection of losers and screw-ups reminiscent of the comic bumblers in *The Doctor, the Widow and the Wardrobe* – according to the credits, the names of the speaking soldiers are Beauty, Brains, Ha-Ha, and

Missy. Apparently they're a "punishment platoon" – sent here to get them out of the way, and not expected to do any real fighting. Essentially they are cannon fodder to prolong the episode, and despite a couple of effective moments it's difficult to feel any sense of horror at their deaths as they get picked off by the Cybermen.

By far the best of the guest cast is Warwick Davis as Porridge, the diminutive operator of Webley's chess-playing "robot" who strikes up an easy friendship with Clara. The two actors work very well together – an early scene where he gives her background information about humanity's wars against the Cybermen gets the necessary exposition across painlessly. Then, when he shows Clara the evidence in the sky of a whole galaxy blown up to stop the Cybermen, Davis sells the moment of introspection well ("I just feel sorry for the poor blighter who had to press the button"), without drawing too much attention to it. The episode builds nicely to the revelation that Porridge is actually the Emperor himself, running away from the pressures of having to make such decisions. He finds himself in a stand-off with the captain of the platoon – the only one of the soldiers who has a more than one-dimensional character – when she realises his true identity, in a strand of the plot that has a subtlety absent from the rest of the episode. Desiring to make up for a past mistake that saw her banished to this punishment platoon, she is willing to use their unit's planet-imploding bomb to destroy the Cybermen, even in the face of orders forbidding it from both Porridge and Clara. Unfortunately, this conflict ultimately comes to nothing when she gets shot by a Cyberman in a muddled scene mishandled by the director (Stephen Woolfenden, a newcomer to *Doctor Who*) – the editing and choice of reaction shots make the sequence of events hard to follow for no good reason.

Gaiman includes lots of fan-pleasing references to past Cybermen stories. Among the most prominent is the idea (used frequently in Cybermen stories of the 1970's and 80's) of gold being used as a weapon against the creatures – seen when the Doctor manages to temporarily wrest control from the Cyber-Planner by using his golden ticket. A couple of passing allusions to cleaning fluid and weather control bring to mind plot elements from 1967's *The Moonbase*; then there's the shot of a triple column of advancing Cybermen that duplicates a memorable cliffhanger in 1982's *Earthshock*, and a lovely wide shot of dozens of them that harks back to *The Tomb of the Cybermen* (also 1967), but on a scale the makers of that story could only dream of. Meanwhile, the Doctor's contest against the Cyber-

Planner continues, as he convinces the soldiers to tie him up before his opponent can regain control of his body, and resumes the chess match. The episode goes to a lot of effort trying to convince us of the high stakes involved in the chess game, in order to justify the amount of screen time devoted to it, but it's very difficult to fully suspend one's disbelief – as the Doctor admits himself, the Cyber-Planner is hardly likely to keep its word and simply leave his mind if it loses.

As ever, Smith and Coleman are excellent at handling the fast-paced banter between the Doctor and Clara. There's a good moment where Clara picks up on the Cyber-Planner's mention that the Doctor thinks of her as "the impossible girl" (only for him to put her off with that old favourite, "I'll explain later"); another nice touch is the scene where the Doctor seems to be expressing deep feelings for Clara, only for her to realize it's actually the Cyber-Planner. (On the other hand, Smith's brief impersonations of his two predecessors, Christopher Eccleston and David Tennant, could charitably be described as loose approximations.) Eventually, the Doctor manages to trick the Cyber-Planner with an insoluble problem (a very old-style "confuse the computer" tactic – another element which would be more at home on children's television) and expel it from his mind, reviving the two children in the process. Particularly amusing is the moment when Clara establishes that he is himself again:

Clara: "Do you think I'm pretty?"
The Doctor: "No – you're too short and bossy, and your nose is all funny."
Clara: "Good enough."

It's clear that the only way to destroy the Cybermen is to use the bomb, but the Cyber-Planner had earlier tricked Clara and destroyed its trigger mechanism. It can also be activated with an authorised voice-print, but the captain is dead – which is the cue for Angie to reveal Porridge's true identity, with an irritating smugness no more attractive than her earlier disdain. A common trope of children's television is that the young protagonists get to show up the lumbering adults, and there's certainly an element of that here. The plot is tidily resolved as the Emperor's confirmation of his identity activates the bomb and simultaneously alerts the nearby ships searching for him of his position, so that everyone gets transported off the planet before the implosion. It's so neat a solution, in fact, that the question is left hanging of why he didn't do it earlier, before so many people started getting killed. The script attempts to paper over this crack by imbuing Porridge with a certain fatalism ("We all die in the end. Does it matter how?") and reluctance to return to the job of Emperor, but once everyone is safe on the imperial flagship this is forgotten, and the story ends on a light-hearted note with Porridge proposing marriage to Clara. The subplot of the lonely emperor, running away from his throne and falling for Clara, could almost have been a separate story in itself. Davis and Coleman are very effective in their final scene, showing a real connection between the two characters. In the end, though, Clara has her own story to get back to.

Nightmare in Silver is certainly one of the season's lesser episodes, consisting of a lot of individual moments which together produce something rather less than the sum of its parts. While it adds new aspects to the Cybermen, it ends up making them too powerful – I suspect the next time we see them, their abilities will be toned down again. It's quite a good vehicle for Clara, but it does the Doctor no favours – while he spends a lot of time centre stage, he plays no part at all in the final resolution. As for the season arc-plot, that has been spinning its wheels for some weeks now, and this episode is no different, simply repeating what has already been established. But, as the online prequel for the next episode hints, all is about to be revealed…

Steven's Classic Who DVD Recommendation: For another Cybermen story that involves their vulnerability to gold and a threat to destroy a planet, check out 1975's *Revenge of the Cybermen*, starring Tom Baker, Elisabeth Sladen and Ian Marter.

***Kevin's review*:** *Nightmare in Silver* is a rather enjoyable renaissance vehicle for the Cybermen. In my review of *Asylum of the Daleks*, I suggested that one way of making the Daleks more interesting would be to make them more evil, and this is something that the Cybermen accomplish in this episode. As Steven notes, Neil Gaiman resurrects the idea that the Cybermen limbs are detachable and can move independently from *The Pandorica Opens* (2010) in order to trick and terrify their human prey. For instance, one of them detaches its hand, which then scurries along the ground like Thing from *The Addams Family* before leaping to attach itself to the mouth of an unfortunate soldier. (I'm not sure why the Cybermen feel the need to stifle the screams of their victims in this episode, since they're so powerful that they don't need to resort to stealth.) However, one thing that Gaiman and the Cyberiad haven't found a way of doing is upgrading the Cybermen so that they have the ability to powerfully engage with the Doctor in dialogue. 21st Century *Who* writers have tended to tackle this same issue with the Daleks by making them progressively madder; here, Gaiman devises a means by which the Cybermen can literally speak through the Doctor. Just as the Cyber-Planner infects the Doctor, so the Doctor, in turn, seems to infect the Cyber-Planner, as "Mr Clever" adopts the Doctor's mannerisms.

Most of my many *Doctor Who* reviews do not mention Matt Smith, an oversight that I must rectify here, as he gives a virtuoso performance in an episode that shows off his formidable acting talent. I'll gloss over Smith's attempt to do Eccleston and Tennant's voices, as impersonation is not one of his many talents. Matt Smith does a fantastic job of portraying the Doctor and the Cyber-Planner's cyberspace chess battle, and making it clear which is in possession of the Doctor's body at any one time (apart from when the Cyber-Planner is trying to deceive Clara). The Cyber-Planner delights in inhabiting the Doctor's alien brain, which allows it to become far more dramatic and demonstrative than usual. The Doctor's threat to rid himself of the Cyber-Planner by regenerating is a real endgame here, for we will see from the next few episodes that this Doctor is the last, and that he will die if he forces regeneration. It's interesting to see that the Doctor chooses not to present an image of the War Doctor as he projects the profiles of his previous bodies. (Although there is a bit of an unexplained yellow fudge in between the Tenth and Eleventh Doctors, which could represent the Tenth Doctor's egotistical choice of retaining his then-current visage when regenerating in *Journey's End*.) An image of John Hurt as the War Doctor might have given *Doctor Who* fans a bit of a surprise prior to the next episode! As it is, this procession of the Doctor's previous faces is a nice touch in an anniversary year story. (How excited we got over such nostalgic clips in the Classic Series in the days before all stories were readily available on videotape!) This cyberspace battle also allows Moffat to highlight the ongoing mystery this series concerning Clara's true nature.

One of several innovations that Gaiman brings to the Cybermen in this episode is the revelation that their collective consciousness is called the 'Cyberiad'. Now, this sounds like something that could have come from *Doctor Who* Cyber-culture all along. However, *The Cyberiad* is also the name of a collection of short stories by the Polish author Stanisław Lem. The protagonists of these tales are two robot engineers who travel throughout a pseudo-medieval universe helping people in need like knight-errants. This is probably why Gaiman sets the showdown with the Cybermen in Natty Longshoe's Comical Castle, as these medieval scenes are very redolent of Lem. However, the exception here is that our knight-errant is very much concerned with preventing the regeneration of a race of godlike warrior cyborgs, instead of creating them, as Lem's heroes do.

Of course, Gaiman is very famous for his graphic novels, and this visual style is very much at the fore in this episode. As I have previously argued, *Doctor Who* during Moffat's reign has seemingly moved from his stated vision of "dark fairytale" to "comic book fantasy". Indeed, I think *Nightmare in Silver* would work brilliantly in comic book form, so I must say that it's fantastic that the visuals of 21st Century *Who* are now usually so brilliant that they can realise anything from even the most vivid imagination. Having written that, there is one very poorly executed visual effect in this episode: that of the horde of Cybermen moving in unison outside the castle. Whenever the production team wanted to show a mass of monsters in the Classic Series (such as the conveyor belt of newly constructed Daleks in 1966's *The Power of the Daleks*), they usually resorted to using commercially produced toys of the monsters. Unfortunately, the horde of Cybermen look like toys instead of threatening monsters when they collectively advance towards the castle. (As Steven writes, the overhead shot of the Cybermen marching is much better, as are the scenes of the Cybermen waking from their tombs.) Perhaps it would have been better to set all of the scenes of the Cybermen attacking during the night, rather than having these daylight scenes at the end. Having written that, I thought that the image of all the Doctors standing together in *The Day of the Doctor* looked similarly fake and toylike, instead of the epochal image that the production team intended.

Gaiman looks to have derived the 'Ludens' part of Porridge's real name from Arkady and Boris Strugatsky's novel *The Time Wanderers*. This in turn is a play on words from the Russian word for humans and Johan Huizinga's concept of Homo Ludens ("Playing Man"), in which Huizinga argues that play 'plays' an integral part in the development of culture. This is possibly why Gaiman has the Doctor play chess with the Cyber-Planner here. Yet there is also more than a hint of Ingmar Bergman's 1957 film *The Seventh Seal* here, in which a doomed knight attempts to delay the inevitable by challenging Death to a game of chess. As previously mentioned, the Eleventh Doctor is literally playing with death here, as we know (from the following two episodes) that he is in his final body, and that to attempt to regenerate to eject the Cyber-Planner would result in his death. Just like the knight in *The Seventh Seal*, the Doctor is playing for time when he suggests the chess match. We know from the beginning of this episode that the Doctor has some good knowledge of chess as he warns Artie that he has made the classic beginner's mistake of falling into a "fool's mate". In the Classic Series, the Seventh Doctor's aptitude for chess came to the fore in *The Curse of Fenric* (1989), while the Fourth Doctor sometimes played (and lost) against his robot dog K9, something that the Doctor appears to have learnt from here. The Doctor demonstrates his higher intelligence here by quickly working out how Webley's Cyber-Mechanical Turk works. (However, the chess masters who played inside the real Turk were of normal size.) The battered Cyberman 'Turk' seems to be one of the alternative Earth Cybus Industries ones from 2006's *Rise of the Cybermen,* as it has a 'C' on its breastplate, unlike the Telosian Cybermen that featured in 2011's *Closing Time*. The rest of Porridge's actual title is quite interesting too. "Kendrick" can mean "greatest champion" or "family ruler" (a fitting name for Porridge's true dynastic origins), while "Nimrod" is Biblical in origin, with Gaiman probably utilising its association with tyranny here.

"Brains", with his oversized spectacles, most likely gets his nickname from the character of the same name in Gerry Anderson's *Thunderbirds*. In the barracks, Brains mentions a problem with the weather control system, which, as Steven points out is a reference to the 1967 Classic Series Cyberman adventure *The Moonbase*. Indeed, this Patrick Troughton serial looks to have made a big impression on the young Neil Gaiman, as the 'Spacey Zoomer' ride recreates some of gravity effects that featured in the beginning and resolution of this adventure. Porridge's nostalgia for dancing snow bears on 'Caspertine' looks to be a jocular reference to Captain Shakespeare's similarly named flying boat Caspartine in Gaiman's splendid 2007 film *Stardust*. It's also interesting that the soldiers' communicator (whose parts the Cybermen have stolen) is an *ansible* one, as this is a term commonly used in sci-fi to depict communication devices that have achieved the seemingly impossible ability to transmit interstellar messages in real time. Ursula K. Le Guin coined the term 'ansible' in her 1966 novel *Rocannon's World*, and other sci-fi writers have adopted it to the extent that David Langford named his legendary fanzine after it. Cyber-Webley says that the Cyber-Planners built a 'Valkyrie' to repair critically damaged units during the Cyber-wars with humanity. However, in Norse mythology, Valkyries were female godlike beings who chose who would die in warfare, sending half of those fallen to Valhalla, where these deceased would prepare for the final great battle of Ragnarök. So Gaiman probably meant to refer to Valhalla, rather than the Valkyries.

In addition to the ongoing mystery about Clara, this episode plays its own riff on other recurring themes from this series. For instance, the Cyber-Planner states that the Doctor has deleted himself from the Cyberiad's databanks in his bid to remove his name from history. (This makes me think that this tactic will only lead to more people asking the oldest question in the universe that will lead to the demise of the Eleventh Doctor, so this is a rather self-defeating move on the Doctor's part.) More of a motif than a theme is the lamp on top of the TARDIS that again stays lit following materialization; since this has happened so often this series, Moffat must have authorized it for some reason. Another ongoing theme is the thoughts, feelings and motivations of those who contemplate 'pressing the button'.

In last week's episode, Mrs. Gillyflower approached her act of genocide (her "wrong hands") with explicit glee, as she anticipated the building of her new dystopia. Here, Porridge is intensely reluctant to 'push the button' as part of his imperial duties. Gaiman makes it clear in this episode that the Cybermen were vanquished a thousand years ago, so it's unlikely that Porridge was the emperor responsible for the destruction of the Tiberion Spiral Galaxy. Although we don't know how long humans can live in the far future presented here, so it is possible that it was Porridge who 'pressed the button' – Gaiman leaves this nicely ambiguous. If Porridge wasn't the guilty party, then he certainly seems to anticipate that he will be required to make the same choice. (Perhaps he received some secret intelligence that there could be some Cyberiad influence in the disappearance of people from Hedgewick's World? And that he then went there to investigate this personally, to the extent of impersonating a Cyberman?)

Steven argues that Porridge could have saved the day much earlier, especially since he knows that his Imperial Flagship will rescue him and any other humans with him prior to the bomb detonating. However, due to his dread of pushing the button, Porridge delays activating the bomb until all the other options have gone. Indeed, such was his fear of being the person responsible for detonating such a bomb that he didn't do anything to stop Alice when she attempted to do so. Even when he does decide to activate the bomb, Porridge still risks everything by choosing to save Artie and Angie from Cyber-Webley first. Indeed, as the avatar Rose will later raise the question of the number of children on Gallifrey as the War Doctor is poised to 'push the button' to destroy them along with the Daleks and the Time Lords, so here it appears that Porridge can't bring himself to kill children. Since the whole purpose of the bomb is to destroy any remaining Cyber-technology, if Artie and Angie had still been part of the Cyberiad, then the Imperial Flagship would not have transmatted them up, just as it later leaves Cyber-Webley to die on Hedgewick's World. Porridge's seeming reluctance to kill innocent children isn't mentioned in the script; however, it is the most likely explanation why he leaves it so long to activate the bomb. Perhaps Moffat thought that it would be unnecessary to make this more obvious in his continuing subtle metaphorical comparison of the Doctor to other genocidal killers this series. (I am presuming that the preponderance of 'pushing the button' moments this series is a deliberate foregrounding of the 50th Anniversary adventure on Moffat's part – not that people wanting to blow up the world have been altogether absent in other series of *Doctor Who*!) Anyway, despite Artie and Angie being a bit obnoxious in the beginning (i.e. despite their being teenagers), both Webley and Porridge seem to bond with them from the start, with Webley being no doubt eager to impress the first child visitors to return to the funfair that is Hedgewick's World of Wonders.

I thought that Jason Watkins did well in what was essentially a cameo character appearance as Webley. (Cult TV fans will have recognised Watkins from his brilliant appearances as Herrick in Toby Whithouse's *Being Human*.) Tamzin Outhwaite does a decent turn as Captain Alice Ferrin, and Calvin Dean (one of Matt Smith's peers from the National Youth Theatre) is excellent in his bit role as the sharpshooting Ha-Ha. Warwick Davis of *Star Wars*, *Willow*, and *Harry Potter* fame is splendid as Porridge (while seemingly stereotypically dressed as Randall from Terry Gilliam's 1981 film *Time Bandits*) although I didn't believe that he could be a tyrant for one moment. Clara goes from being "the woman twice dead" to "the impossible girl" in the Doctor's head. Any initial mistrust that the Doctor may have had towards her seems to have gone now, as he places her in charge of the soldiers while he hunts down the Cyberman. Although not all of Clara's ideas work (such as electrifying the moat), she does a decent job in this leadership role. (Instead, it's Angie that has 'companion clarity' this episode, when she points out that Porridge is the emperor.) This is quite a good episode in terms of Clara's characterisation, especially when she recognises that even if the Doctor does have any romantic feelings for her, then he'd rather die than admit them. However, the fun flirty banter that Oswin and Victorian Clara had are still absent, so making it even more surprising when Porridge proposes to her out of the blue at the end. This kind of 'innocent romance' is reminiscent of how female companions such as Susan, Leela, and Peri left the Doctor during the Classic Series, prior to the flirty banter of 21st Century *Who*.

Nightmare in Silver doesn't reach the heights of Gaiman's previous script, *The Doctor's Wife*, but he never meant it to be more than a fun knockabout adventure, which does indeed achieve his aim of making the Cybermen scarier. Although *Nightmare in Silver* is not amongst the absolute best of this series (like *Asylum of the Daleks*, *The Snowmen* and *Hide*), it is almost there, and I much preferred its more conventional narrative approach to that of the preceding episode. Despite the one visual effect that I hated, this is mostly a visually stunning celebration and fitting revitalisation of the Cybermen during the Anniversary year that I very much enjoyed.

13: The Name of the Doctor

Writer: Steven Moffat
Director: Saul Metzstein
Originally broadcast: 18 May 2013

Cast

The Doctor: Matt Smith
Clara Oswald: Jenna-Louise Coleman
River Song: Alex Kingston
Dr Simeon: Richard E. Grant
Vastra: Neve McIntosh
Jenny: Catrin Stewart
Strax: Dan Starkey
Angie: Eve De Leon Allen
Artie: Kassius Carey Johnson
Andro: Nasi Voutsas
Fabian: David Avery
Clarence: Michael Jenn
Archie: Rab Affleck
Messenger Boy: Samuel Irvine
Young Clara: Sophie Downham
Whisper Man: Paul Kasey

and

The Doctor: John Hurt

Steven's Review: It's been a long haul since this season started with *Asylum of the Daleks* almost nine months ago, but Steven Moffat has finally delivered a tremendous resolution to the mystery of Clara Oswald, the "impossible girl" who the Doctor has encountered multiple times, living apparently unconnected lives in different times and places. *The Name of the Doctor* is a superb finale, providing an ingenious and satisfying payoff for the season plot arc while still ending with a huge twist to lead into *Doctor Who*'s 50th Anniversary Special in November.

Indeed, in many ways this episode feels like an early celebration of that milestone. A frisson of excitement is generated right from the opening scene as a simple exchange between a couple of nameless technicians in a workshop suddenly zooms out to reveal a huge vista of "Gallifrey – a very long time ago". The scope of this story will encompass the Doctor's entire existence, and so we get to see the very beginning of his long journey, with the First Doctor, William Hartnell – in colour, no less – stealing the TARDIS and fleeing his home world. In the course of doing so, he encounters Clara, who is there to stop him from making "a very big mistake." Clara's narrative voiceover which leads into the opening titles makes it clear immediately that this episode is going to be unusual:

Clara: "I don't know where I am. It's like I'm breaking into a million pieces and there's only one thing I remember. I have to save the Doctor. He always looks different, but I always know it's him. Sometimes, I think I'm everywhere at once, running every second just to find him, just to save him. But he never hears me… almost never. I blew into this world on a leaf. I'm still blowing. I don't think I'll ever land. I'm Clara Oswald. I'm the impossible girl. I was born to save the Doctor."

Thanks to a combination of manipulated archive footage and costumed stand-ins, over the course of the episode Clara will be shown encountering all of the previous Doctors. Although the number of times a Doctor rushes past her without clearly showing his face can't help but get a little amusing by the end, it's a lovely gift for the fans in this anniversary year.

The actual story starts (rather like *The Crimson Horror* two weeks ago) as another episode of the non-existent spinoff series starring the Victorian-era trio of Vastra, Jenny, and Strax. In the London of 1893, the Silurian woman visits an imprisoned, insane serial killer, Clarence De Marco, whose mad babblings include boasting about having knowledge of the Doctor's greatest secret. She gathers the others for a "conference call" – effectively, a seance which enables her to reach across time and space to contact other friends of the Doctor. A certain suspension of disbelief is required here – "Time travel has always been possible in dreams" is about the only justification Moffat offers – but really, time travel via seance makes at least as much sense as time travel using mirrors and static electricity, as seen in 1967's "*The Evil of the Daleks*" (set in the same time period), and it somehow seems to fit the whole vaguely steampunk air of Vastra and her friends.

As well as Clara, Vastra has invited River Song – and, appropriately for a seance, River is dropping in from her own afterlife in the Library, as seen in 2008's *Forest of the Dead*. Her presence here is one of a number of touches that help to make this episode a fitting finale to the entire season, and not just the 2013 half of it. (For example, a detail such as having Clara occupied with making a soufflé harks back to Oswin in the season opener.) In particular, River's line about the Doctor – "He doesn't like endings" – which was of poignant significance in *The Angels Take Manhattan*, returns and is just as important here.

There's some clever comedy as Vastra tricks Clara into joining the seance, and while Strax's jokes are starting to become somewhat repetitive, it's still funny when his confusion about gender compounds River's annoyance that the Doctor never mentioned to Clara that Professor Song was a woman. But things turn serious as Vastra tells them of Clarence's information – in particular, his knowledge of a place called Trenzalore, first heard of as part of an ominous prophecy at the end of the 2011 series. But before they can talk further, they are attacked. Vastra and Jenny receive some good character development in this episode – their relationship, previously used mostly as a punchline, is deepened and treated seriously. It's a moment of genuine horror as Jenny says "Ma'am… I think I've been murdered," as the enigmatic faceless creatures known as the "Whisper Men" enter the house and surround their sleeping bodies. They are revealed to be servants of the Great Intelligence, the bodiless entity seen in *The Snowmen* and *The Bells of Saint John*, which has sent them to capture the Doctor's friends.

The Doctor himself finally enters the story as Clara wakes up, back in the present day. Matt Smith is excellent here as he shows the Doctor's shockingly uncharacteristic reaction to Clara's mention of Trenzalore. He rushes back to the TARDIS, and when she follows him inside, he tells her what it was about Clarence's declaration – "The Doctor has a secret he will take to the grave… and it is discovered" – that has so rattled him. When he's on top form, Moffat is amazingly adept at taking the viewer by surprise with a sudden twist that sheds a whole new light on a previous scene or line. He does it several times in this episode, including here, where the Doctor points out that "it is discovered" does not refer to his secret:

The Doctor: "When you are a time traveller, there is one place you must never go. One place in all of space and time you must never, ever find yourself… Trenzalore is where I'm buried."

Nevertheless, the Doctor realises he must try and save Vastra and her friends, in repayment for their looking after him during his dark time following the loss of Amy and Rory (as seen in *The Snowmen*). He and Clara eventually arrive on Trenzalore, after overcoming the protests of the TARDIS, which recognises that he is about to endanger his whole timeline. They find themselves in a vast graveyard – the aftermath of the Doctor's final battle, the "fall of the Eleventh" as prophesied at the end of 2011's *The Wedding of River Song*. Director Saul Metzstein creates a lovely sombre, funereal atmosphere in these scenes, making it easy to believe that we have indeed arrived at the time and place that holds the final end of the Doctor's journey, just as earlier we saw the very beginning. In a very striking image, his tomb and monument is the dead TARDIS ("What else would they bury me in?"), which has grown to enormous size after its interior dimensions "leaked" to the outside when it expired.

The Doctor spots a headstone with River Song's name on it, but he knows that it cannot be real – as both he and we have known from her first appearance, she died far away from here. River herself is present, still linked with Clara after the seance, but can be seen and heard only by her. She prompts Clara to realise that the false gravestone is actually a secret entrance to the tomb. Chased by a group of Whisper Men, they make their way through some catacombs into the corridors of the ruined TARDIS. The similarity of their situation to that in *Journey to the Centre of the TARDIS* starts to cause memories of that adventure to break through to Clara – even though at the end of it, events were changed so that it never really happened. The Doctor explains that the wrecked TARDIS's telepathic circuits are spilling the information into her mind, with a fan-pleasing reference to 1982's *Castrovalva* ("the dimensioning forces this deep in the TARDIS can make you a bit giddy") thrown in for good measure. What Moffat is actually doing, though, is ingeniously making an ostensibly throwaway episode a crucial part of the season arc; the memory of the Doctor's confrontation with Clara in *Journey* where he told her of his encounters with multiple versions of her provides her with information vital to the climax of this story.

Elsewhere, Vastra and Strax wake up, and Strax manages to revive Jenny. The Doctor and Clara meet up with them, as they are all surrounded by the Whisper Men, and the Great Intelligence finally appears in person – at least, to the extent that that phrase makes sense in connection with a creature that is a mind without a body. It demonstrates this by taking over one of the Whisper Men and transferring its features to it in a sequence of nicely realised effects. In a story that revolves around the revealing of previously secret information, the Intelligence certainly makes an appropriate antagonist, with its arrogant declaration to Vastra, "I *am* information." It attacks the Doctor's friends in order to force him to open the sealed tomb chamber, the doors of which are keyed to the answer to the oldest question in the universe (and the series): "Doctor Who?" – the question which, according to the 2011 prophecy, must never be answered. But the Doctor is spared the necessity of revealing the answer when the doors open apparently of their own accord – actually triggered by the invisible River Song, the only other person who knows his real name (as she amusingly told Clara earlier, "I made him [tell me]. It took a while…"). With an air of resignation, the Doctor leads them all inside.

The developments in the show's mythos that Moffat introduces here have never been hinted at before (at least, on television – some of them are similar to ideas advanced in various novels produced in the 1990's while the show was off the air), but somehow feel utterly fitting. The concept of time travel causing damage to the fabric of the universe is particularly apt, as is the revelation that the remains in the tomb (formerly the TARDIS console room) are not a body, but a forever revolving, unfathomably intricate and convoluted light-sculpture that represents all the scars in the universe created by the Doctor's uncountably many journeys through time – a fact demonstrated as more old sounds and sights are resurrected from the archives. Perhaps neatest of all is the idea that the reason the Doctor's grave must remain unknown is that otherwise an enemy could get into this "open wound" and corrupt the Doctor's entire history.

It's something of a stretch on Moffat's part to have the Great Intelligence so enraged by its previous defeats at the hands of the Doctor that it's willing to destroy itself in order to poison the Doctor's timeline, but Richard E. Grant really sells the idea, portraying the creature as the very personification of malevolence. Its minions, the Whisper Men, are another case (like the titular monsters of *The Snowmen*) of Moffat inventing a striking monster more for the sake of an episode's trailers than the episode itself. Dressed as creatures from a Victorian nightmare, with their blank, eyeless faces and whispered, nursery-rhyme style of speech, they are nicely creepy, but once they have served their purpose of drawing the Doctor to Trenzalore and getting him to open the tomb, the story simply discards them.

As the Doctor's life gets rewritten, amid a welter of more modified archive clips, there are brief mentions of whole star systems vanishing, and so on, to convey the universal scale of the disaster. But as always with Moffat's season finales, the focus remains firmly on our regular characters, at the centre of the maelstrom. Neve McIntosh effectively shows Vastra's panic and grief when Jenny suddenly vanishes and she is forced to kill a hostile Strax, who turns back into an unreconstructed Sontaran warrior without the Doctor's influence – it's only a brief moment, but Dan Starkey generates a surprising amount of menace. Finally, with Vastra and the Doctor helpless, only one person is left who can reverse the situation – Clara.

Thanks to her position at the centre of the season's mystery, Clara has often been kept at a distance from the audience, as much a plot device as a real individual. This has probably done no favours for Jenna-Louise Coleman, but she has certainly dealt admirably with everything she has been given to do so far, and has shown that she works very well opposite Matt Smith. With the mystification now at an end, Clara will hopefully be free to develop as a more normal companion character to the Doctor in future stories. Coleman is very good here at the climax of the episode, which provides the inspired resolution of the season-long contradiction between Clara being a perfectly ordinary human girl and yet also more closely connected to the Doctor than any previous companion. She realises that her destiny is to enter the Doctor's timeline, despite River's warning that she will be torn into a million "echoes" existing throughout time, to counteract the damage caused by the Intelligence.

It seems to me that, more than either of Moffat's previous season finales, this one succeeds at both plotting cleverness and emotional depth. The climax of 2010's *The Big Bang* was emotionally very satisfying, but its logic was that of a fairytale, while the explanation of the season-long tease of the Doctor's apparent death in the following year's *The Wedding of River Song* made sense from a plotting point of view, but could not avoid being something of a let-down on the emotional level. Here, Moffat makes excellent use of the technique I mentioned above, where a small twist changes our understanding of a previous moment. With the addition of one final word to Clara's line that we have already heard twice before – "Run, you clever boy… and remember me" – everything falls into place as Clara makes her sacrifice.

As Clara's narrative voiceover returns to round off her story, we once again see footage of her encountering previous Doctors, but this time with a full knowledge of what is going on (and the idea that it's Clara who was responsible for saving the Doctor from the infamous "literal cliffhanger" in 1987's *Dragonfire* is hilarious). The opening scene with the First Doctor is resumed and completed, as we find out that the "very big mistake" she saves him from is stealing the wrong TARDIS: "Steal this one instead. The navigation system's knackered, but you'll have much more fun." It's an astoundingly successful piece of writing chutzpah by Moffat, as he completes a plot which touches on the entirety of the Doctor's travels, from Gallifrey to Trenzalore.

But the emotional climax of the episode takes place after Clara's story is completed, as the Doctor and his friends are restored. The Doctor proposes to enter his own timestream in order to retrieve Clara. River protests at the danger – and the Doctor reveals that he knew she was there all along. Matt Smith and Alex Kingston have always shown great chemistry in this improbable pairing, but their scene here may be their best moment yet, as two characters who so often dance around each other are reduced to complete honesty:

The Doctor: "You are always here to me, and I always listen. And I can always see you."
River: "Then why didn't you speak to me?"
The Doctor: "Because I thought it would hurt too much."
River: "I believe I could have coped."
The Doctor: "No, I thought it would hurt *me*… and I was right."

Despite a delightfully unexpected shaft of humour when they kiss ("Since nobody else in this room can see you, God knows how that looked"), and one last chance for River to tease him with "Spoilers," this scene is written and played as a final goodbye. The Doctor is forced to face the fact of her death squarely, rather than leaving a ghost of her in the Library ("like a book on a shelf") to fade away out of his sight while he moved on. In turn, River's final "Goodbye, Sweetie" neatly bookends her opening line from her first appearance in 2008's *Silence in the Library*. Given her time-travelling nature, there's no reason River cannot appear in future stories, but if this does turn out to be the last time we see her, it was a good ending. The moment is underlined by the absence of the expected "Geronimo" catchphrase as the Doctor enters his timestream – he simply turns to face it, takes a deep breath, and steps into the light.

A final voiceover from Clara ("I'm the impossible girl, and my story is done") heralds the epilogue, as she finds herself lost in an indeterminate, fog-shrouded environment representing the Doctor's timestream. Frightened, she hears the Doctor's voice as he sends her the leaf that was her own beginning (as seen in *The Rings of Akhaten*), to help her find the way back to him. This rather perfunctory rescue sequence then becomes something else entirely, as Moffat uses it to kick off a whole new phase of the story. In this metaphorical landscape populated only by versions of the Doctor ("There's only me here, that's the point"), Clara sees a figure she doesn't recognise. The Doctor's true secret is finally revealed, as a final instance of Moffat's ingenious perspective-shifting technique is applied to the very title of the episode:

Unknown: "What I did, I did without choice… in the name of peace and sanity."
The Doctor: "But *not* in the name of the Doctor."

That little word "in" makes all the difference. It's clear now that the question "Doctor Who?" will never be answered with anything so prosaic as his "real" name – which is as it should be. One of the first decisions made when *Doctor Who* was devised fifty years ago was to not give the title character a name. Perhaps Moffat's greatest achievement in an episode called *The Name of the Doctor* is to avoid revealing an actual name (which could never live up to the mystique generated by half a century of anonymity), without it seeming in any way a cop-out. What he has really been getting at is the far greater importance of our hero's choice long ago to *take* the name of the Doctor ("The name you take, it's like a promise… He's the one who broke the promise"). The credits may say "Introducing John Hurt as the Doctor," but this is not the Doctor we know – this manifestation has done things so terrible that he has been hidden away and denied the name. It's a powerful ending, perfectly designed to keep anticipation for the next episode at fever pitch. It's going to be a long six months to wait.

Steven's Classic Who DVD Recommendation: For another story dealing with tangled timelines and weird, surreal environments, see the striking imagery of *Warriors' Gate* from 1981, starring Tom Baker, Lalla Ward and Matthew Waterhouse.

***Kevin's Review*:** Just like Christmas Specials, it must be very difficult for *Doctor Who* showrunners to devise an end of series finale that is just as epic as the preceding ones. The threat that Steven Moffat portrays here of star systems being snuffed out due to the erasure of the Doctor's timeline is quite a powerful one. However, despite there being excellent pieces in the jigsaw that is *The Name of the Doctor*, they do not all fit together that well. *The Name of the Doctor* is quite a good bookend to *Asylum of the Daleks* in visual terms. This series began in a colossal statue of a Dalek on a wrecked Skaro, and ends in an equally colossal fossil of the TARDIS on the scorched earth of Trenzalore.

The Asian feel to Vastra's new conference call desktop is a bit of a giveaway that Moffat derived this sequence from Christopher Nolan's 2010 movie *Inception*, which also featured characters that could interact powerfully and emotionally with each other while sharing the same dream. Added to the dreamlike intensity are the various rhymes that herald the appearance of the Whisper Men, the faceless Victorian undertakers that summon the Doctor's companions to his grave. Moffat has used this poetic device before, of course, such as the 'Tick tock' rhyme that featured throughout the previous series. Indeed, Moffat famously utilised the traditional wedding rhyme "Something old, something new, something borrowed, something blue" to great effect in 2010's *The Big Bang*. Just as Clara will become millions of echoes when she enters the Doctor's time stream, so we hear echoes of phrases that have already occurred in the series: "Soufflé girl", "Impossible girl", "The Doctor doesn't like endings", "Run, you clever boy, and remember", and "I don't know where I am". Readers may recall that I wasn't too convinced by Jenna-Louise Coleman's rendition of "I don't know where I am" in *The Bells of Saint John*, as I thought that she didn't sound terrified enough. Yet again, when Jenna Louise-Coleman repeats this phrase here, its repetition loses resonance, as her delivery is again not emotional enough. This could be a problem with her acting, or an issue with Moffat's repetition of this device, because there is always a danger that some of these echoes will not reverberate as powerfully as others have done. However, there is an exception at the very end of the episode, when Clara reiterates, "I don't know where I am". Clara is also visibly distressed at this point, when she is lost in the Doctor's timeline, so it is possible that Moffat wanted Coleman to sound most terrified reiterating this phrase while in the underworld of the Doctor's subconscious.

Like the magicians in Christopher Nolan's 2006 film *The Prestige*, Moffat spends a lot of time misdirecting the audience's attention. For instance, the *She Said, He Said* minisode prequel to *The Name of the Doctor* specifically mentions Trenzalore, while the preview of *The Name of the Doctor* at the end of *Nightmare in Silver* revealed that this episode features the asking of the "oldest question". Moffat compounded this by entitling the episode "The Name of the Doctor", as the oldest question is supposed to be "Doctor who?" (When I first watched this preview of the series finale at the end of *Nightmare in Silver*, I was under the misapprehension that Strax was asking "Doctor who?" and so concluded that he would somehow stupidly contribute to the Doctor's demise!) Consequently, some fans would have anticipated that this episode was going to feature the "fall of the Eleventh", although they would have been puzzled as to why Richard E. Grant was present as the Great Intelligence, and why the Silence looked different, when they saw the similarly designed Whisper Men. Indeed, if this episode did concern the "fall of the Eleventh", then some fans would have been asking how Matt Smith could also be in the 50th Anniversary episode as advertised.

Like the Silence, the Whisper Men very much resemble the Gentlemen from the excellent 1999 *Buffy the Vampire Slayer* episode *Hush*, who (in Moffat-like fashion) steal the voices of everyone in Buffy's hometown so that they can rip their victims' hearts out without provoking a loud scream. Indeed, the Whisper Men's pale skin tone and their preference for wearing black suits mean that they do very much look like the Silence. Like the Shakri orderlies in *The Power of Three*, I suspect that not much else went into their design than the necessity for them to look creepy. However, unlike the Silents, there is a good reason why the Whisper Men wear suits, for, as the Great Intelligence later reveals, they are some kind of echo of its Simeon persona, and so are dressed like him to enable him to adopt one of them as his latest avatar with the greatest of ease. Like the eponymous beasts of *The Snowmen*, the Whisper Men have sharp, feral teeth, which add to their fear factor. (Then again, as I wrote in our previous book, I guess Moffat meant the Silence to resemble the legendary

'Men in Black' of ufology.)

At the beginning of this episode, Moffat mercilessly quashes my theory that Susan, the Doctor's granddaughter, could have been a baby when the Doctor first escaped from Gallifrey. This idea first occurred to me when the Doctor produced his cot in *A Good Man Goes to War*, as I couldn't think of any other reason why someone would choose to take something from their childhood nursery when they went on the run. Here, in a brief glimpse, Moffat clearly represents the First Doctor leading the figure of the teenaged Susan into a TARDIS, much as we first saw her in *An Unearthly Child*. The Doctor isn't carrying a cot or any other luggage, so one can only presume that the Doctor took his cot on one of his subsequent, brief trips home to Gallifrey. Moffat doesn't provide any explanation as to why the Doctor and Susan ran away, just as he does not reveal the Doctor's real name. Although there is a bit of a boo-boo here, as Moffat shows the First Doctor responding to Clara's calling out of "Doctor? Doctor?" The original person to call our favourite Time Lord "Doctor" was Ian Chesterton in his first adventure in 1963, *An Unearthly Child*. Upon being called "Doctor Foreman" (as Ian presumed that the Doctor had the same surname as Susan), the Doctor became the first person in the series to ask the oldest question, "Doctor who?" So, the First Doctor should not have responded to Clara calling him "Doctor", as he had not adopted this name yet. Then again, given that the First Doctor was in the process of clandestinely attempting to steal a TARDIS, it is possible that he would have responded in the same way upon discovery by someone who is clearly not a security guard. Since joyriders do not tend to take their grandchildren with them, one can only assume that the Doctor and Susan were running away due to her innocently getting into some kind of deadly trouble on Gallifrey. As we saw throughout the Classic Series, despite their high-mindedness, the Time Lords were prone to corruption and political intrigue, something that Susan's parents (and therefore one of the Doctor's children) have evidently fallen victim to. Obviously, the footage of William Hartnell as the First Doctor here is from the Classic Series, so this limits what he can say and do. Also, the First Doctor is dressed up in his traditional 'Victorian' garb, instead of as a Time Lord, so one can only postulate that he always intended to head for Earth for some reason. Anyway, given that the 50th Anniversary adventure and the Eleventh Doctor's demise will revolve around Gallifrey, it was a good idea for Moffat to bring the Doctor's home world to the fore here, as well as showing the

Cyber-Planner's excitement about the Doctor's secret knowledge relating to the Time Lords in the previous episode.

It's amusing to see that throughout Clara's interactions with the Classic Series Doctors, she is mostly dressed in period clothes relating to each Doctor's era (rather than the age in which a story is set). For instance, Clara is wearing 80's clothing when she calls out to the Seventh Doctor during his infamous cliffhanger in 1987's *Dragonfire*. (Perhaps Clara ended up there due to the same time storm that transported Ace to Iceworld? Clara's not the first *Doctor Who* companion to end up displaced in time and space due to the machinations of one of the Doctor's enemies, as the Great Intelligence's plot here is comparable with that of Fenric, who the Seventh Doctor subtly battled during Ace's time with him in the final years of the Classic Series. Like Fenric, the Great Intelligence has no physical form, but despite this, it can still exert influence over people and events. However, despite certain similarities between the 50th Anniversary, and the 25th Anniversary era, especially with regards to the chess motif of the previous episode that also featured strongly in his battle against the Seventh Doctor, Fenric does not make an appearance here, as the Great Intelligence has far more resonance over the five-decade history of *Doctor Who*.)

Of course, in the Classic Series, the Great Intelligence's monster of choice was a kind of robotic yeti, yet Moffat's only subtle reference to them here is the Second Doctor's incongruous wearing of his 'yeti' coat while running for no apparent reason on what appears to be Venice Beach in California. (Perhaps the Second Doctor is there to prevent the debacle that was *Torchwood: Miracle Day*.) The Second Doctor wore this coat in his first encounter with the Great Intelligence in 1967's *The Abominable Snowmen*, and again when he encountered a Yeti in the 20th Anniversary adventure, *The Five Doctors* (1983). We know that Moffat had reservations about resurrecting the Ice Warriors as he didn't think that their costume design would look that impressive in 21st Century *Who*, so this must be the reason why he chose not to bring back the Yeti along with any of the Great Intelligence's appearances this year. Indeed, following the recent rediscovery of missing episodes from *The Web of Fear*, my wife laughed at the clips of the Yeti in news stories, so it is probably just as well that Moffat replaced the Yeti with the Whisper Men here. Going back to Clara's clothes, one detail that I thought was unusual was that Clara's modern-day dress appears to have the same tartan pattern that Strax's suit incorporates in this adventure.

Given the funereal atmosphere of this episode, it was brilliant to see Alex Kingston reprise her role of River Song here, especially as the River that features in this episode is her dead spirit, which we saw the Doctor save to "a database in the biggest library in the universe" in 2008's *Forest of the Dead*. Consequently, the dead River is a very appropriate guest for Madame Vastra's séance. (Like Steven, I didn't think that Strax's inability to guess gender had much further to run, but it does get more mileage here when the Sontaran comically relates that he didn't realise that River was a woman either. It's even more perversely funny when Strax shouts "Speak to us, boy!" to Jenny as Vastra's consort dies in front of them.) I thought the only off-note in River's return was when the Doctor says her name upon seeing her fake gravestone, as it's clear from the tone of Matt Smith's voice that he's not acknowledging her ghostly presence. As Steven writes, it seems as though this will be the last appearance for River, even though she would be an appropriate paramour for the Twelfth Doctor, as Alex Kingston's only a few years younger than Peter Capaldi. The emotional drama that River and the Doctor play out at the end is very powerful, to the extent that 'sentimental me' felt a trickle of a tear at the thought that this could be River's last goodbye. There is also some good comedy timing here, as the Eleventh Doctor finally intercepts a slap to his face this series! River's presence also allows for one of this episode's most startling visuals – that of a Whisper Man bursting through her ghostly image in the spectral catacombs. River is also useful as a plot device, for it's she who says the Doctor's name to open the tomb and save his friends. (The Doctor's real name is probably Sesame!) Of course, this compassion for the Doctor's friends, which the Doctor taught his one-time would-be assassin, could also lead to the Doctor's death and eradication from history… Although the Doctor has been intent upon eradicating his name from every database in the universe, his love for his wife would obviously always prevent him from deleting River's 'data'. As we have seen from *The Power of Three*, the Doctor will always live on in the sentiments of those people that have known him, attaining a soufflé recipe-like immortality. Besides, as we see in this episode, a universe without the Doctor would be a very bleak place indeed. However, without the sacrifice of River in *Forest of the Dead*, and Clara here, the Doctor wouldn't be there to have this final meeting with his wife. Although there is a hint that there may be further revelations about River, as she still has "spoilers" that possibly relate to a future as yet inconceivable to the Doctor (i.e. beyond his current body, as the Time Lords will gift him a new regenerative life cycle in *The Time of the Doctor*).

Indeed, given that the Doctor was previously paralysed by the paradox of being so exposed to his future life, he has recovered a great deal after Clara enters his time stream to save him from the Great Intelligence. Otherwise, the Doctor wouldn't have been able to engage in this powerful scene with his dead wife. However, as we know, this Doctor (although he will live many more years in *The Time of the Doctor*) doesn't have much of a future. This idea of a companion entering the Doctor's time stream, and continually saving his life throughout the decades, probably won't sit well with many *Doctor Who* fans, who will feel that this 'companion clarity' diminishes the Doctor. However, the local star systems only 'go out' of existence once the Great Intelligence begins its attack on the Doctor, so suggesting that it is the Doctor's influence that has previously saved them. Then again, with Vastra on hand to provide Clara with cue cards as to what is happening during the Great Intelligence's attack, Clara realizes that she was always meant to enter the Doctor's time stream and save him. Moffat compounds this with Clara's memory of that startling scene in *Journey to the Centre of the TARDIS* where the Doctor demanded to know who she was. Thanks to the TARDIS's telepathic circuits (to which the Doctor hooks her up to get DeMarco's coordinates for Trenzalore) Clara now remembers the events that the Doctor had previously rewritten from time. However, as in Christopher Nolan's *Inception*, although there are millions of echoes of Clara throughout the Doctor's time stream, it is still very difficult for any of these echoes to have any influence on events or to plant an idea in the Doctor's subconscious. The Great Intelligence's influence looks to be enough to tip things over whenever the Doctor's life is in the balance (which it has often been throughout his lifetime). However, Clara's presence in the time stream is enough to counter-balance the Great Intelligence's threat, even although Moffat shows that she is not in direct confrontation with it most of the time. (It's interesting that Moffat presents Clara most 'in the flesh' while battling Dr. Simeon in *The Snowmen* and *The Bells of Saint John*.) Although we do see Dr. Simeon in the place of Clara in the Classic Series clips when he usurps the Doctor's time stream, it's likely that he only appears onscreen as a symbolic avatar, rather than being physically present in these scenes, unlike the more corporeal echoes of Clara. In this way, Clara's entry into the Doctor's time stream restores its natural path without unduly influencing it otherwise.

There is a large element of Moffat's 'dark fairytale' in this story. For instance, Moffat doesn't explain how Dr. Simeon and the Whisper Men transport the Paternoster gang from 1893 Victorian London to the Trenzalore of the far future. However, the Great Intelligence must have a rapid, advanced form of transport if it can get Jenny there so that Strax has enough time to save her. Previously, we'd seen the Great Intelligence travelling to Earth in the early Victorian era in a metaphorical snow storm during *The Snowmen*, but a less ethereal vehicle would be required to transport the Paternoster gang. (Unless, of course, Dr. Simeon transports the Paternoster gang in time and space by tricking our heroes into thinking that they have left the dream world of the conference call, as would befit a tribute to Christopher Nolan's *Inception.* Although this would mean that all the events of *The Name of the Doctor* just occur within a dream.) When the Doctor turns off the TARDIS's anti-gravs, so that they can crash land on Trenzalore, it's interesting that Moffat conveys the trauma of the crash on the TARDIS by having one of the glass panels on its doors shatter. I made sure to check if this same crack appears in *The Day of the Doctor* and *The Time of the Doctor* (which it doesn't), because Moffat makes this apparently insignificant detail more important by replicating this crack in the glass on the outer shell of the TARDIS that contains the Doctor's tomb. Since the TARDIS's outer shell is essentially an illusion, there isn't a real glass panel in the door to crack, so this crack in the glass is Moffat's metaphorical allusion to the damage that the TARDIS suffers on its crash landing. In the same light, it's amusing to see that the chameleon circuit is still working on the dead Doctor's TARDIS even though its dimensional dams are breaking down. Then again, the chameleon circuit *isn't* actually working, as it is still looks like a 1960's London police box. It's interesting that the entrance to the Doctor's tomb isn't actually through the TARDIS's main doors; instead, everyone enters via the stairway at the base of the time rotor, possibly close to the panel that the Doctor opened to enter the heart of his ship in *Journey to the Centre of the TARDIS.* As I previously noted in my review of that episode, Michael Pickwoad designed the new TARDIS console room to be a lot more flexible than previously, as Moffat's narrative demanded the removal of the entire time rotor here. It's interesting that there is a lot of ageing vegetation in the console room. It's possible that these were funerary flowers left by the Doctor's mourners before they sealed his tomb or that these creeping vines represent some kind of entropic invasion from outside vegetation. (Not that Trenzalore looks like a fertile planet otherwise.) As River stated in *The Impossible Astronaut*, alien empires are prepared to rip worlds apart to get their hands on the miracle that is a Time Lord's body, so it is likely that the Doctor left instructions for his mourners to burn his body upon his death. Yet even a disembodied Time Lord corpse is invaluable to the Doctor's enemies here. Had Gallifrey still been in existence, the Doctor would have headed home to die, so that the Time Lords could dispose of his body properly and make a record of his brain scan to upload to the APC Net in the Matrix. Since the Doctor and Clara were able to enter the depths of the TARDIS via the catacombs leading from River's fake grave, and then reappear to confront Simeon outside the Doctor's tomb, this must mean that the TARDIS has fractured. The Doctor's tomb is not the TARDIS itself per se, but the console room specifically. Another indication of the kind of detail that Moffat has put into this episode is the iron bar that lies on the ground outside the Doctor's tomb. Someone has evidently tried to use this bar to break into the tomb before Strax uses it as a weapon. Writing about Strax and weapons, I must point out that Archie would have found it easier to knock Strax out by striking his probic vent instead of just hitting him repeatedly on the head; then again, I'm sure Strax wouldn't want his sparring partner to know what his Achilles heel is.

I'm not quite sure why Vastra is left standing while Jenny disappears, and Strax forgets the Doctor's influence, as the Doctor affected her life just as much as the other members of the Paternoster gang. Since Vastra has previously implied that she tracked down and ate Jack the Ripper, it is also a bit inconsistent that she is content to hand over Clarence DeMarco to the police, despite the fact that he's killed 14 women, far more than the Ripper ever did. It's interesting that Vastra calls out "Oh, dear Goddess" when Simeon attacks the Doctor's timestream, as I think that this is a dead giveaway that Moffat alludes here to the Na'vi goddess Eywa from James Cameron's 2009 film *Avatar*, especially her similar symbolic representation (to the Doctor's time stream) as the Tree of Souls on Pandora. The Na'vi communicate with their ancestors via the Tree of Souls (which is akin to the Time Lords' APC Net), just as the Doctor's time stream is a link to his previous bodies. Eywa keeps Pandora in equilibrium; in a similar manner, Clara restores equilibrium to the Doctor by entering his time stream to counter the Great Intelligence's malevolence. Elsewhere, Vastra cries out "God" when Jenny vanishes, as other characters do throughout this episode at moments of stress as an essentially meaningless cliché, so I do think that it is significant that she cries out for a more maternal deity (like Eywa) in the face of the Doctor's collapsing time stream. (Or maybe Vastra's just covering all her bases when it comes to the prospect of her seemingly imminent afterlife.) It's also interesting that when equally stressed out about Jenny's earlier 'death' on Trenzalore, Vastra is very hostile to Strax (and he in turn reciprocates) until he manages to revive Jenny. This hostility turns into reality when the Great Intelligence removes the Doctor's positive influence on Strax, to the extent that Strax attacks Vastra.

I found the conclusion of this episode quite irritating. Moffat builds up the tension and the stakes for both Clara and the Doctor's entry into his time stream, and then promptly jettisons the conclusion of Clara's story to make way for a foreboding prequel to the 50th Anniversary adventure. The more casual viewers of my family were going "Wow! How can John Hurt be the Doctor?" However, my reaction was "Erm… How did the Doctor and Clara escape from the Doctor's time stream?" Perhaps critics like Steven and I are to blame for allowing Moffat too much dramatic licence in the conclusion of the 2010 series finale, *The Big Bang*, which relied much upon Moffat's concept of the "dark fairytale" to work. Usually, I don't mind when an author requires the reader/audience to do some work to imaginatively fill in the gaps in a narrative, as this can be very intellectually pleasing, and can lead to some great debates between fellow readers/viewers. However, in this instance, the gaps are too huge to be satisfactorily filled by the audience, especially when you consider that the whole series of events in this episode are effectively 'retconned' out of existence only two episodes later when the Doctor doesn't die at the end of *The Time of the Doctor*. Since the Doctor doesn't die at the end of his regenerative life cycle, this means that there is no time stream for Clara to later enter in *The Name of the Doctor*. We can't even say that Peter Capaldi's Doctor will later choose to be buried on Trenzalore at the end of his whole new life cycle, as the only Doctors that Clara sees are from the Doctor's original lives.

However, there is still a way for *The Name of the Doctor* to both happen and not happen, and that is for the whole adventure to be the result of lucid/shared dreaming in the style of *Inception*. As I argued in our previous book, Christopher Nolan's 2000 film *Memento* clearly influenced Moffat's depiction of our heroes keeping a record of the number of the Silence they had seen by writing tally marks on their faces with marker pens. In this reading, although everything that occurs happens in a dream, the results are still psychically real for the participants. So, when the Whisper Men invade Vastra's conference call, River takes control of the dream. We have already seen that River can influence events in this dream world by turning the tea that Vastra gave her into champagne. River allows the Great Intelligence to think that it has successfully gained control of the conference call. Since River is actually dead, the Great Intelligence is probably not aware of her psychic presence throughout this narrative. River then pulls the Doctor into the dream by making Clara think that she has woken up in the real world, and Clara then pulls the Doctor into the 'conference call'/dream world when she touches the Doctor's head with her soporific stained hands while removing his blindfold. Like Vastra in the conference call, Clara then makes tea for the dream's new participant, the Doctor. Since this is 'only a dream', this probably explains why River thinks that it will be okay to open the Doctor's tomb, and why she does nothing to stop Simeon from entering the Doctor's time stream. However, the Great Intelligence's psychic attack on the Doctor has real consequences for the Time Lord, causing him physical pain, and River loses control of the dream. Clara then takes over the shared dream, and enters the Doctor's time stream to save him. Following Clara's departure, the Doctor then takes over the shared dream, which enables him to lead Clara to safety. Although 'it was only a dream', this shared dream has real effects in the physical and psychical worlds that our heroes inhabit.

Indeed, this kind of virtual reality battle is not without precedent in *Doctor Who*, for the Doctor fought a similar conflict in the Time Lord Matrix during 1976's *The Deadly Assassin*. (As I mentioned earlier, this seminal Classic Series adventure quite possibly influenced the Wachowski brothers' 1999 movie *The Matrix*.) During *The Deadly Assassin*, Engin warned the Doctor that if he died in the dream world of the Matrix that he shared with his mysterious assailant, then the Doctor's physical body would also die. In this way, the Great Intelligence's psychical assault on the Doctor looks to have similar effects on his physical body here too.

Clara explores the Doctor's consciousness in the dream world, exposing the part of the Doctor's personality that he has kept deeply hidden within his subconscious: the War Doctor. Until the Doctor locates Clara, she is effectively lost in some kind of limbo. With the Doctor's assistance, Clara begins to see this as a simulacrum of Hades, albeit based in Trenzalore's graveyard. In Greco/Roman myth, only heroic mortals such as Theseus and Heracles could enter the underworld to converse with the deceased (in this case, Clara), and only such heroes would then be allowed to leave Hades. It's just as well that the Doctor is such an heroic figure too. The Doctor is able to lead the psychically 'dead' Clara to safety by utilising the Oswald family myth of the leaf that blew her into the world. As I previously discussed, the etymology of Clara means 'clear/bright', as she has often led the Doctor to safety in his psychical and physical reality, like removing his blindfold in this episode. Now the Doctor returns the favour by taking Clara 'home'. In this dream reading, the Doctor then finds a fissure that leads them home to the Maitlands' house, just as the Greco/Roman Hades had exits into the physical world. The Paternoster gang will then discover that they were still engaged in the conference call all along, which Vastra will then end. Although most of the events in this episode happened in a dream world, they appear real to all our heroes, not least because Clara's echoes resulted in her achieving corporeal existence on at least two occasions in *Asylum of the Daleks* and *The Snowmen*; i.e. Clara's echoes really did travel in time and space in this dream world. This was also a result of Simeon's psychic attack on the Doctor, for, as we saw in *The Snowmen*, the Great Intelligence had the capacity to give the monsters in people's nightmares corporeal existence, so in turn, the Great Intelligence's presence in the Doctor's time stream seems to amplify the corporeal presence of Clara's echoes. Although the 1893 Simeon 'dies' here, in reality the Great Intelligence still exists to summon Yeti to invade London during 1967's *The Web of Fear*, and to upload people to the wi-fi during *The Bells of Saint John*.

Curse you Moffat! You've kept me up most of the night while I imagined how the events of *The Name of the Doctor* can be both real and unreal. Then again, it was no less than Sigmund Freud who first came up with the idea that people could influence each other's dreams via 'dream telepathy'. Now, whether or not you regard psychoanalysis as a 'proper' or a 'pseudo' science, there is no doubt that Freud's imaginative approach to healing the psyche (with its groundings in Classical myth) has been hugely inspirational to modern-day mythmakers. If anything, the cultural phenomenon that is *Doctor Who* is proof positive that there is such a thing as 'shared dreaming', which showrunner Steven Moffat and the production team direct, with the active engagement and participation of fans like us.

50th Anniversary Special: The Day of the Doctor

Writer: Steven Moffat
Director: Nick Hurran
Originally broadcast: 23 November 2013

Cast

The Doctor: Matt Smith
The Doctor: David Tennant
The Doctor: Christopher Eccleston
The Doctor: John Hurt
The Doctor: Paul McGann
The Doctor: Sylvester McCoy
The Doctor: Colin Baker
The Doctor: Peter Davison
The Doctor: Tom Baker
The Doctor: Jon Pertwee
The Doctor: Patrick Troughton
The Doctor: William Hartnell
Clara: Jenna Coleman
Rose: Billie Piper
Tom: Tristan Beint
Kate Stewart: Jemma Redgrave
Osgood: Ingrid Oliver
Time Lord Soldier: Chris Finch
Androgar: Peter de Jersey
The General: Ken Bones
Arcadia Father: Philip Buck
Time Lord: Sophie Morgan-Price
Elizabeth I: Joanna Page
Lord Bentham: Orlando James
McGillop: Jonjo O'Neill
Atkins: Tom Keller
Zygons: Aidan Cook, Paul Kasey
Voice of the Daleks & Zygons: Nicholas Briggs
Dalek 1: Barnaby Edwards
Dalek 2: Nicholas Pegg
Voice Over Artist: John Guilor

Uncredited cast

The Doctor: Peter Capaldi

Steven's Review: An episode made to commemorate a show reaching its golden anniversary could be forgiven for merely being an excuse for a party, a nostalgic stroll through the high points of the previous five decades. In *Doctor Who*'s last big anniversary celebration, *The Five Doctors* back in 1983, so many elements and characters from the past were thrown in – all the Doctors, plus five companions (with half a dozen more making cameos), with Time Lords, a Dalek, a Yeti, a whole troop of Cybermen, and the Master – that the result was more of a parade than a story. Tremendous fun to watch, but of no lasting significance; indeed, the end of that story explicitly puts all the toys back in the box and assures the viewer that the show will continue on unchanged. With *The Day of the Doctor*, Steven Moffat successfully pulls off something far more ambitious – an ingeniously constructed episode that provides plenty of celebratory spectacle, but also marks a turning point in the continuing story of the Doctor. This is an episode that, as Moffat emphasised in several interviews, is pivotal to the future of the show, looking forward to the next 50 years as much as to those just past.

The series' rich history is certainly not neglected – there are innumerable touches that pay homage to the past, right from the top of the episode. Instead of the standard titles, we start with an abbreviated version of the original black-and-white *Doctor Who* opening, leading into a sequence of the Doctor's companion Clara working at Coal Hill School in London – the location where the whole story began 50 years ago. The actual credits appear only when Clara and the Doctor are literally picked up and deposited into the story by helicopter in a spectacular, exhilarating stunt sequence. The TARDIS is put down in Trafalgar Square on the orders of Kate Lethbridge-Stewart, leader of UNIT, the military organization dealing with alien threats to Earth that the Doctor has frequently worked with before. Introduced in last year's *The Power of Three*, Jemma Redgrave made an immediate impression as the daughter of the Doctor's old friend Brigadier Alastair Lethbridge-Stewart, and her return is very welcome.

In the National Gallery, the Doctor finds himself facing an impossible painting – apparently titled either *No More* or *Gallifrey Falls*, it is somehow showing a three-dimensional image of his home planet. This episode marks the first time *Doctor Who* has been filmed in 3D (and possibly the last time as well, given that the fascination with 3D film and television seems to have peaked), and the incorporation of this technical innovation into the story itself works very well, thanks to some excellently realised visual effects. The Doctor explains that the image is an example of Time Lord art ("bigger on the inside – a slice of real time, frozen"), and it's holding in stasis a particular moment of tremendous significance to him. It shows the last day of the Time War, when the Doctor made his fateful decision to end the war by destroying both sides – wiping out both the Daleks and his own people, the Time Lords.

In reality, of course, the decision that left the Doctor as the last of the Time Lords was actually taken by Russell T Davies when *Doctor Who* was revived for the 21st century. For over eight years now, the Doctor's status as the lone survivor of a cataclysmic conflict has been a fundamental part of his nature, and has provided a rich source of inspiration for plot and character development by Davies and his successor Steven Moffat. Christopher Eccleston, David Tennant, and now Matt Smith have all shown the Doctor haunted to a greater or lesser extent by this shattering event in his past. The culmination was the reveal earlier this year of a previously unknown incarnation of the Doctor – the one who actually fought in the Time War, and whose action to bring about its end resulted in him being hidden away in shame, denied the right to be known as the Doctor. This story brings a resolution to this long-running character arc, as the Tennant and Smith Doctors (regrettably, Eccleston was either unable or unwilling to take part) finally face up to their past decision, and as a consequence gain the precious chance to revisit it.

The scenes depicting the actual war are – unavoidably, I think – the least effective part of the episode. A conflict that spans the entire universe ("Every moment in time and space is burning") is essentially unfilmable. On the previous occasion we visited the Time War, in David Tennant's finale, *The End of Time* (the Gallifrey scenes of which are presumably happening more or less simultaneously with those of this story), the action of the war was deliberately kept off-screen. Only a list of evocative names ("the Nightmare Child, the Could-Have-Been King with his army of Meanwhiles and Never-Weres…") hinted at the mind-twisting horrors involved. Here, it was necessary to show *something* at least, but the shots of a few people scurrying around debris-filled streets, with a handful of Daleks pushing their way through the rubble, or scenes of some worried Time Lords standing around a table, can't help but seem prosaic and lacking in impact. Even the CGI images of the enormous Dalek battle fleet surrounding Gallifrey, firing a continuous rain of energy bolts down on the whole planet, don't convey a fitting scale for such an apocalypse.

It's only through its effect on the Doctor that the Time War can be made to provoke a response in the viewer. This is shown clearly by the two short "prequels" released online before the broadcast of this episode. *The Last Day* is a brief vignette showing a nameless soldier's experiences on the front lines, and is completely uninteresting. By contrast, *The Night of the Doctor* is a beautiful and moving piece; in a lovely surprise, it brings back the Eighth Doctor, Paul McGann – the last of the "Classic" Doctors, only seen previously once, in the 1996 TV movie which failed to lead to a new series. In just seven minutes, Steven Moffat brings the Doctor (who until now had refused to be involved in the war) to the realisation that he can no longer avoid taking an active part. With the help of the Sisterhood of Karn (a perfect reuse of an element from 1976's *The Brain of Morbius*) he regenerates, becoming transformed into the "War Doctor" – as he needs to be referred to, to avoid having to renumber the later ones. (At the end of *The Day of the Doctor*, the War Doctor regenerates again, though we don't see the completion of the process – it's a great pity that Eccleston was not there to help close the last gap in the story linking the old series and the new.)

It was a wonderful coup for the show to be able to cast John Hurt in the role of the War Doctor. The episode doesn't show anything of him actually fighting – the most violent thing we see him do is use a soldier's blaster rifle to carve the words NO MORE into a wall. It's entirely Hurt's acting talent – the air of exhaustion created with his pained eyes and wheezing voice – that gives such a strong impression of a man who has seen and done terrible things, reached the end of his tether, and can see no remaining course of action but to use the sentient super-weapon known as "the Moment" (the name of which is another reference back to *The End of Time*).

There's no compelling reason why the Moment communicates through an interface that looks like Billie Piper, but it provides a clever way for the image – albeit not the character – of Rose Tyler, so central to the first years of the revived series, to return in this commemorative episode. (It also provides a charmingly ingenious retrospective suggestion, for those who want it, for why the Doctor seemed so drawn to Rose from the moment he met her in 2005.) The Moment is willing to allow itself to be used to end the Time War, but its price is that the Doctor must live on, contrary to his own wishes. Acting as the War Doctor's conscience and guide (throughout the episode, the image of Rose is seen and heard by no one else), it opens up "time fissures" that allow him to visit his own future selves – to discover the kind of man he will become after making the decision he is contemplating. In this way, Moffat makes the multi-Doctor nature of the episode intrinsic to the story he is telling, and of far more significance than just an anniversary celebration. The Doctor is effectively debating within himself his proper course of action – but thanks to *Doctor Who*'s unique format, we get to see the various aspects of his psyche portrayed by three different actors.

With such a strong central spine to the episode, the surrounding plot fizzes along with all of Moffat's usual inventiveness, keeping up a constant stream of twists and reversals. As is often his method, he presents us with a series of deliberately disjointed jigsaw puzzle pieces, and part of the enjoyment is watching him link them together into a coherent narrative. Thus, we have the Eleventh Doctor and Clara in the present day, brought to the "Undergallery" (a repository for art "deemed too dangerous for public consumption") by Kate following centuries-old secret orders from Queen Elizabeth I. They are shown more three-dimensional paintings whose glass has been shattered from the inside – and the figures that used to be in them have vanished. Elsewhere, in the year 1562, David Tennant slips seamlessly back into the role of the Tenth Doctor, having an amorous adventure with Elizabeth herself, and ending up accidentally proposing marriage to her (as was alluded to a couple of times during his era) in the course of foiling a plot by the shape-stealing alien Zygons.

One of the most successful and memorable creature designs of the Classic Series (despite appearing in just one story in 1975), the Zygons provide this episode with the "monster" element that has always been so much a part of *Doctor Who*. As the title of their previous story (*Terror of the Zygons*) implies, it was a dark, atmospheric tale of threats lurking in the shadows, full of the tension and paranoia inherent in the idea of creatures that can transform themselves into perfect copies of human beings. Here, though, they are treated much more light-heartedly, with Moffat having fun exploiting the comic potential of mistaken identity (the Doctor twice directs a stream of insults at what he thinks is a Zygon masquerading as Elizabeth, only to discover to his consternation that it's the real one). Joanna Page's girlish version of Elizabeth, seemingly owing as much to the *Blackadder* version of the character as to actual history, adds to the impression of the story suddenly taking a turn into comedy sketch territory. As for the Zygons themselves, the costume design of 38 years ago (by future Academy Award winner James Acheson) needed no changes to work just as well in 2013, with the oversized head making the creature look like a grotesque parody of a human fetus. It's not quite as successful outdoors in bright sunlight (something that never happened in the original story), but when we see them in dimly-lit interiors like their base under the Tower of London, the Zygons retain all their old menace. Hopefully they will be brought back in a future story where they can properly take centre stage, rather than a subsidiary role.

When the time fissures open, the Eleventh Doctor, half-remembering his previous experience of these events, jumps through and meets the Tenth. They are soon joined by the War Doctor, amid some comic business with a fez that gets thrown from one time-zone to another (and which eventually forms one of Moffat's patented closed loops of cause and effect when it's brought to Elizabethan England, where it presumably gets stored in the Undergallery where the Doctor picked it up in the first place). For the remainder of the episode, the Doctors are together, and the interaction between them is full of laugh-out-loud funny moments. All three actors are on top form, showing wonderful comic timing as the Doctors can't resist throwing out barbed comments about each other's idiosyncrasies. The jokes fly thick and fast about Tennant's footwear and accent ("Brave words, Dick Van Dyke," retorts Smith after Tennant makes a crack about the "posh, gravelly thing – very convincing" that Hurt has going), or Smith's hyperactive physicality ("Are you capable of speaking without flapping your hands about?" snaps Hurt). One of my favourites was Hurt's acerbic comments on the other two's habit of brandishing their sonic screwdrivers at people like weapons ("What are you going to do, assemble a cabinet at them?"), or their propensity to use terms like "timey-wimey" (with Tennant commenting, deadpan, "I've no idea where he picks that stuff up").

Meanwhile, the subplot is proceeding, as UNIT scientists Osgood and McGillop discover that the creatures that escaped from the 3D paintings were Zygons, preserved there since Elizabethan times via "stasis cube" technology. Osgood, with her Fourth-Doctor-style multicoloured scarf, clearly carries on the tradition of Malcolm in 2009's *Planet of the Dead* of UNIT scientific staff being big fans of the Doctor. (In fact, Malcolm gets a couple of mentions in this episode, including one where Kate asks him to retrieve one of her father's old incident files for her: "70's or 80's depending on the dating protocol" – a lovely in-joke for fans, referring to the hopelessly screwed up chronology of the Classic Series, which has irreconcilable contradictions when it comes to the dating of the UNIT stories.) She evidently knows her *Doctor Who* well, using her scarf to trip up an attacker in the same way Tom Baker did in his first story *Robot* nearly forty years ago.

Captured by Elizabeth's troops, the Doctors are thrown into a cell in the Tower of London. Since that very building is the present-day headquarters of UNIT, Kate heads back there to rescue them. She takes Clara into UNIT's "Black Archive" – a collection of forbidden alien technology, not unlike that in the now-defunct spinoff series *Torchwood.* Appropriately, the archive contains a vortex manipulator that once belonged to Torchwood head (and former companion of the Doctor) Captain Jack Harkness, and they are hoping the Doctor will send them the activation code for it. The Eleventh Doctor obliges, scratching the code into a pillar in their cell, to be found four and a half centuries later. (In a lovely touch, close inspection shows the code to be "17 16 23 11 63" – which encodes the date and time of *Doctor Who*'s first broadcast, at 5:16 p.m. on November 23, 1963.) This section ends with another twist, as Kate is revealed to be a Zygon duplicate; Clara grabs the vortex manipulator and uses it to escape, leaving the Zygons in control of the Black Archive.

In the cell, the conversation between the three Doctors becomes more serious as the War Doctor begins to probe the others for information about his future. When he first met them, he could hardly believe that these youngsters were his future selves ("Am I having a mid-life crisis?"). Now, observing the uncomfortable way they look at him (since they don't realise that he has yet to make the fateful decision), he asks whether they ever found out how many children were on Gallifrey that day (as the Moment had suggested earlier that his future self would do). Although the emphasis on the children is a slightly facile shorthand tactic, too easily tugging at the heartstrings, it does lead to a terrific exchange, with some real conflict between the Doctors. The Tenth Doctor reveals that he did go back to find out the number of children who died – knowledge that he is appalled to discover his successor no longer remembers.

The two Doctors are left looking angrily at each other – in the Moment's poetic phrase, "The man who regrets… and the man who forgets." The War Doctor finds it difficult to recognise himself in these men, but the Moment encourages him to see in their different sonic screwdrivers a metaphor for his own situation ("Same software, different case"). This gives him the idea to use his screwdriver to start the calculations needed to disintegrate the door of the cell – calculations that will take centuries – whereupon the Eleventh Doctor looks at his own screwdriver and sees that the calculations are finished. The whole sequence is a brilliantly flowing piece of multi-layered writing, drawing the Doctors apart and then bringing them together again. And as a perfect capper, the sense of triumph is comically undermined when Clara barges in, revealing that the door was unlocked all the time.

Elizabeth takes them to the Zygons' base, where the creatures are storing themselves in the paintings, ready to be hidden away until their revival in the 21st century. It turns out that this is the real Elizabeth, playing the part of her Zygon duplicate. In a clever twist on a famous quote from the historical Elizabeth I, she explains that she managed to kill her counterpart in their earlier confrontation: "I may have the body of a weak and feeble woman… but at the time, so did the Zygon." This strand of the story is neatly concluded as the Tenth Doctor is left with no choice but to go through with the marriage ceremony. Throughout the episode, Moffat has a lot of fun with the Tennant version's reputation as the "ladies' man" of the Doctors; here, he receives a passionate kiss from his new bride while the others look on. ("Is there a lot of this in the future?" "It does start to happen, yeah.")

They all pile into the Tenth Doctor's TARDIS to journey back to 2013, leading to some more fun as the console room's appearance keeps changing, going from the Eccleston/Tennant version (the "grunge phase," as the Eleventh Doctor calls it), to one for the War Doctor that harks back to the Classic Series, with the white roundel patterns on the walls. Finally it settles on the most recent console room, prompting a line from Tennant which is traditional in these multi-Doctor stories: "Oh you've redecorated. I don't like it…" Meanwhile, Kate (having escaped from Zygon captivity) precipitates a confrontation with the aliens. Locking both groups in the Black Archive, she threatens them with mutual destruction and sets off a countdown to a nuclear detonation. It finally becomes apparent why the episode has spent so much time on the Zygon plot against Earth, which previously seemed like something of a distraction from the Time War and the Doctor's externalised introspection. Moffat has carefully set up a thematic parallel between Kate's determination to remove the Zygon threat and the decision that the War Doctor is contemplating.

Using a "space/time telegraph" that he gave to her father long ago (another callback to *Terror of the Zygons*), the Doctor tries to dissuade Kate from carrying out her threat, but fails. They can't land in the Tower directly because it's been TARDIS-proofed, but the War Doctor comes up with a solution – use the Zygons' stasis cube to store themselves in the *Gallifrey Falls* painting. In another typical Moffat trick of time-crossed plotting, the mystifying coda of the earlier sequence when the Eleventh Doctor and Clara were first shown the painting – where we saw the scientist McGillop receive an unexplained phone call – is revealed to be the Doctor telling him to have the painting transported to the Black Archive.

Emerging from the painting, the Doctors force the humans and Zygons to cancel the self-destruct countdown and work together by using the Black Archive's memory-wiping technology to remove their knowledge of which side they're on – a practical demonstration of the "veil of ignorance" thought experiment developed by the American moral philosopher John Rawls. Rather surprisingly, we don't see the conclusion of this plot strand – the episode leaves us to assume that a satisfactory peace is reached between the two sides (as hinted at by the scene where Osgood and her duplicate come to their own agreement). Once the point has been made that the avoidance of mutual destruction is possible, the Zygon subplot has served its purpose.

Jenna Coleman (as she is now credited, having dropped the "Louise" part of her professional name) has not really been at the forefront of the episode to this point – natural enough, with three Doctors hogging the limelight. Even so, it is very noticeable that Clara's relationship with the Doctor has changed; it is far more warm and open than before. With the mystery of her origin and significance resolved, the distance between them has gone and they are now clearly good friends. When she gets a quiet scene alone with the War Doctor, Coleman has a chance to shine. Clara has realised that his "young eyes" give away the fact that he has not yet made his choice – reminding us that the youthful Matt Smith is actually playing by far the oldest of the Doctors. She tells him that her Doctor very much regrets his decision, but the War Doctor counters with how much good that regret has driven him to. This glimpse of his future selves carrying on with the work of "the Doctor" has resolved his doubts. Hurt beautifully conveys the bittersweet nature of the moment (no pun intended) as he declares that "All things considered, time I grew up" and tells his watching guide that he is ready.

The direction by Nick Hurran – one of the best directors to come into the show in the last couple of years – is exemplary throughout the episode, but apart from the three-dimensional paintings rarely draws attention to itself. An exception is the striking image of the War Doctor standing before the Moment's "big red button" – a large red gem balanced atop a beautiful metallic flower. The emotional crux of the story arrives as he prepares to push the trigger ("Great men are forged in fire. It is the privilege of lesser men to light the flame... whatever the cost"), but the other two Doctors, having been alerted by Clara, arrive to join him, and formally release him from his banishment:

Tenth Doctor: "All those years, burying you in my memory..."
Eleventh Doctor: "Pretending you didn't exist. Keeping you a secret even from myself."
Tenth Doctor: "Pretending you weren't the Doctor, when you were the Doctor more than anybody else."
Eleventh Doctor: "You were the Doctor on the day it wasn't possible to get it right."
Tenth Doctor: "But this time..."
Eleventh Doctor: "...you don't have to do it alone."

Unlike the endless sea of books and websites dealing with the series available today, prior to the 1980's the reference library of a *Doctor Who* fan consisted entirely of one slim volume: *The Making of Doctor Who* by Terrance Dicks and Malcolm Hulke. Dicks in particular was a crucial contributor to the success of the show from 1968 right through to *The Five Doctors* in 1983, with a gift for storytelling structure and crystal-clear prose. The Moment's "wheezing, groaning" description of the TARDIS sound is a nod to his use of that phrase in dozens of novelisations of Classic Series stories. In the revised edition of *The Making of Doctor Who* in 1976, he managed to capture the essential character of the Doctor in a few memorable sentences:

> He never gives in, and he never gives up, however overwhelming the odds against him. … Though often caught up in violent situations, he is a man of peace. He is never cruel or cowardly.

Tennant and Hurt quote from the above passage as, prompted by Clara's distress (a great wordless performance from Coleman), the Smith version of the Doctor looks within and reconsiders what his name really means. A true happy ending for the story arrives as the latest Doctor, with his extra centuries of experience, is finally able to figure out a way to end the Time War without destroying his own people. The whole planet will be snatched away in an instant, frozen in a pocket universe (and the delight with which Hurt's Doctor shares the idea with Clara – "Like a *painting*!" – is a wonderful moment), leaving the surrounding Daleks to destroy each other. In another clever parallel from Moffat, the comic sequence earlier with the Doctors' sonic screwdrivers becomes a prefiguring of the climax, where we find out that the Doctor has been working on the calculations that will preserve Gallifrey throughout his whole life. The entire history of the show is brought to bear on the moment, including shots of *all* the Doctors – even a quick flash of the Doctor-in-waiting, Peter Capaldi, due to take over the role at Christmas.

The quiet aftermath, back in the National Gallery, is tinged with sadness as neither of the earlier Doctors will remember these events when they return to their proper places and times. This contrivance ("The time streams are out of sync – you can't retain it") is, of course, absolutely necessary so as to not invalidate the great journey the Doctor has taken over the past eight years. The long story of the Time War has now been told, from first to last, and although the War Doctor's moment of relief ("But for now, for this moment, I am the Doctor again") will be transitory, the same sentiment could be expressed by the current Doctor going forward, at last free of its shadow.

Finally, the Doctor is left alone to contemplate the painting that started it all, and the episode presents the most marvellous of its gifts to long-time fans, with a cameo from Tom Baker as the curator of the gallery, who acquired the painting "in remarkable circumstances". The erstwhile Fourth Doctor may be a little older (okay, a lot older), but the magnificent screen presence is still there as he reveals Moffat's final twist – the painting's true title, *Gallifrey Falls No More* – in that resonant voice. The delight of the moment is only increased by the teasing hints that maybe he really *is* the Doctor after all – but as he says, perhaps it doesn't matter either way.

What matters is what the Doctor chooses to do next. This episode, which so beautifully utilised the show's past, ends by firmly looking to the future. The Doctor, knowing now that he succeeded in saving Gallifrey, is on a quest to find it again. It remains to be seen just how committed he will be to that quest – it's conveniently free of urgency, meaning that future production teams will be able to focus on it or not, as they choose. Whatever happens, the great adventure in space and time, 50 years old and still going strong, is guaranteed to continue, as the Doctor sets out toward his new goal: "Home – the long way round."

Steven's Classic Who DVD Recommendation: Back in 1973, *Doctor Who* celebrated its tenth year with *The Three Doctors*, a story whose stars – William Hartnell, Patrick Troughton, and Jon Pertwee – are all no longer with us. The interaction between Smith, Tennant, and Hurt in *The Day of the Doctor* was very reminiscent of what happened when the original three Doctors got together, all those years ago.

Kevin's Review: *The Day of the Doctor* harks back to *Doctor Who*'s origins with its opening shot of the shadow of a policeman in front of a wooden advertising sign for I. M. Foreman's junkyard, the location of the Doctor's TARDIS in his first televised adventure, *An Unearthly Child*. The policeman is a bit more stocky than his 1963 counterpart, a reflection perhaps of our modern-day obesity epidemic. Then again, since Coal Hill School appears to be so close to the junkyard, Ian Chesterton must have been a bit lazy to drive there with Barbara Wright while following their errant pupil, Susan Foreman, during *An Unearthly Child*, although there was a pea souper of a fog that night. Either that or Totter's Lane is a longer road than its name suggests. From the Coal Hill School sign, we learn that Ian Chesterton is now chair of the school governing body, and that W. Coburn is head teacher. Now, most fans have taken this to be a reference to Anthony Coburn (the scriptwriter of *An Unearthly Child*) – which it is. However, there is a reason why the Steven Moffat lists the Headteacher as "W. Coburn" instead of "A. Coburn", as this is also a reference to "Wendy Coburn", a character in Kim Newman's *Doctor Who* novella *Time and Relative* (which was published on 23rd

November 2001, the 38th anniversary of *Doctor Who*). In Newman's novella, Wendy Coburn was a Coal Hill pupil, in the same year as the Doctor's granddaughter, Susan Foreman. Therefore, Wendy Coburn would be the right age to be a Headteacher in 2013. Perhaps Moffat's obscure allusion is also a nod to the man credited with the creation of *Doctor Who*, producer Sydney Newman, although Kim Newman is not a relative of his. Another reference to *An Unearthly Child* is the clock showing the time as 5.15 p.m. when Clara leaves the school on her motorbike, as this is the time that *Doctor Who*'s first episode aired. (Clara must have been teaching an after-school class, as most British schools end their day at 3.30 p.m.) Clara seems to be teaching a Philosophy class, since she said in *The Rings of Akhaten* that she hated History [at school]. Indeed, Clara will later state in *The Time of the Doctor* that she is an English teacher, much as Steven Moffat used to be. The Marcus Aurelius quote – "Waste no more time arguing about what a good man should be. Be one." – is an apt one for the beginning of this adventure. However, the Doctors essentially ignore this stoical advice, and do debate "what a good man should be" as a fundamental part of this drama. As for wasting time, well, I did quite a bit of that while trying to decipher what Clara had written on the whiteboard, as I thought she had written in the first line "No more time Arcadia", which led me to an online essay bank treatise on Tom Stoppard's 1993 play *Arcadia*. Since Moffat likes to place obscure Easter eggs onscreen to tease and please fans, I thought that he might have been referring to Stoppard's play. While there is much that would interest a *Doctor Who* fan in Stoppard's work, this was a dead end, as I eventually realised that Clara had just written the Marcus Aurelius quote on the whiteboard, and nothing else.

However, Moffat possibly solves one mystery left over from *The Bells of Saint John* here, when he shows that Kate Stewart has the TARDIS's emergency external phone number listed on her phone as belonging to the Doctor. (Great to hear that Kate uses the TARDIS materialization noise as the Doctor's ringtone on her phone.) We see later on in this episode that Kate has previously taken Clara to the Black Archive to check her out, and then deleted Clara's memory of this event via the automated memory filters. Whoever gave Clara the Doctor's phone number must have had a premonition that Clara would meet the Doctor. Angie and Artie will later conclude at the end of *The Crimson Horror* that Clara is a time traveller from the period photographs that they have found of her and the Doctor in the public domain. Consequently, it would not be a huge surprise if the more sophisticated UNIT had discovered that Clara was going to become a companion of the Doctor via Kate taking the simple precaution of scanning the Eleventh Doctor's features during her first encounter with him in *The Power of Three*. It would then be simple enough for UNIT to uncover any previously unknown activities of the Eleventh Doctor by running facial recognition software on photos in historical records. (His chin, by itself, would be a big giveaway.) While Clara's mind was still blurry from the memory filter, Kate would then have given her the Doctor's phone number.

Obviously, it would be unusual for Kate to precipitate Clara's 'first' meeting with the Doctor, but then these were unusual circumstances with the Great Intelligence's control of so many people over the wi-fi. UNIT did arrive suspiciously quickly in the wake of the Great Intelligence's defeat in *The Bells of Saint John*, and Kate probably only tried this tactic in desperation after the Doctor did not respond to an attempt to communicate with him via the Space-Time Telegraph while in his reverie about the 'woman twice dead'. Admittedly, the Doctor did look surprised when the phone started ringing in *The Bells of St. John*, but then he uses the same phone to call Kate when UNIT rudely grapples with his TARDIS. Since Kate has given this phone number a TARDIS materialization ringtone, the Doctor has obviously rung her from this phone before. (However, from Peter Capaldi's opener, it is evident that Moffat is a couple of steps ahead of the fans as usual, as he suggests in *Deep Breath* that it was the previously unseen character of Missy who gave Clara the Doctor's phone number.) We have seen the Doctor having phone calls from within the TARDIS prior to his redecoration of the console room, so the Doctor looks to have thrown out the multitude of phones that he previously had in there. Although, obviously, the only reason why the Doctor calls Kate from the TARDIS exterior phone in the beginning is because this makes for a more spectacular opening to the show. Indeed Moffat, in *The Time of the Doctor*, creates quite a poignant moment of drama when the Doctor asks that Handles remind him to patch the TARDIS phone back through the console, as making phone calls from the exterior phone while the TARDIS is flying through space is quite a hassle! It's interesting to note that when all three Doctors are in the TARDIS, the update of the console room 'desktop' also temporarily affects the ship's external appearance, as the Eleventh Doctor has to hang outside the door again to ring McGillop, despite this being the

Tenth Doctor's TARDIS.

Another more obvious link to the events of the preceding series is the Doctors' hiding of Gallifrey in a parallel pocket universe. We saw from *Hide* how dangerous and difficult it was for a TARDIS to enter a pocket universe, so this means that it will be next to impossible for the Doctor to track down the hidden Gallifrey, or for the Time Lords to escape from the pocket universe. Another reference to *Hide* occurs when the Eleventh Doctor calls upon Clara to impersonate the "Wicked Witch of the Well", as the spectre of Hila Tacorian was also called this name. (Moffat probably named the Tudor lord here after Jeremy Bentham, who was the co-founder of the *Doctor Who* Appreciation Society in 1976, and also the lead writer of Marvel's *Doctor Who* magazine in its early years.) One of the main themes of the Anniversary Special is the Doctor's regret at committing an act of genocide to end the Time War, which Moffat also examined at length throughout the previous series. Kate Stewart's threat to destroy the Black Archive (and London along with it) to prevent the Zygons getting their hands on the technology that will allow them to subvert humankind is not unlike the reaction of Porridge's people to implode planets and star systems whenever there's Cyber-technology on the loose during *Nightmare in Silver*. Kate is not malevolent in her desire to save billions of people by killing millions, and certainly far less aggressive than her own father's reaction to the prospect of Homo Reptilia's escape from their caves at the conclusion of *Doctor Who and the Silurians* (1970). The only bum note about this is when Moffat has the Tenth Doctor pleading with Kate not to do this grievous act as "This is not a decision you will ever be able to live with." Given that Kate will be dead when the nuclear warhead explodes, she won't be around to have any regrets. However, as the War Doctor observes, the Doctor's regret at his own act of mass destruction has led to a lot of good in the preceding series of 21st Century *Who* and beyond, and so this perversely confirms his justification of his murderous crime. Most of the time in the series, an instance of 'companion clarity' helps the Doctor save the day, but although Clara is perceptive enough to realise that the War Doctor has yet to 'push the button', her articulation of the great pain that his doing so will cause the Doctor does not dissuade the War Doctor. However, thankfully she is more persuasive later on with her own Doctor, firstly through the pain in her eyes (which, as Steven also writes, is an excellent performance by Coleman), and then by stating that she'd never pictured the Eleventh Doctor being the one to press the button.

Although Clara doesn't have much to do in this episode, what she does do is very important. There is a sense here that Moffat is comparing the Doctor to the Moment when the General states that, "According to legend, it developed a conscience." The Doctor is certainly far more moral and ethical when he has a travelling companion to question his decisions. In this way, it is regrettable that the War Doctor seems to have dispensed with the need for a companion. As Amy said in *A Town Called Mercy*, "See, this is why you shouldn't travel alone." Clara's moral disapproval of the Eleventh Doctor's action is what makes the Doctors reconsider, to see if there is another way out of this dilemma, no matter how crazy it is.

It's very possible that Moffat has Clara working in Coal Hill School only as a device to reflect the beginnings of the Doctor's televised adventures, and that we may never see her working there again. (Of course, we now know that Clara's job at Coal Hill will continue into the next series.) Like Rory's work as a nurse, Clara's profession doesn't seem to be an ideal one for constant interruptions. Then again, I suppose that time off in the TARDIS would give her more time to prepare for lessons than other teachers would have. It also seems as though Clara is still not the Doctor's constant travelling companion, and that she is in control of when the Doctor picks her up for a jaunt.

Of course, Coal Hill School was also the setting for another adventure in an anniversary year, for it featured in *Remembrance of the Daleks* in 1988. This story featured the Hand of Omega, a Time Lord stellar manipulator that, like the Moment, had sentience, and could be a fearsome weapon in "the wrong hands". Since the Hand of Omega was in a box that looked like a coffin, and the First Doctor supposedly took it with him along with his cot, then one could say that the Doctor preparations for leaving Gallifrey ranged from the cradle to the grave. (There is a British joke about people who pack too much on holiday also taking the 'kitchen sink' with them, so perhaps the Doctor took this too!) *Doctor Who*'s official 25th Anniversary story was *Silver Nemesis*, which featured a living metal, Validium, which Rassilon and Omega created as an ultimate weapon to defend Gallifrey. Like the Moment, it too was sentient and capable of speech. Validium is likely to be one of the forbidden weapons in the Omega Arsenal that have ultimately proved ineffective against the Daleks in *The Day of the Doctor*.

The end of *Remembrance of the Daleks* featured the Hand of Omega destroying Skaro. Davros had deployed the stellar manipulator to turn Skaro's sun into a power source for time travel akin to what the Time Lords enjoyed. However, the Seventh Doctor, in anticipation of Davros' scheme, altered the Hand of Omega's programming so that Skaro's sun went supernova, destroying Skaro in the process. Although this was a suitably epic ending to *Remembrance of the Daleks*, the destruction of Skaro (and possibly the many Daleks on it) struck most fans as a wrong note, which led to author John Peel's retconning of this act in his novel *War of the Daleks* (1997). In this book, the Dalek Prime claimed that the Hand of Omega only destroyed a sun that looked similar to Skaro's. Likewise, *The Day of the Doctor* is a retcon of the Doctor's destruction of Gallifrey in his bid to end the Time War. However, Moffat has put a great deal of thought, effort, and ingenuity into pulling this off, rather than just relying on a "one-liner" as John Peel did.

Indeed, one could argue that *The Day of the Doctor* sees the resolution of the Cartmel Masterplan that began in *Remembrance of the Daleks*, which involved the previously comic Seventh Doctor becoming far more dark and mysterious, and possibly 'more than a Time Lord'. Fans named this 'the Cartmel Masterplan' after Andrew Cartmel, script editor of *Doctor Who* during the final years of the Classic Series, who felt that the Doctor had lost some of his essential mystery during the previous 25 years. Cartmel devised the idea of the Doctor being a reincarnation of 'the Other', a shadowy figure that co-founded Time Lord society with Rassilon and Omega, but who may not himself have been Gallifreyan. The Doctor's decision to destroy Gallifrey later as part of his bid to end the Time War was perhaps an inevitable consequence of Cartmel's decision to make the Doctor darker and more Machiavellian.

I liked the dark, brooding part of the Cartmel Masterplan at the time, although one aspect that I didn't particularly like was the Time Lords' sterility due to an ancient curse. This seemed particularly silly to me at the time, especially as Andrew Cartmel, Ben Aaronovitch and Marc Platt apparently devised this idea because no children had ever appeared on screen during the Doctor's return visits to Gallifrey. However, I believe that the final producer of the Classic Series, John Nathan-Turner, ultimately devised this concept of the Time Lords being sterile as part of his bid to have no "hanky panky in the TARDIS". This reached the ridiculous extreme of the production team asking Carole Ann Ford not to call the First Doctor 'Grandfather' during the 20th Anniversary adventure, *The Five Doctors*, as to do so would raise the spectre that the Doctor had once copulated. Ford rightly refused this idiotic suggestion, as this did not fit in with the character of Susan. Indeed, the Cartmel Masterplan never satisfactorily incorporated the conundrum that was Susan. Therefore, I was quite happy to see that Moffat has retconned this aspect of the Cartmel Masterplan by conveying that there is a multitude of children on Gallifrey during the resolution of the Time War.

Unlike Steven, I don't think that Moffat's emphasis on children is facile here. I know that in the previous books, I have moaned about Moffat's tendency to incorporate children in his scripts and the series as a whole, since children did not feature strongly in the Classic Series. As an adult *Doctor Who* fan, I suppose this makes me quite defensive against the age-old accusation that it is "a children's programme", while forgetting that Susan Foreman was supposed to be a teenager from the very beginning, along with Vicki, Dodo, and possibly Jamie. However, since older actors played these characters, it is easy to forget that they are teenagers. The only actors who were teenagers when they first appeared in the Classic Series were Sarah Sutton as Nyssa and Mathew Waterhouse as Adric. As I was very young at the time, I didn't mind Adric, but many older *Doctor Who* fans disliked the character of this teenage genius on board the TARDIS, much as I later abhorred his counterpart on *Star Trek: The Next Generation*, Wesley Crusher. Many fans disliked Artie and Angie's brief trip in the TARDIS this year for much the same reasons, although these teenagers, while naturally arrogant, were clearly not geniuses like Adric and Wesley Crusher.

As a parent, I now try to avoid news stories where young children are the victims of crime or war, because it is all too easy to imagine the same happening to my child. Therefore, I now regard it as being entirely natural that the Doctor would have most regret over his killing of innocent children. Note that when he escapes from Arcadia in his TARDIS at the beginning, the War Doctor does take out some Daleks that had been threatening to exterminate children in the process, instead of dematerializing straight away. This seems to be a subtle reminder on Moffat's part that the Doctor was once a father. However, the Tenth Doctor's estimate that there may have been 2.47 billion children on Gallifrey at the end of the Time War is a startlingly large amount. I think perhaps that Moffat had chosen the exact same number of children that are currently on Earth to make Gallifrey more analogous to our planet in this instance, so that we would identify more with the Time Lords' plight. (There were about 2.2 billion children in the world under 18 in 2010, according to the *International Herald Tribune*.) The only reason why I think this is an incredibly large number of children for a planet like Gallifrey is due to the fact that the Time Lords, with all their regenerations, have incredibly long life spans, so I would have thought that this would cause a more or less permanent dip in the birth rate. Then again, the birth rate could still be this high if each Gallifreyan had only one child. Perhaps the population of Gallifrey is far greater than that of Earth? Incidentally, since the Doctor changes character and appearance quite a bit with every regeneration, a Time Lord marriage would probably have some quite interesting dynamics in dramatic terms! Having written that, River Song always appears to love the Doctor, no matter what face or mood he's in.

There is a curious scene in *The Day of the Doctor* where the Moment shows the children of Arcadia dancing around a maypole in the wake of a possible reprieve by the War Doctor, and as a possible sign of hope and renewal. When the Tenth Doctor told the Cult of Skaro that he was "there at the fall of Arcadia" in *Doomsday* (2006), the first impression is that the Daleks had destroyed some heavenly paradisiacal planet during the Time War. In Classical and Renaissance myth, 'Arcadia' was a rural idyll and utopia unspoilt by civilization. The Gallifreyan Arcadia, in contrast, is a concrete jungle, although it was possibly more paradisiacal when first named. The wastelands outside Arcadia don't appear any more inviting than the city itself. So Moffat's incorporation of Arcadia as a Gallifreyan city at the end of the Time War has some minor terminological problems. As an interesting aside, some scholars believe that maypoles are a continuation of the pagan Norse cosmology that viewed the universe as a World Tree, which connects the earth to the heavens and the underworld via its high branches and its low roots. Janie Aire, in her blog *In Praise of Thirst*, has written a very interesting breakdown of *Hide*, in which she writes that the TARDIS is quite redolent of the World Tree:

> The TARDIS is herself a kind of World Tree, in that she facilitates travel between the worlds. She goes to Upperworlds (like *The Rings of Akhaten*) and Underworlds (like in *Cold War)* and every place in-between. She has her

> own *axis mundi*, the Time Rotor, which now has a lovely carousel above it, and many pretty lights and Gallifreyen [*sic*] hieroglyphs that evoke a "celestial" atmosphere.

Janie Aire has also written an excellent treatise of *The Name of the Doctor* on her blog that is well worth checking out. I'm not sure that it would be possible for Moffat to ensure that every director on the show realises the symbolism that Aire sees in her view of *Doctor Who*, but if he does, then this would make Moffat's narrative far more complex than even I had previously considered. The Doctor's time stream, in particular, did seem very much like a World Tree in *The Name of the Doctor*, with its roots into the heavens, the here and now, and the underworld where Clara was momentarily lost. At first, I thought that Moffat was influenced by James Cameron's depiction of Eywa in *Avatar* (which he probably was), but ultimately, both Eywa and the Doctor's time stream in *The Name of the Doctor* are representative of the Norse pagan myth of the World Tree.

You may recall that in my review of the previous episode, I made a mental note to look out for the crack in one of the glass panels in the TARDIS doors that the Doctor caused by making his ship crash land on Trenzalore in the previous episode. This 'crack in the glass' is no longer visible from the exterior of the Eleventh Doctor's TARDIS. Indeed, when UNIT picks up the Eleventh Doctor's TARDIS in the beginning of *The Day of the Doctor*, some of the glass panels in the TARDIS door are coloured white. When we see the Eleventh Doctor's TARDIS later on in the 50th Anniversary adventure, these white glass panels are no longer there. This was no doubt due to the production team using a different TARDIS model in the beginning of the episode, one which could withstand being knocked about on a crane. So, given that the production team gave little thought to continuity regarding the glass in the TARDIS doors during *The Day of the Doctor*, the fact that the future TARDIS crypt also has a crack in its glass panelling must have been deliberate on Moffat's part. Moffat probably meant this to signify that the main events in *The Name of the Doctor* happen in a Dream World. (Since I first wrote this paragraph, I watched *The Day of the Doctor* again, and can now see that the white coloured window panels are consistently there after all in this episode and before. These white coloured panels are more noticeable in *The Day of the Doctor*, because they are not so visible when the TARDIS windows (like the lamp on the roof) are fully illuminated. Indeed, since the Doctor did not have the TARDIS windows illuminated at the beginning of the episode, UNIT presumed that the Doctor was not 'at home', which led to their decision to move the TARDIS by helicopter.)

I previously speculated that the Doctor and Clara must have escaped from the 'underworld' at the end of *The Name of the Doctor* via some tunnel. Given that this underworld is reflective of Trenzalore's surface, the Doctor and Clara probably escaped via the Doctor's time stream in this underworld's symbolic representation of the TARDIS. The Doctor then took the Paternoster gang and Clara home in the dream TARDIS, with the dream itself only ending when each of our heroes next woke up. Remember that at the end of the 50th Anniversary adventure, the Doctor tells us that Clara has previously asked him if he dreams. The Doctor relates that he does indeed dream, despite the Fourth Doctor's pronouncement in *The Talons of Weng-Chiang* (1977) that "sleep is for tortoises". Consequently, it would seem that none of our heroes realise that most of the events of *The Name of the Doctor* happened in a dream, although the Doctor and Clara should begin to suspect this, given that the Doctor does not die on Trenzalore in *The Time of the Doctor*. In my review of *Nightmare in Silver*, I criticised the ensemble image of all the Doctors at the end of this episode, as I thought that it looked too fake. However, now that I remember that it is supposed to represent one of the Doctor's dreams, I am more forgiving of it, since it is only natural that the Doctors that the Eleventh has recently met should look more vivid in contrast to rather idealised images of his other predecessors.

Other than this, I thought that the visual effects in *The Day of the Doctor* were mostly brilliant. The Dalek assault on Arcadia in the beginning is truly spectacular and cinematic. However, I didn't think that the three Doctors' entrance into the Black Archive via *Gallifrey Falls* worked very well, as you only get the impression of them stepping out of the picture, instead of actually doing so. I guess that this must have been quite tough for Nick Hurran to realize, especially as it involved a Dalek crashing out of the picture too. To reinforce what has actually happened, Hurran had to have a shot of Clara with her hand on the picture frame, in the process of walking out of it. The War Doctor's 'cup-a-soup' moment that led to this was also a bit off, unless the Eleventh Doctor had given the War Doctor some behind-the-scenes exposition of what he had been doing when interrupted by the time fissure. Otherwise, it's a bit strange that the War Doctor suddenly knows about *Gallifrey Falls*. I guess the War Doctor could have suggested that they use some other picture from Elizabeth I's collection first, as he was present when they saw a Zygon's 'translation' into one of these, and then the Eleventh Doctor came up with the idea of using *Gallifrey Falls* instead. Of course, it's necessary for the plot development that the War Doctor comes up with this idea, so that the other two Doctors begin to see that he is "an alright sort" after all, rather than the figure of dread that they first viewed him as.

It's also a bit strange that the Zygons lead Clara to Captain Jack's vortex manipulator in the Black Archive. Presumably, the Zygon leader wanted to impersonate Clara and use the vortex manipulator to stop the Doctor's interference with their plans, and as a quicker route to the more comfortable future than hanging around in paintings for centuries. However, just as they had chauvinistically underestimated Elizabeth I earlier, so they do with Clara here. Also, the Zygons were a bit more threatening in their original appearance in *Terror of the Zygons* (1975), for in that adventure, they had a sting that could incapacitate humans. Then again, this does not invalidate Elizabeth I's ability to kill a Zygon when in human form. When I first watched *The Day of the Doctor*, I was a bit irritated that the Zygons only had a cameo appearance that soon seemed forgotten and inconsequential to the plot. However, it's only when you watch every episode several times (and in order) that you begin to discern more of Moffat's nuances, such as his regular comparison of the Doctor to the other 'press the button' merchants this series, like Kate Stewart in her standoff with the Zygons here.

As for the War Doctor, I suppose Moffat's decision to devise a new, previously hidden incarnation of the Doctor should really irritate long-time fans. However, he has taken some pains to ensure that the numbering of the Doctors hasn't changed, which would have made most previous *Doctor Who* reference books (such as ours) automatically out of date otherwise! Another factor in Moffat's decision is that it means that the Eleventh Doctor is the final incarnation of our favourite Time Lord, especially as the showrunner pedantically includes the Tenth Doctor's partial regeneration in *Journey's End* (2008). With tongue firmly in cheek, one hopes that the showrunner for *Doctor Who*'s 100th Anniversary won't be in such a hurry to finish off the new regenerative cycle that the Time Lords grant him in the *Time of the Doctor*! Having written that, Moffat has compensated for this by making the Eleventh Doctor's life probably the longest of any of the incarnations, with plenty of gaps in the narrative for Moffat's successors to exploit. Beyond this, in the brilliant prequel minisode to the 50th Anniversary adventure, *The Night of the Doctor* (which finally allowed Paul McGann some more screen time as the Eighth Doctor), the reflection of the War Doctor's face following the regeneration is that of a youthful John Hurt. This means the War Doctor incarnation also had a long life span, just like that of the Eleventh Doctor. In the end, I guess one cannot get too angry at Moffat's liberties here in light of all these safeguards. Also, I would have thought that it would be impossible for any viewer to fail to warm to and empathise with the gravitas of a 'national treasure' like John Hurt. By having an older Doctor here, Moffat is most likely paving the way for the imminent depiction of the Doctor by another older actor who, unlike Doctors Ten and Eleven, is unlikely to talk like a child. It was especially brilliant of Moffat to include a fierce shot of Peter Capaldi's Doctor-to-be in the finale.

Doctor Who's previous two big Anniversary specials have revolved around Gallifrey, so it is natural that Moffat would want to do the same here. Admittedly, there was the added complication this time around that the Doctor had destroyed Gallifrey in the Time War. However, the prospect of saving Gallifrey from destruction after all is a very fitting justification for all the incarnations of the Doctor to work on screen together for the first time. A plot to save Earth from a similar kind of threat would not have had the same resonance. Some viewers may have wondered why the Doctor felt compelled to destroy Gallifrey at all, since the Time Lords don't appear to be doing anything wrong here apart from being defeated by the Daleks, and would probably have forgotten the Time Lords' attack on Earth during *The End of Time* (2010). However, the General does imply that the Time Lords have used various unethical weapons against the Daleks. It's good that the Doctor is finally able to take the "I destroyed Gallifrey" monkey off his back. Moffat's depiction of the Eleventh Doctor as "the man who forgets" has more than an element of truth about it, as the Doctor's character has changed a great deal from the 'wounded warrior' that he first appeared to be in 21st Century *Who*.

It was a wise decision on Moffat's part to concentrate mostly on celebrating the Revived Series since 2005, as this is still quite fresh in most viewers' minds, instead of trying to fulfil the fantasies of those few viewers who have watched the series for the full 50 years. In particular, I thought that Billie Piper's performance as the Moment's Bad Wolf/Rose interface was brilliant – she's certainly a more accomplished performer than she was in her early years in the programme. Moffat's presentation of the Moment's 'big red button' as an elegant, bejewelled *rose* is a great example of how subtle and poignant he can be. However, I did get a real buzz when I heard Tom Baker's unmistakeable voice, the last surviving of the first four archetypal Doctors. (Not that Peter Davison ever did anything wrong, I hasten to add.)

How do we explain how the Curator has the appearance of an aged Fourth Doctor? I've fantasised that he could be the Zygon leader Broton, who survived the aftermath of *Terror of the Zygons*, albeit crippled when the Brigadier shot him. Having previously taken a sneaky body scan of the Doctor while our hero was on the Zygon ship, Broton escaped by pretending to be the Fourth Doctor. Unable to summon up the Zygons' ultimate weapon, the Skarasen, Broton decided to become a curator upon his retirement, and developed an empathy with the owner of the body whose image he'd stolen. In the wake of humanity's historic peace deal with the Zygons, the Fourth Doctor/Broton then decides to make amends with the peacemaker. However, as written here, the Curator is most likely some kind of parallel Fourth Doctor from the pocket universe where Gallifrey now lies. Indeed, since Elizabeth I wanted the Doctor to be the Curator of her collection, and since the Curator looks like an aspect of the Doctor, the suggestion here is that the Curator is somehow the Doctor. As the Curator says that he acquired the painting in "remarkable circumstances", and that Elizabeth I knew about it, then the Curator must have been looking after *Gallifrey Falls No More* for nearly 500 years, something that only a Time Lord can really do. (Incidentally, I thought the *Gallifrey Falls/No More* title debate was rather a false dichotomy, as unlike most of Moffat's riddles, its resolution was obvious.) Although the Eleventh Doctor gives some foreboding hints about his future to the Tenth (and hence to himself), these do not seem so ominous now that the Doctor has already been to Trenzalore. The Curator hints that the Doctor may soon revisit a few familiar, favourite faces… Just as the Doctor gives 'hope' to Gallifrey, so the Curator offers hope to the Doctor of a future beyond Trenzalore. So, with hints of further nostalgia imminent, *Doctor Who* fans have good reason to look forward to the future, as well as to the past here.

2013 Christmas Special: The Time of the Doctor

Writer: Steven Moffat
Director: Jamie Payne
Originally broadcast: 25 December 2013

Cast

The Doctor: Matt Smith
Clara: Jenna Coleman
Tasha Lem: Orla Brady
Dad: James Buller
Linda: Elizabeth Rider
Gran: Sheila Reid
Colonel Albero: Mark Anthony Brighton
Abramal: Rob Jarvis
Marta: Tessa Peake-Jones
Barnable: Jack Hollington
Colonel Meme: Sonita Henry
Voice of Handles: Kayvan Novak
Young Man: Tom Gibbins
Voice: Ken Bones
Cyberman: Aidan Cook
Voice of the Daleks & the Cybermen: Nicholas Briggs
Dalek 1: Barnaby Edwards
Dalek 2: Nicholas Pegg
Silent: Ross Mullan
Sontaran: Dan Starkey
Weeping Angel: Sarah Madison

With Karen Gillan as Amy Pond, and introducing Peter Capaldi as The Doctor

Steven's Review: With *The Time of the Doctor*, Steven Moffat completes a loose trilogy of episodes which have focused on *Doctor Who*'s title character perhaps more deeply than any others before them. *The Name of the Doctor* saw the Doctor discover how his life was fundamentally entwined with that of his friend Clara, while *The Day of the Doctor* revealed and resolved the secrets of the great Time War that was such a huge part of his past. Now, as the show completes the year of its 50th Anniversary with yet another milestone – by a happy coincidence, *The Time of the Doctor* is the 800th episode of *Doctor Who* to be broadcast – and the era of Matt Smith's Doctor comes to an end, Moffat gathers up plot threads from the whole of Smith's time as the Doctor and provides a fitting wrap-up for the mysteries that have stretched over the last four years. It's not the stellar piece of work that the 50th Anniversary episode was, but with an outstanding central performance from Smith himself it still delivers quite an emotional punch at the end, and looks forward with confidence to the show's future.

The first half of the episode, however, does suffer from a certain staleness – it's a parade of previous Moffat ideas and characters that for a long time resists coalescing into an actual story. The opening sequence, with the Doctor investigating a huge gathering of ships from all manner of species surrounding a planet broadcasting a message to the entire universe – a message which is untranslatable, but provokes fear in all who hear it – inevitably calls to mind the convocations in previous season finales *The Pandorica Opens* and *The Wedding of River Song*. The planet is shielded and protected by the Church of the Papal Mainframe, the far-future organisation of militant clerics Moffat has used a number of times since *The Time of Angels* in 2010. On board the Church's ship, Clara encounters the strange memory-wiping Silence that were a major part of the 2011 series. Eventually, the Doctor discovers that the planet is actually Trenzalore – the place where, as he saw in *The Name of the Doctor*, his life is fated to end. Later, when he and Clara manage to get down to the planet to investigate the small human settlement from which the signal is emanating, there's an extended action sequence involving the Weeping Angels (complete with music recycled from their first appearance in *Blink*) which serves no purpose but to provide an indulgent cameo for the famous monsters. (I did, however, admire the ingenuity with which Moffat makes use of the fact that, for the first time, the Doctor's quiff is artificial – Matt Smith having shaved his head earlier this year for his part in Ryan Gosling's *How to Catch a Monster* before returning to film his *Doctor Who* finale.)

One element that does provide some novelty is the Doctor's new assistant. With Clara still living her own life on Earth rather than travelling full-time with him in the TARDIS, he has acquired a mechanical companion, a disembodied Cyberman head ("The organics are all gone, but there's still a full set of data banks") which he nicknames "Handles". With his fussy literal-mindedness and propensity for spouting information, Handles provides a light-hearted touch in the portentous initial scenes that recalls the fondly remembered robotic dog, K9, from Tom Baker's time as the Doctor. (Amusingly, during his tenure Baker once proposed the idea that his Doctor didn't actually need a human companion, and could work just as well with a talking cabbage on his shoulder to explain the plot to – not dissimilar to the idea of Handles.) But he's a source of pathos as well, when the Doctor casually orders Handles to remind him to take a certain action in the future, without specifying when. It's not a hard payoff to see coming, but it's still an affecting moment when, after slowly deteriorating over the long course of the story, Handles' last act before shutting down completely is to produce a long-since irrelevant reminder.

When it's not recalling the past, this first part of the story is getting bogged down in some laboured comedy involving the Church requiring all visitors to be naked, necessitating the use of illusionary clothing by the Doctor and Clara. Admittedly, the scene where the Doctor meets Clara's family (having absent-mindedly forgotten to extend the projection of his clothing to anyone apart from Clara) was funny, but once they get on board the Papal Mainframe the idea falls as flat as the rest of the Doctor's innuendo-laden banter with the Church's leader, Tasha Lem. Orla Brady does her best with what's there, and will get some better moments later, but initially Tasha comes over as a caricature, a pale imitation of River Song at her shallowest – which is particularly grating after the depth of emotion in River's last appearance just two episodes ago.

Another favourite idea of Moffat's (used beautifully in *The Girl in the Fireplace* in 2006, and many times since) is that of two individuals with vastly different but intersecting timelines. For the Doctor, literally centuries pass in the course of this episode – which unfortunately means that his scenes need to be inelegantly stitched together with some gratuitous voiceover narration from Tasha (who is she telling this story to, exactly?). But for Clara, the entire story takes place in the course of a single Christmas dinner with her family – she only gets involved at all because she phones the Doctor for help in cooking the turkey. This is *Doctor Who*'s ninth consecutive Christmas special, and incorporating festive motifs into the story in ways that haven't been done before is evidently starting to get a little challenging. The town on Trenzalore at the centre of the story is named Christmas, for no real reason ("How can a town be called Christmas?" "I don't know, how can an island be called Easter?"), and the snowy environment and pseudo-Victorian costume and production design deliberately echo previous Christmas episodes (in particular, last year's *The Snowmen*) in a rather strained attempt to justify the name.

The best moment of this set-up phase of the episode is the unexpected reappearance of the "crack in the universe" which loomed so large throughout the 2010 series. (In passing, a thread left hanging from 2011's *The God Complex* is resolved, as we learn that the crack is what the Doctor saw in the room supposedly containing his greatest fear – "I always knew it wasn't over," he says as he sees it again.) It is now ingeniously linked with the fate of Gallifrey, as revealed in *The Day of the Doctor*. The mysterious signal is from the Time Lords, attempting to re-enter this universe through the weak point represented by the crack. In a deft homage to 1983's *The Five Doctors*, the Doctor suddenly whips out the Seal of the High Council which he took from the Master in that story and has apparently carried in his pocket ever since, using it to give Handles the capability to translate the message. The last piece of the jigsaw is revealed as the message turns out to be the oldest question in the universe – "Doctor Who?"

Only once the pieces are all in place, around twenty-five minutes in, does the story start to become compelling. Moffat has carefully constructed a situation in which the Doctor is boxed in, forced to adopt a position of stasis. A "truth field" emanating from the crack means that he cannot answer the question with anything but his real name – which would act as an indication to the Time Lords that they have found the right place to re-enter this universe. Given the massed alien forces above, the emergence of the Time Lords would mean immediately reigniting the Time War. And so the Church dedicates itself to Silence (one of Tasha's better lines is "There will now be an unscheduled faith change") – to making sure that the Doctor does not speak his name. They assist him in keeping Christmas safe from the aliens that manage to penetrate the Church's shield (as shown in an amusing scene with a couple of Sontarans), so that he won't be pressured into answering the question out of desperation, but at the same time they are prepared to destroy him if he tries to answer it voluntarily, leading to an uneasy triangular stalemate.

The Doctor: "It's a standoff. They can't attack in case I unleash the Time Lords, and I can't run away because they'll burn this planet to stop the Time Lords. After all these years I've finally found somewhere that needs me to stick around."

In a clear echo of Christopher Eccleston's final story, *The Parting of the Ways* in 2005, he uses a small deception to send Clara home in the TARDIS, out of danger. She manages to get back to him, but by the time she returns, three hundred years have passed for him. The Doctor is now noticeably older, but still the proud protector of Christmas, equally adept at fixing toys for children and standing up to the never-ending stream of aliens attacking the town. He may be feebler now, and need the aid of a walking stick, but the Doctor's mind is still as sharp as ever when he is confronted with the bizarre threat of a wooden Cyberman, cleverly making use of the town's truth field to defeat a creature that his sonic screwdriver won't work on.

The warmth in Clara's relationship with the Doctor which emerged in the previous episode is just as strong here. Jenna Coleman and Matt Smith are particularly good in the extended quiet scene where they look out over the town at dawn (it's also the scene in which Handles suffers his aforementioned poignant death), and the Doctor finally explains to Clara why he is reconciled to living out the rest of his existence here – he's a Time Lord at the end of his time. When writer Robert Holmes casually dropped into his 1976 story *The Deadly Assassin* the notion that a Time Lord can regenerate no more than twelve times, the Doctor was still only in his fourth body, and the possibility of the show surviving long enough for the limit to matter was not remotely a consideration. Later writers (particularly in the time of the Fifth and Sixth Doctors) took the idea and built further stories on it. *Doctor Who* has never been reluctant to disregard inconvenient parts of its past, but the twelve-regeneration limit had established too great a hold in the public consciousness (despite the best attempts by the showrunners of the new series to ignore or downplay it) to be simply swept aside. It had to be addressed, and the revelation this year of John Hurt's previously unknown "War Doctor", together with the regeneration used up by David Tennant's Doctor in 2008's *The Stolen Earth*, which restored him after a Dalek blast but did not change his appearance ("I had vanity issues at the time," comments his successor), provided Moffat with the opportunity to establish that Matt Smith was in fact playing the Doctor's final incarnation.

Unusually for a Moffat script, there are few real twists in the progression of the story once the siege of Trenzalore begins. But the absence of plotting pyrotechnics leaves room for Matt Smith to, appropriately, take centre stage throughout his last episode. He is given a huge variety of material to play and, as has generally been the case all through his time as the Doctor, he is never less than compelling. A particularly good example of his talent for subtlety arises when Clara, upset that he has got himself stuck in this situation for centuries rather than leaving the planet, apologises for starting an argument:

The Doctor: "Clara, I've been having that argument for the last three hundred years, all by myself."
Clara: "But you didn't have the TARDIS."
The Doctor: "Ah, yes. Well, that made it easier to stay… true."

That last hesitation is exquisitely judged by Smith, leaving it impossible to tell whether the Doctor is being simply wry ("to stay, true") or thankful to have escaped the temptation to be selfish ("to stay true"). Also worthy of note is the avuncular relationship the Doctor develops with Jack Hollington's Barnable – the latest in a long line of good child actors that Smith has been able to strike a rapport with.

When the Doctor and Clara meet up with Tasha Lem again, the story pauses while the remaining loose ends from the past four years are cleared up. Some of the explanations are more convincing than others; we discovered during the 2011 series that the mysterious Silence was a religious movement, so learning how that movement arose from the Church of the Papal Mainframe made sense. But the idea that the Silent creatures are simply genetically engineered "confessional priests" of the Church doesn't work at all, reducing a memorable monster to a throwaway gag. More satisfyingly, the "Kovarian chapter" (which was behind the attempted assassination of the Doctor in that series, and the creation of River Song) is revealed to be a breakaway sect which wanted to attack the Doctor earlier in his timeline rather than try to contain him on Trenzalore. They were also the ones responsible for the blowing up of the TARDIS in the 2010 series – the event which created the very crack in the universe the Time Lords are now attempting to exploit. ("The destiny trap – you can't change history if you're part of it.")

The only real surprise in the plot occurs here, as it is revealed that the Doctor has walked into a trap – the Daleks have gained the upper hand in the battle over Trenzalore, converting all the Church operatives, including Tasha, into Dalek agents. As in *Asylum of the Daleks*, the horror moment when Tasha realises her true status, and a Dalek eyestalk erupts from her forehead, is nastily effective. On the other hand, the Doctor and Clara escape rather easily, as he provokes Tasha's strong-minded nature enough for her to resist the Dalek conditioning, enabling them to get back to the TARDIS.

Again, the Doctor manages to send Clara back to her normal life through a subterfuge, this time successfully. The parallel with *The Parting of the Ways* continues, as Clara's family vainly try to console her over the loss of her "boyfriend". Unlike Jackie and Mickey in that story, however, we have never met Clara's family before now, and they remain thin sketches rather than fully-fledged characters – social climbing mother, easy-going father, and slightly dotty grandmother (played by Sheila Reid, who Classic Series fans may recognise from her role as Etta in 1985's *Vengeance on Varos*), who is clearly the most sympathetic to Clara's feelings. The point of this interlude is simply to get Clara out of the way while another long stretch of time passes for the Doctor; eventually, Tasha Lem arrives on Earth, piloting the TARDIS (another characteristic she shares with River Song) to retrieve Clara and return her to Trenzalore, because "he shouldn't die alone."

By this point, the Doctor is an ancient figure, and Matt Smith gives a great performance through the extensive old-age makeup, his long white hair swept back in an echo of the original Doctor, William Hartnell. He conveys wonderfully how the Doctor is finally losing his grip, both mentally and physically, no longer having the strength to even pull open a Christmas cracker, and confusedly thinking that a townsman who comes to warn him the Daleks are coming is the long-dead Barnable. When asked what his plan to deal with them is, he can only fall back on the humorous, "Talk very fast, hope something good happens, take the credit. That's generally how it works." The protector of Christmas can now only ask Clara to stay inside while he goes to confront the Daleks; his last victory will be to keep her safe, if only for a few extra minutes. Coleman and Smith are both exceptional in this scene, as the Doctor and Clara share what they think will be their last moments together. This story leaves Clara in a similar position as another companion of the Doctor's back in the 1980's – Peri (played by Nicola Bryant), who quickly formed a lovely partnership with one Doctor, only to lose him after two stories. (Of course, Clara has been in many more than two stories this season, but as I've mentioned before, her earlier appearances saw the Doctor treat her as a puzzle as much as a person; only with *The Day of the Doctor* did a true, unguarded friendship between them finally emerge.) While the Doctor is resigned to his fate, Clara is still hoping for a way out:

Clara: "Change the future."
The Doctor: "Ha. I could have, once. When there were Time Lords. Not any more."

All sorts of speculations and suggestions were made as to how the Doctor might ultimately evade the regeneration limit; in the event, Moffat goes with the straightforward idea of the Time Lords granting him a whole new regeneration cycle (a capability they were revealed to have in *The Five Doctors*). In some ways it's regrettable that he ends up having to be saved by an outside agency; on the other hand, it is entirely appropriate that the Doctor, dying of old age – the one thing even he can't defeat – and having given everything of himself to protect the town, receives an unlooked-for reward. In a satisfying payoff for the "Doctor Who?" question that Moffat has been highlighting for years, Clara speaks directly to the Time Lords – and with the aid of Murray Gold's music, which from here to the end of the episode is outstanding, Coleman makes the moment a convincing emotional high point in spite of having to deliver an impassioned address to a wall:

Clara: "You've been asking a question. And it's time someone told you, you've been getting it wrong. His name… is the Doctor. All the name he needs, everything you need to know about him. And if you love him – and you should – help him…"

In a final confrontation atop the clock tower at the centre of Christmas, the Doctor is frail and helpless (although he takes some pleasure from the fact that the Daleks still have trouble working up the nerve to shoot him) until the Time Lords at last intervene. Then Smith gets to indulge in one last big speech and hyperactive outburst as, with a literal eruption of energy, the Doctor is able to wipe away the enemies besieging Trenzalore and cheat his fated death. Director Jamie Payne, who did so well with the small-scale episode *Hide* earlier in the season, here constructs a suitably apocalyptic climax, with huge explosions and Gold's music combining memorably with the clock symbolically striking midnight as the Doctor disappears behind a vortex of whirling energy reaching into the sky.

It would have been more logical, perhaps, for the new Doctor to have emerged at this point. But that would have deprived us of the lovely coda in the TARDIS, when the Doctor gently prepares both Clara and himself for the impending change. It was much better that Matt Smith's final moments as the Doctor should feature his true face – the face of the man who many worried was far too young to play the Doctor when he was announced back in January 2009, but ended up doing so brilliantly. He has maintained the show's success not only in Britain, but throughout the world – in particular, its profile in the United States has never been higher. Smith had an almost impossible job taking over from David Tennant, who had been an incredibly popular Doctor for four years. No better compliment can be given than to observe that he has left his own successor with exactly the same problem.

But as he says, in almost his final words to Clara, "Times change – and so must I." The emotional final scene is capped by a lovely brief appearance from Karen Gillan as Smith's Doctor imagines his first companion, Amy Pond, returning to bid him goodbye. (It's a curious coincidence that each episode of this Moffat trilogy involves the Doctor having an important interaction with a figure from his past that only he can see and hear.) To the strains of the gorgeous anthem previously heard at the climax of *The Rings of Akhaten*, the Eleventh Doctor's time runs out. He pulls off his signature bow tie, letting it fall to the floor, indicating that the moment is upon us. Then Moffat catches us out with one final surprise: unlike the protracted fireworks of previous regenerations, the change is over in a flash – in an eye-blink we're facing the fierce stare of Peter Capaldi, leaving us as shocked as Clara is.

Plenty of other shows have presented multi-year story arcs, but I can't think of any other that has tried to tell one in reverse order. The concept of the Eleventh Doctor's final episode reverberating back through his life, so that everything from *The Eleventh Hour* onward would find its eventual explanation here, is perhaps the ultimate demonstration of Steven Moffat's plotting capabilities. Not all of it fits together perfectly, and this finale suffered a little from the sheer number of plot points from the past to get through, many of which were no longer directly relevant. But with Matt Smith's fantastic central performance tying it all together, this era of *Doctor Who* reaches a satisfying conclusion, wrapped up as neatly as previous showrunner Russell T Davies did with his own tenure at the beginning of 2010. Unlike what happened with that complete changeover four years ago, a certain continuity will be maintained as Moffat is continuing on into the new era, as is Jenna Coleman, but it is already clear that when the show returns with a new Doctor it will feel quite different, and deliberately so. As always in *Doctor Who*, change is the only constant. The Doctor is dead; long live the Doctor.

Steven's Classic Who DVD Recommendation: In 1966, *Doctor Who* went through its first change of lead actor with William Hartnell's final story, *The Tenth Planet* – also notable as the story that introduced the Cybermen. Unfortunately, its last episode remains missing from the BBC archives, so the DVD release provides an animated version which is still quite effective. I'd also strongly recommend Mark Gatiss's recent docudrama *An Adventure in Space and Time*, which tells the story of the Hartnell years, with the man himself portrayed brilliantly by David Bradley. After seeing what happens to Matt Smith's Doctor in this episode, the final scene of *Adventure* is now even more poignant.

***Kevin's Review*:** At first, I was a bit grumpy while watching *The Time of the Doctor* when it became apparent that this was not going to be a set-piece showdown between the Doctor and the Silence. Perhaps, when it came down to it, Steven Moffat decided that the Doctor's most fitting adversary in his finale (let alone the Eleventh Doctor's) would be the Daleks. We can't know for sure when Moffat first devised the War Doctor, which meant that Matt Smith's departure would be the end of the Doctor's first regeneration cycle (while also pedantically including the Tenth Doctor's 'vanity regeneration' in *Journey's End*). Of course, this all started at the very beginning of this incarnation, when Prisoner Zero and the Atraxi warned the Doctor "Silence will fall" during the resolution of *The Eleventh Hour* (2010).

Matt Smith's second series featured the Silence and the prediction of the Doctor's end on Trenzalore, so fans reasonably expected the Eleventh Doctor's fate to be in the very rubbery hands of their monstrous acolytes, the Silence. Indeed, perhaps because those hands are so very perceptibly 'rubbery', Moffat decided that they were the "wrong hands" to mete out the Doctor's fate, and so went with the sink plungers instead. This may be another reason why Moffat chose the Weeping Angels as the Doctor's adversaries in *The Angels Take Manhattan* instead of the Daleks, so ensuring that the evil pepper pots would not be overused this year, given that they also played a pivotal role in the 50th Anniversary adventure. Yet, since the Silence played such a huge role during the 2011 series, it is a bit disappointing to see the Doctor relegating them to the position of confessional priests in an off-the-cuff remark. When I first watched the episode, it sounded as if the Doctor was saying that people would forget making a confession to a Silent, which meant that when they next saw it, they would confess again, having forgotten their first confession to it. However, what the Doctor means is that when people confess to a Silent, it takes away the memory of whatever sin is that is troubling them. Although in this instance, such forgiveness derives from prosaic genetic engineering, instead of divine grace.

As Steven writes, this does diminish the Silence a great deal. Not only are they no longer the Doctor's main adversary at Trenzalore as expected, but the Silence's role in shaping and influencing humanity throughout the centuries seems diminished. (Unless, of course, they still did this out of 'plain sight' within the confines of the confessional box.) This also makes you wonder why the Saturnynians said that they fled from "the Silence" during *The Vampires of Venice* (2010). Of course, we don't know whether the Saturnynians fled from the creatures called 'the Silence', or from Tasha Lem's call for *Silence* here. Indeed, although most creatures find the message that rings out at the beginning of this episode fills them with dread, they seem incapable of ignoring its call, so one would have thought that the Saturnynians would have found some relief at the prospect of silence. Anyway, back in *Let's Kill Hitler* (2011), according to the Teselecta's records, the Silence was a "religious order or movement". However, in a brilliant example of one of Moffat's numerous ingenious wordplays, it turns out here that the Silence is literally a religious *order* and "unscheduled faith change" issued by Tasha Lem, instead of a religious community that shares the same beliefs.

Obviously, Tasha Lem is the head of a religious order, as she is the "Mother Superious" of the Papal Mainframe. By presenting a female head of the Church, Moffat is as deliciously subversive here as he was in his presentation of the Thin/Fat Gay married Anglican Marines from *A Good Man Goes to War* (2011). This is because it seems that the Catholic Church will never have a female primate, while the Church of

England has only just allowed women to become bishops. Just like 'Oswin' and 'Oswald', Moffat adopts a masculine name for his Mother Superious, as 'Lem' seems to be a contraction of 'Lemuel', the boy's name that means (appropriately enough) 'devoted to God' or 'belonging to God'. Tasha's surname could also be a reference to the Polish science fiction author Stanisław Lem.

I don't think Janie Aire has written a critique of *The Time of the Doctor*, but now that I've read her reviews of *Hide* and *The Name of the Doctor*, I do see quite a lot of the symbolism that she writes about. For instance, Michael Pickwoad does a brilliant job of subtly representing the Church's Christianity by displaying a red cross on the carpet in front of Tasha's chapel. The doors of the chapel represent Christ's head, while the circular series of lights above represents the crown of thorns that Christ wore. Pickwoad brilliantly conveys this future Christian crucifixion iconography. No doubt Janie Aire would consider the crucifix to be just another example of the World Tree that I discussed in my previous review. An additional representation of the World Tree appears as a pagan emblem on the doors of the bell tower that the Doctor lives in on Trenzalore.

Although the settlement is called "Christmas", this is mainly due to it resembling a Dickensian Yuletide seen on many a seasonal card from the Victorian era onwards, instead of being due to any Christian sentiment. Indeed, the Doctor's propensity for fixing toys in his tower workshop is analogous to Father Christmas, instead of Jesus Christ. It's probably just as well that the Doctor doesn't grow a white beard and wear red, as this would have taken things too far... Having written that, I do like the fact that the Doctor has decorated his workshop with the pictures that children have given him. Presumably, children have sent these pictures to the production team during Matt Smith's time as the Doctor. If so, then this is a lovely gesture for Moffat to make to the show's younger fans. Like Steven, I think that the incorporation of seasonal elements into the Christmas Special has gone as far as it possibly could, so I think it would be better if the production team just concentrated on producing a rollicking adventure at this time of year without pandering to the seasonal memes. For me, Moffat's only truly satisfying Christmas Special was the previous one, *The Snowmen*, as that was set in the proper traditional Victorian Christmas era, instead of the pseudo one we see here. Then again, I'm sure all of us have either discovered for ourselves or seen how stressful preparing Christmas dinner can be, so Moffat's juxtaposition of Clara's anxiety at cooking for her family to the Doctor's stress at fleeing from Cybermen is very funny.

Continuing with the theme of symbolism, Moffat is also very subversive in his depiction of the Dalek puppets. There has long been an esoteric tradition concerning the "Third Eye": the belief that humans have an invisible extra eye on the forehead that allows some of us to achieve higher consciousness. Of course, the Daleks would argue that by giving their puppets a "third eyestalk" on their foreheads, that they are indeed enabling them to have a "higher consciousness", albeit one that is hugely at variance with traditional mystical and New Age beliefs concerning the "Third Eye". When Tasha manages to fight off the Dalek within her, her "third eyestalk" retreats, leaving a scar on her forehead that is reminiscent of traditional representations of the Third Eye in Eastern art. As for how the Dalek nanocloud managed to get on board the Papal Mainframe's ship, it is possible that Colonel Meme was infected when she wasn't on board. Indeed, Colonel Meme appears to be the main Dalek puppet on the Papal Mainframe prior to the eruption of Tasha's third eyestalk. If so, then it would seem that Moffat is playing another of his subversive linguistic games with us, for a 'meme' is a behaviour, idea or style that spreads from one person to another within a culture in an evolutionary way, much as the Colonel's Dalek infection would have done. Indeed, the British evolutionary biologist and religious sceptic Richard Dawkins first devised the word 'meme' in his 1976 book *The Selfish Gene*. This is probably a deliberate and affectionate nod to Dawkins by Moffat here, as our showrunner will know that former legendary *Doctor Who* script editor Douglas Adams introduced Dawkins to his wife, Lalla Ward, who played the second incarnation of the Fourth Doctor's Time Lady assistant Romana. Richard Dawkins, of course, appeared as himself in *Doctor Who* during *The Stolen Earth* (2008).

Contrary to Steven, I quite like Tasha's voiceover here. I much preferred it to Eldane's narrative in *Cold Blood* (2010), not least because it's relatively straightforward (i.e. not misleading, unlike Eldane's). Since Tasha has a more privileged position than Eldane, she has much more authenticity. In many ways, it reminds me of Princess Irulan's narrative in Frank Herbert's *Dune* (1965), which David Lynch incorporated at the beginning of his 1984 adaptation. Like Irulan, Tasha is part of a religious order, although Irulan is not an integral member of the mystical female sisterhood (the Bene Gesserit) in *Dune*. Tasha's voiceover has the effect of making the Doctor's 'final stand' seem more epic in scope. In addition to her narrative voiceovers, Tasha also seems quite potent and godlike when addressing the Doctor as a huge hologram in the sky. Although when Tasha states in her voiceover that the Silence fought with the Doctor, it is perhaps a bit unfortunate that they are standing behind him, so that he would not have realised that they were there! As Steven writes, it would perhaps have been preferable to have River Song perform these roles here, as Tasha also has a flirtatious relationship with the Doctor, but we know from *The Name of the Doctor* that River was not present (or alive) during the Doctor's final stand on Trenzalore. I guess River could have been present in spirit form, but I think that this would have complicated things too much, as Moffat wanted to present the Papal Mainframe as being on much friendlier terms with the Doctor here than the Kovarian Chapter had been. Anyway, since Peter Capaldi has stated that he isn't keen on his Doctor being flirtatious (with a younger companion at least), I guess the Doctor's banter with Tasha could represent a final fling on his part. Besides, someone always has to give the Eleventh Doctor his traditional slap on the face, and Tasha performs this role admirably here. Like Alex Kingston, Orla Brady isn't much younger than Peter Capaldi, so she could return (along with her flirtatious banter) to the show in the future.

While watching this episode, I was wondering who could have buried the Doctor in the TARDIS (had he died) as we saw in *The Name of the Doctor*. Tasha would appear to be the obvious choice to lead the funerary honours, as she is still living at the end, and she can gain entry to the TARDIS. The Daleks (and all the other monsters that have previously infiltrated the Church's shield) seem to ignore the native human inhabitants for the most part. If I lived in Christmas, then I would probably be livid that this stranger had turned up, especially when all that threatening alien trash followed him. At this point, the episode seems to echo 2012's *A Town Called Mercy*, with the Doctor playing both the sheriff and the kindly alien fugitive Kahler-Jex. However, unlike Gary Cooper in *High Noon* (1952), the people of Christmas do not forsake the Doctor as the clock moves from Eleven to Twelve. Instead, the Doctor tries to shake off Clara, but she holds onto the TARDIS firmly during her impromptu exposure to the time vortex. (It's great to see that the TARDIS now has a more positive attitude to Clara, which is shown by the Doctor's ship extending its force field to protect her.) I guess it helps that the Doctor has such a great relationship with the children of Christmas during the early years of his arrival and beyond, so that they grow up viewing him as their protector (especially as the aliens above will burn their planet to prevent the return of the Time Lords if the Doctor does ever leave). The Doctor becomes a living myth to the children of Christmas, which Moffat demonstrates via a Punch and Judy show that apparently dramatizes the Doctor fighting off a Monoid (a poorly realized monster from the 1966 adventure *The Ark*) with his sonic screwdriver!

It's a bit of a shame that the production team recast Clara's dad in this episode, although Michael Dixon did admittedly look too young while standing next to Clara as she mourned at her mother's grave in *The Rings of Akhaten*. Then again, the *Doctor Who* costume department is very good at conveying ageing via prosthetics such as those sported by Matt Smith in this episode, along with Amy's reading glasses, which, instead of nostalgia for his lost companion, now basically signify that the Doctor is ageing whenever he needs to use them to read. I wasn't too convinced by Clara's outburst that she has a "Bubbly personality masking bossy control freak", as we haven't really seen this so far, not even when the Doctor gave her command of the soldiers during *Nightmare in Silver*. It's possible that she gets her 'control freakery' from her father. Clara does roll her eyes when she recalls how detailed her father's emailed instructions to cook the turkey were. Perhaps we will see the 'control freak' aspect of her nature when she next appears in front of a classroom? If Clara is indeed a control freak, then she must have thought that she had literally died and gone to heaven in *The Name of the Doctor*, when she entered the Doctor's time stream to put him back on the right path! However, if Clara is a computer genius following the events of *The Bells of Saint John*, then she should have been able to work out how to use iPlayer by now!

The most obvious way that the TARDIS could have saved Clara's turkey was by the Doctor transporting her further back in time so that she could put the turkey on earlier. However, I guess even the Doctor seems to regard this as being a too dangerous and frivolous way of rewriting time. Instead, the doors at the bottom of time rotor get another (inconsistent) function: this time, one of them operates as an impromptu turkey oven. There is so much hopping around here that it looks as though Moffat uses some shorthand tricks to keep the narrative flowing. For instance, there is also an inconsistency in the way that Trenzalore appears on the TARDIS scanner, even although the TARDIS is then outside Clara's block of flats on Earth. Later, when Tasha invites the Doctor to parley, she offers to transport the Doctor to her ship, which the Doctor refuses, as he now has the TARDIS back thanks to Clara. After Tasha's revelation that she is a Dalek puppet, the Doctor and Clara escape via Tasha's teleport, yet arrive back on Trenzalore in the TARDIS. (I guess this could be explained away by the Doctor teleporting them directly to the TARDIS.) Trenzalore itself looks a world away from the dark hellfire it appeared as in *The Name of the Doctor*. Obviously, a lot of time has passed since *The Time of the Doctor* and the would-be events of *The Name of the Doctor*, so that the TARDIS has begun fracturing and the planet has aged in the meantime. Yet the gravestones of the soldiers in *The Name of the Doctor* do not seem to have aged, and there is no sign of any structure from Christmas, such as the stone bell tower in which the Doctor lives during this episode. If anything, this confirms my suspicion that the Trenzalore in *The Name of the Doctor* was nothing but a nightmare that the Great Intelligence's imagination built. However, there is a very pleasing consistency in the production team's use of Ken Bones' voice as that which asks the oldest question here, for he played the Time Lord General that the Doctor interacted with in *The Day of the Doctor*. On the other hand, it's a bit disappointing to see the Sontarans' comic turn here – since the hilarious Strax's advent, it seems that the Sontarans will never be a serious threat to the Doctor again.

There's a nice bit of Eleventh Doctor nostalgia when he states that he procured Handles from the 'Maldovar Market', which Dorium must have established prior to his 'death'. Obviously, there is even more at the end when the Eleventh Doctor makes his final farewell. Like Steven, I must praise Murray Gold's music here (as well as Moffat's writing and the acting), for Matt Smith's final scenes did bring a tear to my eyes. It's a pity that Caitlin Blackwood could not resume her role as the young Amelia Pond (as she must be too old now), because it did look a bit odd that we could not see the young Amelia's face as she ran along the console gallery. As we know from the events of *The Angels Take Manhattan*, the Doctor could not go to see Amy again, so it is wonderful take she comes alive again here in his imagination. Then again, this is also a reminder that actors do not tend to play the Doctor for long, since it does not feel like such a long time ago that we said goodbye to Amy. In this way, it is good that Moffat has chosen an older actor to reboot *Doctor Who*, as, unlike a younger thespian, Peter Capaldi is unlikely to have his head turned by Hollywood. Given that

Capaldi was a *Doctor Who* fan in his youth, it is likely that he will choose to stay in a role for longer. It may seem a risk to make the Doctor a bit more menacing and prickly (according to the advance publicity for the eighth series of 21st Century *Who*) as a similar kind of approach did not work for Colin Baker as the Sixth Doctor. Then again, Capaldi is already approaching 'national treasure' status, so I am sure that audiences will forgive him for being more 'in your face'.

Clara's is the first face that the Twelfth Doctor sees, so we are certain to see more of Jenna Coleman in the future, especially since she is obviously in Series Eight. Coleman's performance in this episode was excellent – she's really warming to her role as Clara now, and it's good for Clara's character development that she is so pivotal to the Time Lords' decision to cut the Doctor some slack. It will certainly be interesting to see how Clara will adjust to the new challenge of dealing with a pricklier Doctor. However, the episode ultimately belongs (appropriately enough) to Matt Smith, who is literally in sparkling form here. I think my favourite part of the episode was seeing the revitalization in the Doctor's eyes as he realized that the Time Lords had gifted him a completely new life cycle – Smith brilliantly acted this, despite the heavy prosthetic makeup. Sometimes the Eleventh Doctor's over-exuberant zaniness has got on my nerves, but this is mostly due to Moffat's characterisation of the Doctor (which it seems that he will rein in for Capaldi), instead of being due to any error on Matt Smith's part. So, it is sad to think that this brilliant, wide-ranging actor will not be in the show anymore, but I wish him all the best for the future, especially since I am sure that this is not the last of Matt Smith in the role of the Doctor. For instance, there's the 10th Anniversary of the Revived Series in 2015, and we all know from this year how *Doctor Who* likes a big party!

Steven Cooper and Kevin Mahoney are also the authors of:

Steven Moffat's Doctor Who 2010

&

Steven Moffat's Doctor Who 2011

the HOUSE NEXT DOOR

http://www.slantmagazine.com/house/

SLANT MAGAZINE

http://www.slantmagazine.com

29409299R00137

Printed in Great Britain
by Amazon